Transport for a Sustainable Future

Transport for a Sustainable Future

The Case for Europe

John Whitelegg

Belhaven Press
London and New York
Copublished in the Americas by Halsted Press,
an imprint of John Wiley & Sons, Inc.

Belhaven Press
(a division of Pinter Publishers Ltd)
25 Floral Street, Covent Garden, London WC2E 9DS, United Kingdom

First published in 1993

Co-published in the Americas by Halsted Press, an imprint of
John Wiley & Sons, Inc., 605 Third Avenue, New York, NY 10158-0012

John Whitelegg is hereby identified as the author of this work as provided under Section 77 of the Copyright, Designs and Patents Act, 1988.

British Library Cataloguing in Publication Data

A CIP catalogue record for this book is available from the British Library.

ISBN 1 85293 145 0 (hb)
     1 85293 146 9 (pb)

Library of Congress Cataloging-in-Publication Data

Whitelegg, J. (John)
    Transport for a sustainable future: the case for Europe / John Whitelegg.
       p. cm.
    Includes bibliographical references (p.   ) and index.
    ISBN 1-85293-145-0 (Belhaven Press) – ISBN 1-85293-146-9 (pbk.: Belhaven Press)
    – ISBN 0-470-21936-X (Halsted Press). – ISBN 0-470-22018-X
    (pbk.: Halsted Press)
    1. Transportation – Environmental aspects – Europe.
  2. Transportation and state – Europe. 3. Transportation – Social aspects – Europe.
  I. Title
    TD195.T7W47   1993
363.73'1–dc20   93–14989
                                                                                    CIP

ISBN 0 47021 936 X (hb) (in the Americas only)
     0 47022 018 X (pb)

Typeset by Mayhew Typesetting, Rhayader, Powys
Printed and bound in Great Britain by Biddles Ltd, Guildford and King's Lynn

CONTENTS

List of figures   vi
List of tables   viii
Preface   x

Introduction   1

1. Transport and sustainability   4

2. Global warming   14

3. Air pollution   36

4. Noise   60

5. Time pollution   76

6. Transport and health   97

7. The cost of transport   127

8. Transport and Europe   146

9. Conclusion   154

Appendix 1: Chemicals present in vehicle exhausts   163

Appendix 2: Air pollutant factsheets   174

References   185
Index   195

LIST OF FIGURES

2.1   Contribution of different gases to global warming   20
2.2   Carbon dioxide emissions by source, 1988   20
2.3   Road transport carbon dioxide emissions: low forecast   21
2.4   Road transport carbon dioxide emissions: high forecast   22
2.5   All transport carbon dioxide emissions   23
2.6   Global carbon dioxide emissions from cars under different
      growth rates   24
2.7   Average car fuel consumption against engine capacity   26
2.8   Carbon dioxide emission characteristics of a range of car
      types   27
2.9   Diesel and petrol-engined cars and fuel consumption   28
2.10 Projected carbon dioxide emission reductions from
      passenger cars   33
3.1   Relationship between OSHA workplace limits and UK road
      source emissions for a number of potentially hazardous
      compounds   44
3.2   Road transport NO_x emissions: low forecast   51
3.3   Road transport NO_x emissions: high forecast   51
3.4   Road transport CO emissions: low forecast   52
3.5   Road transport CO emissions: high forecast   52
3.6   Road transport HC emissions: low forecast   53
3.7   Road transport HC emissions: high forecast   54
3.8   All transport NO_x emissions: low forecast   55
3.9   All transport CO emissions: low forecast   55
3.10 All transport HC emissions: low forecast   56
3.11 Different modes of passenger transport in terms of energy
      use and pollution   57
3.12 Different modes of freight transport in terms of energy use
      and pollution   58
4.1   Examples of noise levels   61
4.2   Noise impact from different sources in West Germany, 1985   62
4.3   Noise impact by size of urban area in West Germany, 1985   63
4.4   Noise levels recorded for different groups of vehicles under
      differing speed conditions   65

4.5   Speed and noise in urban areas   66
4.6   Comparison of noise output of different modes of road
      transport   67
4.7   A German view of noise and the citizen (cartoon)   68
4.8   Speed measurements before and after speed limit zones   71
5.1   Consumption of space by different modes of transport,
      occupancy and speed   79
5.2   Average social speeds of the bicycle and the car   81
5.3   Travel times in urban areas from door to door   82
5.4   Waiting times and crossing speeds at pelican crossings   84
5.5   The relationship between speed and injury and fatality rates   86
5.6   Injuries and fatalities in Hamburg road accidents before and
      after the introduction of 30kph speed limit zones   87
5.7   Fuel consumption and emissions from petrol-engined cars at
      constant speeds   88
5.8   Comparison of nitrogen dioxide emissions from cars in
      identical driving conditions at different speeds   88
5.9   Fuel consumption and noise levels under 50kph and 30kph
      speed limits   89
5.10 Emission levels under 50kph and 30kph speed limits   90
5.11 Accident balance programme: Nippes   91
5.12 Accident balance programme: Agnesviertel   92
5.13 Paris – southeast routes: evolution of passenger traffic,
      1980–89   93
6.1   San Francisco: traffic hazard on three streets   100
6.2   San Francisco: noise, stress and pollution on three streets   101
6.3   San Francisco: social interaction on three streets   102
6.4   San Francisco: home territory on three streets   103
6.5   Independent mobility of English children by age, 1971 and
      1990   105
6.6   Method and supervision of English children's journeys, 1971
      and 1990   107
7.1   Environmental damage and costs of different modes of
      transport   134
7.2   The inadequacy of present fuel taxation levels   135
7.3   Inventory of costs associated with car ownership   138

LIST OF TABLES

1.1   Worldwide growth in selected human activities and products   4

2.1   Key data: greenhouse gases   15

2.2   Specific heat output and carbon dioxide emissions at point of use: various fuels   30

2.3   Potential for reducing carbon dioxide emissions from road transport   31

3.1   Transport's share of total pollution   37

3.2   EC directives relevant to air quality and vehicles   39

3.3   Emissions from tyre abrasion on a variety of road types   45

3.4   Hourly concentrations of nitrogen dioxide at selected UK sites during 1987   47

3.5   Carbon monoxide concentrations at four London sites in 1988   47

3.6   Typical urban concentrations of atmospheric pollutants associated with transport   49

4.1   The effect of traffic calming measures on noise levels in Köln   70

4.2   Schedules of directives for vehicle noise limits in the EEC   72

4.3   Noise levels for town planning in Germany   73

4.4   Noise standards in Switzerland   74

6.1   Ways in which transport influences health   97

6.2   Average costs per casualty and per accident in Great Britain, 1990   110

6.3   Risk of accidents to pedestrians and cyclists   112

6.4   Fatal and serious injury rates from RTAs in Manchester and Köln   113

6.5   Summary of the health effects of the major air pollutants   114

6.6   Summary of atmospheric levels, health effects and WHO guidelines   117

7.1   An environmental damage balance sheet   131

7.2   Total costs and taxation income for lorries in West Germany, 1987   132

7.3   Total costs and taxation income for cars in West Germany, 1987   132

7.4   Social costs in relation to transport modalities   133

7.5 The contribution of public transport in Bremen to improving
     the environment   136
8.1 Proportionate contribution to increased road freight activity
     in Germany, 1987–2000   153

PREFACE

This work is dedicated to John Roberts who died in July 1992. For twenty years, as the person who ran, indeed was, TEST (Transport and Environment Studies), John produced a large number of reports that exposed the fallacies underlying a motorised society and pointed towards a solution that was equitable, environmentally friendly and sustainable. John described the elements of a 'sustainable' transport policy long before the word was linked to transport and this book has been heavily influenced by his original and creative contributions.

The book has benefited enormously from two years of exposure to transport thinking in the *Land* of North Rhine–Westphalia in Germany. During this time I worked with Helmut Holzapfel in Dortmund and this work owes an intellectual debt to his highly original approach to transport problems. In spite of these sound precursors the book doubtless contains some flaws, and for these I take full responsibility.

The book was written during the time when I was head of the department of Geography at Lancaster University, and would not have been completed but for the splendid support and friendship of Sheila Hargreaves, Sandra Irish, Claire Jarvis and Matthew Ball. Matthew did all the diagrams.

Finally I would like to thank Iain Stevenson of Belhaven who was remarkably patient during many delays and Midge Whitelegg who produced the index.

John Whitelegg
July 1992

INTRODUCTION

The 1980s have witnessed two very clear and interrelated trends. On the one hand there has been an intensification of awareness of environmental problems and issues at all geographical scales, culminating in the 'Earth Summit' in June 1992, and on the other an accelerating deterioration in environmental quality. The key areas of such deterioration have been documented by the Worldwatch Institute (Brown, 1992) and transport figures significantly in this catalogue. Our propensity to travel longer distances by car and our reliance on lorries to carry large amounts of freight on which our lifestyle depends have created a land-use structure and a set of expectations that make transport policies one of the most intractable of policy areas.

Adams (1992) estimates that each of us in the UK travels on average 120 miles per week and accounts for 60 tonne-km of freight by road per week. Most of us make journeys that we regard as essential and most of us are involved in patterns of consumption that are only possible because of the work done by lorries. The consequences of this societal dependence on motorised transport are wide-ranging and are a central concern of this book. Transport is an important source of greenhouse gases and one which is likely to experience most difficulties in meeting targets for reduction (Hughes, 1992); global warming is discussed in chapter 2. Chapter 3 is concerned with air pollution in its regional and local manifestations and chapter 4, similarly, with noise pollution.

Transport has far wider impacts on society than can be summarised under the usual list of pollutants. It has a major say in what is possible and what is not possible in society and in determining the ways in which space and time are moulded for the advantage of some to the detriment of others. These issues are tackled in chapter 5 where the thesis is advanced that the use of space through the desire to minimise or eliminate time constraints is a major source of pollution and community disruption.

Transport clearly has a major impact on health and this is reviewed in chapter 6. These health impacts extend beyond air pollution and respiratory problems and raise important questions about the design of healthy cities and public health strategies. It follows from the catalogue of environmental and health impacts that transport imposes a cost burden on society that is not picked up in any direct sense but forms part of larger public and private expenditures on health care, environmental improvement and infrastructure provision. Chapter 7 looks at these wider costs as part of a discussion about cost-recovery or environmental taxation to steer the economy and spatial structures towards forms which are less environmentally damaging.

The impact of transport on society is better understood through a general appreciation of the links among consumption, economic growth, environmental impact and sustainability. The demand for transport is closely linked to measures of economic growth (Simonis, 1990) and the sustainability debate raises fundamental questions about the viability of a long-term increase in the demand for transport and the possibility that transport might in some way be curtailed (ie demand reduced) while the economy continues to grow. It is also possible that sustainability as documented, for example, in the EC's statement on 'sustainable mobility' (EC, 1992a) is based more on a desire to see the status quo maintained than a commitment to achieve levels of resource consumption far less than those currently prevailing. Transport provides an ideal test bed for the examination of sustainability concepts as found in chapter 1. An analysis of transport offers extra insight into the concept of sustainability and an analysis of sustainability offers the possibility of new ideas for transport policies.

Just as sustainability provides a useful analytical framework for looking at the demand for transport, so Europe provides a logic in terms both of scale and of critical policy influences on transport and the environment. Europe is increasingly important in setting the pace of transport and environmental policy developments. The completion of the internal market and the changes to be brought about as a result of the Maastricht treaty completely redefine market conditions and the range over which goods and people will move. More importantly these changes will produce a substantial increase in passenger and freight activity. This is the subject of chapter 8. In addition to the policy-making and spatial restructuring roles of European-level developments there is now a substantial involvement in basic infrastructure provision. The European Community has plans to establish a high-speed rail network (Whitelegg, Hulten and Flink, 1993) as well as to complete a number of links in the European motorway system. The plans for motorways or similar high-quality roads (EC, 1992b) indicate routes through the Snowdonia National Park and Pembrokeshire in the UK as well as extensive new construction in Spain, Portugal, Greece, Ireland and France.

European developments are likely to increase in their significance for national transport and environmental policies as well as for local environmental quality. If economic and fiscal instruments become important for achieving transport and environmental policy objectives (see chapter 7) they will have to be implemented at the EC level if major disparities between member states are to be avoided.

European-level developments in logistics (see chapter 8) will ensure that any issues related to freight movement will have to be addressed at that level as will the future of European railways outside of the high-speed net. A fully internationalised and liberalised road freight industry will present a formidable challenge to the railway system which will not be up to the competitive struggle in its present national compartments. New forms of co-operation to use the road mode sensitively whilst fully involving rail will demand European-level organisations and new forms of working.

The arguments in support of the importance of European-scale issues are explored in chapter 8. At a more fundamental level Europe has a variety of transport problems and solutions that have been shaped by a common European heritage and are significantly different from those experienced in North America, Australia or Africa. This book ranges widely over the European experience to provide examples of both problems and solutions. Inevitably it is heavily influenced by a period of two years in which I worked for the Ministry of Transport of the State of North Rhine–Westphalia in Düsseldorf and by subsequent exposure to mainland European transport arguments.

Europe has a large number of transport problems, many of which look intractable, but also has a large variety of initiatives and solutions. This book aims to emphasise the solutions as much as the problems and to show that a Europe conditioned by the single market and assumptions about the advantages of economic growth and the spread of development 'benefits' can also be a Europe in which the movement of freight and passengers is reduced and/or shifted to more benign modes and environmental quality is increased. Sustainable transport policies are likely to reduce resource consumption (including distance) and increase real economic welfare (Ekins, 1992). Chapter 1 explores the concept of sustainability and its relevance to a better understanding of transport.

1 TRANSPORT AND SUSTAINABILITY

UK traffic forecasts indicate that by the year 2025 we can expect an increase in vehicle miles of between 83 and 142% (Department of Transport, 1989). Average travel speeds in central London have altered very little since the turn of the century (Mogridge, 1990). Average peak traffic speeds in central London fell from 20.7kph in 1972 to 17.6kph in 1990 (Church, 1992). Americans spend about two billion man-hours per year stuck in traffic jams and by the year 2000 there will probably be one car for every person aged 20–64 (*Economist*, 1992). The annual rate of growth in vehicle numbers in Germany exceeds the growth rate for world population and the installed horsepower of German automobiles is greater than the population of the world (Holzapfel, 1992). The UK road construction and widening programme over the next ten years will cost £20 billion and add 5% to total road space. Meadows, Meadows and Randers (1992) in their discussion of global limits and 'overshoot' reproduce some basic data shown in table 1.1.

Table 1.1 Worldwide growth in selected human activities and products

	1970	1990
Human population	3.6 billion	5.3 billion
Registered automobiles	250 million	560 million
Kilometres driven/year in OECD countries		
passenger cars	2584 billion	4489 billion
trucks	666 billion	1536 billion
Oil consumption/year (barrels)	17 billion	24 billion
Soft drinks consumption (per year/US only barrels)	150 million	364 million

Source: Meadows, Meadows and Randers, 1992

The growth in vehicle numbers and distance driven is the starting point for any assessment of transport's environmental impact and the growth rates are very high indeed. The growth in soft drink consumption, for instance, is also indicative of trends in transport. The growth in consumption of products of this kind is a major source of the growth in road freight (Cooper et al, 1991) and clearly demonstrates the interdependencies of transport, consumption and economic growth.

The growth in distance travelled and vehicle numbers is relatively modest in comparison with the liberation of suppressed demand now occurring in Eastern Europe and the third world. Growth rates of over 600% in the distances travelled by car are being forecast for Eastern Europe by the year 2010 (Rothengatter, 1991) and a movement towards quite modest car ownership rates by European standards (300 per 1000 population) would deliver 300 million Indian-owned vehicles and 300 million Chinese-owned vehicles. In terms of both resource consumption and pollution levels these vehicle populations and the distance they travel are not sustainable. Only 8% of the world's population owns a car. Whatever sustainability means in terms of a detailed definition there is not enough room to build the highways to take the traffic that would be implied by this 8% doubling or trebling. The demands on energy, raw material resources and space would be overwhelming. The air pollution, noise pollution and climatic change consequences would be dramatic and fall well within the description painted by Meadows et al (1992) of 'overshoot'. More important perhaps is the social implication of this overshoot. Not only do we have resource exploitation on a scale that is not sustainable, especially if we associate sustainability with the concept of 'overshoot', but we have it in support of something which benefits only 8% of the world's population.

The World Commission on Environment and Development (1987) defined a sustainable society as one 'that meets the needs of the present without compromising the ability of future generations to meet their own needs'. Daly (1991) argues that a physically sustainable society should satisfy three basic conditions:

1 its rates of use of renewable resources do not exceed their rates of regeneration;
2 its rates of use of non-renewable resources do not exceed the rate at which sustainable renewable substitutes are developed;
3 its rates of pollution emission do not exceed the assimilative capacity of the environment.

From a transport point of view, with rates of growth over twenty years identified in table 1.1 and use of resources which are in the main non-renewable, the first condition is not met. Condition 2 has enormous potential in the transport sector since it is perfectly possible to carry out the same set of activities but over shorter distances and to switch from environmentally damaging modes to modes which are relatively benign.

It is however another condition which is not met as road-based modes win an increasingly large share of the market for both passenger and freight transport (Roberts et al, 1992). The third condition is not met in the transport sector. Carbon dioxide emissions from the transport sector continue to rise (Hughes, 1992) and the available evidence on human health and transport pollutants (chapter 6) indicates that critical thresholds have been tripped.

A sustainable society 'would not freeze into permanence the current inequitable patterns of distribution . . . it would certainly not permit the persistence of poverty' (Meadows et al, 1992, p210). One of the most obvious characteristics of personal transport is the wide variation in car ownership levels between places at all geographical scales and among social groups. At global extremes we have car trips in developed countries for journeys of less than 500m and in third world countries daily searches on foot for fuel and drinking water of up to 30km. Disparities of this kind and of a less dramatic nature fuel the desire and determination which leads to car ownership. Normally a desirable thing in itself for a complex mixture of reasons (Bayley, 1986; Sachs, 1992), the situation in Eastern Europe shows how quickly the trading up process can proceed when political and market forces liberate the demand that has festered unsatisfied for many years. The Indian middle classes are not far behind the newborn consumers of the former German Democratic Republic in this important respect.

It follows that a strategy to reduce car ownership or the distance travelled by car must involve devoting similar amounts of effort to reducing 'excess' consumption and dealing with the transport deficit in those countries and amongst those social groups who are disadvantaged in this respect. Whilst these concepts might be difficult to define it is clear that sustainability does involve an equity dimension and that the removal of global and local inequalities is one of the few ways to stem the process of trading-up to whatever level of consumption is characteristic of the developed world.

The concept of sustainability is poorly defined and is described as a 'story line' by Hajer (1991) and as 'not only an attempt to provide solutions to improve the objective state of the environment but also an effort to accommodate latent social conflict'. Its widespread use at a time when there is still considerable disagreement about targets for reducing greenhouse gas emissions (chapter 2) is indicative of its social and political status as much as it is of its relevance to environmental improvements.

It is much more convenient for everyone to continue to behave in very much the same way as in the past, allowing technology to give us clean cars and clean power stations and maybe substituting renewable energy for fossil energy here and there and renewable softwoods for tropical hardwoods, than it is to move to significantly lower levels of per capita consumption of energy, transport and manufactured goods. Sustainability is above all else a very convenient concept because it allows us to defer facing the unthinkable: that maybe we ought to consume less and shift consumption and wealth to third world countries reversing the traditional flow of benefits.

A detailed description of the sustainability argument can be found in *Blueprint For a Green Economy* (Pearce et al, 1989). The concept has been a major concern since the UN symposium on Interrelations among Resources, Environment and Development, held in Stockholm in August 1979, but has its origins in population and resource debates going back at least to the *Limits to Growth* debate of Meadows et al (1972).

Sustainable development was a key concern of the World Conservation Strategy published by the World Conservation Union (IUCN), the United Nations Environment Programme (UNEP) and the World Wide Fund for Nature (WWF) in 1980 and even more so of the World Commission on Environment and Development (Bruntland) Report published in 1987. The Bruntland Report (*Our Common Future*) had at its centre the concept of sustainable development. The UN General Assembly accepted a resolution in 1987 which advocated sustainable development as a guiding principle for the UN, government and private sector.

In June 1988 the leaders of the G7 countries adopted the concept and in the summer of 1988 the Secretary General of the UN initiated a special task force to monitor progress on institutionalising the idea of sustainable development. In November of the same year the OECD commenced a survey of how environmental considerations could be integrated in a system of national accounts. The concept is now widely accepted as a kind of shorthand for environmental concerns and political responsibility but there is still very little sign of progress towards a translation of sustainability into tangible targets and values relevant to consumption and pollution. Indeed Hajer suggests (1991, p21) that support for sustainability arguments may have much to do with their 'relative superficiality and ambiguousness' and Redclift quoted in Hajer (p25) expresses the view that sustainable development is 'more than a pious hope but rather less than a rigorous analytical schema'.

In a similar vein O'Riordan and Rayner (1991) identify sustainability as a 'predictable synthesis' out of the thesis and antithesis of prevention and adaptation. Prevention reflects the view that nature is very fragile and it is morally wrong to abuse it. The prevention response is quite literally to prevent whatever might threaten this fragile system. Adaptation reflects the view that nature is very robust and that it is morally wrong to curtail development. The environment is flexible, resilient to change and 'cornucopian in its ability to provide resources for human use' (ibid, p100).

Sustainabilty has at its centre the notion that it is possible to avoid global catastrophe by careful stewardship of the limited opportunities that nature provides for controlled growth. It is possible, therefore, to carry on very much a business-as-usual strategy or as O'Riordan and Rayner describe it: 'It is to be expected that hierarchical organisations will favour a response to environmental uncertainty that allows them to have their cake and eat it – the strategy of sustainable development.'

There are further problems with the concept of sustainability. Some of these are described in the work of Ekins et al (1992). Ekins focuses attention on the dilemma created by societies based on consumerism and on the tyranny of the relationships among population, consumption and technology. He describes the environmental crisis as the crisis of unsustainability '[which] must be laid squarely at the door of Northern industrial lifestyles and their imitations now in nearly all countries of the Third World'. He uses the equation $I = PCT$ to represent Impact on the environment (I) as a product of population (P) $\times$ consumption (C) $\times$ technology (T). The equation originates in the work of Paul and Anne Ehrlich (1990).

Ekins assumes that I is currently too high. This is in line with other observers of global environmental change (Brown, 1990; Von Weizsacker, 1990). Interestingly, both authors and the institutions they represent implicate the development of motorised transport in the growing environmental and ecological crisis.

Population is increasing and is likely to stabilise at 10.2 billion, approximately double the 1991 figure (United Nations medium variant quoted in the *Economist*, 20 January 1990). A fuller discussion can be found in Keyfitz (1992) who identifies the relationship between population growth per se and consumption per capita as an important variable in discussions of environmental impact. It is certainly central to an understanding of sustainability.

If population is to double then the product of consumption and technology has to halve to maintain I at its present level; and its present level is too high. Proponents of sustainability and 'green growth' argue that technology can help to overcome these obstacles; but technology would have to deliver a reduction of 93% of the environmental impact of each unit of consumption over the next fifty years to halve I (which Ekins assumes equates with sustainability). This is clearly not possible.

Ekins argues that over the next fifty years we can assume a 3% annual growth in economic output (green or otherwise) which will double global consumption over twenty-five years even if we do not take fully into account the catching up of third world countries in their consumption. So, over the next fifty years, I must be halved to achieve sustainability, P will double, C will quadruple and T cannot deliver the goods. The result is that 'green growth' and possibly sustainability is an illusion.

Ekins uses the growth in motor vehicles to illustrate his point. With an annual growth rate of 5.1% for trucks and buses and 4.7% for cars, vehicle stocks double every fifteen years so that just to keep emissions from this source constant the fuel efficiency of vehicles must double every two generations of vehicles (approximately every sixteen years).

The illusion lies in the abstraction of small parts of a much larger reality and its reduction to small technical problems. Cars, transport and the environment highlight the illusion more than most sectors of the economy. The conversion of a vehicle to lead-free petrol or the fitting of a catalytic converter do not render vehicles 'green'. The use of environmentally friendly paints and solvents and the broadcasting of the fact through expensive advertising does not produce an environmentally sound product. The centre of the 'green growth' illusion and much of the sustainablity argument is that it does. Just as there is (as yet) no such thing as a 'green' car so there is no such thing as 'green growth'. Vehicles with zero emissions, zero fuel consumption and virtually zero impact on pedestrians, cyclists and urban population densities might be 'green' but then we might as well have rediscovered the bicycle or feet. The introduction of 'clean' vehicles in California has not produced reductions in air pollution because gains from individual vehicle performances are rapidly negated by growth in the size of the total fleet. The switch to 'zero-emission' vehicles in California (ie electric vehicles) is, in effect, a transfer of pollution to the site of electricity generation and the final balance sheet for its pollution effects is far from clear.

Pearce et al (1989) are guilty of a technological optimism which is uninformed by social realities and the realities of interconnections in social and economic life. When they state that the environment might be integrated into capital investments and other decisions (p22) and use unleaded petrol as an example they overlook the overwhelming evidence that the car itself is a major environmental problem. It consumes vast amounts of energy in its manufacture, is used for only 5% of the time and when in use is occupied by an average of 1.2 people. It creates enormous problems of waste disposal which are particularly serious for tyres, exhaust systems and batteries, is manufactured and sold on the basis that it can and does break speed limits when average traffic speeds in many cities are much slower than 30mph, and initiates environmental damage on an enormous scale to provide itself with roads, car parks and artefacts to generate even more cars (eg out-of-town shopping centres). Many of these effects are documented in TEST (1991).

Measures of physical environmental impact, whilst important, do not convey the whole picture. Motorised transport has a serious effect on human health (chapter 6) including road traffic accidents, loss of independence for children and destruction of communities as a result of urban road construction. Child freedoms and child mobility have been severely curtailed by the growth in traffic and the perception of danger by parents (Hillman, Adams and Whitelegg, 1990). Children are now less likely to walk or cycle to school alone than at any time since the introduction of compulsory education and are accustomed to escorts and car journeys for everyday social and leisure activities. This deprivation of social and spatial learning experiences in their immediate neighbourhoods is a major change in child behaviour with implications for both health and development. It also adds to traffic volumes and pollution for journeys which can easily be made by non-motorised modes.

In Germany the rallying cry for motoring organisations in response to the threat of speed limit imposition on motorways has been 'Frei Fahrt fur frei Burger' (free travel for free citizens). There is no equivalent campaign for children's freedom. This is a measure of the degree to which the car can expect to consolidate its position and grow in importance and the degree to which land use patterns can develop to build in energy expensive and car-dependent structures (Owens, 1991). With this kind of ideological baggage there is no possibility of achieving sustainability and in this respect the car allows us to see through the illusion of the essentially consumerist 'green growth' argument and the political expediency of the 'green economy' propositions.

The car and the lorry are symbolic of the central problem of unsustainability. Their incorporation into behavioural and land use structures and their role in extending the daily commute, the trip to the shops and the area served by warehousing and distribution companies is at the core of understanding sustainability.

They represent consumption on a vast scale and this consumption is embedded in societal structures, land use structures and ideological structures which render it almost impregnable. It supports a global economy to serve its needs stretching from the oil wells of Kuwait to the tyre dumps of Ontario and the breakers' yards which adorn the rail and road routes into every city. It thrives on status and competition rather than co-operation and altruism and it is a potent image of economic progress and development that is desired as much by 100 million middle-class citizens of India as it is by poorer groups in the USA and those robbed of local goods and services by the mobility gains of car owners. The real problem of unsustainability is the future spread of German car-ownership levels (456 per 1000 people) or even worse, American (626 per 1000) to the citizens of Poland, Hungary, the former Soviet Union and then India and China. This process is now firmly underway amongst the 17 million inhabitants of the former territory of the German Democratic Republic and will not be contained within that small geographical area.

Transport, sustainability and the third world

There can be no understanding of sustainability at any level other than global. This means including the third world in all discussions of transport policy and the environmental impact of transport. This is necessary because transport is implicated in global environmental threats (chapter 2). More importantly most of the world's car manufacturing capacity is in the North whilst most future demand is likely to be in the South. Traditional concerns for jobs and economic growth in the North are likely to coincide with the release of suppressed demand in the South to increase dramatically the size of the world's vehicle population. Transport policies in the North that cannot conceive of a reduction in vehicle numbers, journey length or number of trips will reinforce the aspirations of third world countries and their elites for car ownership and use. Transport policies will increasingly come under scrutiny from an equity point of view and it will not be convincing to argue for less car dependency in the third world than exists in the developed world.

Presumably Europe could move towards sustainability based on the conversion of vehicles to biomass fuels (eg ethanol, methanol) supplied from Africa and South America. This would deliver some of the gains to be had from sustainability, for example cleaning up urban air quality, but it would do little for the source countries denied adequate land for food crops and forced back into the kind of survival behaviour which currently destroys fragile environments through overexploitation of forests or marginal agricultural land. Sustainability 'purchased' in this way might provide temporary relief to cities in Europe or North America but would represent a new kind of cash crop to be exported at enormously disadvantageous rates. The search for new ways of supporting our car based societies as in the Californian zero-emission vehicle programme involves shifting the problem elsewhere and continuing to exploit raw material resources. If sustainability is dealt with as a global problem then the full impact of transfers of waste, pollution or energy around the planet can be seen.

What then are our assumptions about third world countries, development and vehicle populations? Sustainability looks very silly if our assumption is that EC vehicle ownership and use norms are acceptable but not in the third world. Equally, sustainability is a nonsense if it depends on reducing emissions at a rate which is constantly overtaken by the growth in vehicle numbers. The small amount of smugness which creeps in when Europeans compare their population growth rates with India and Bangladesh rapidly evaporates if the calculation is done again for who consumes what share of what resources with what environmental impact. Whilst overworked as a metaphor it is nevertheless instructive to compare the impact of the US or German citizen with two or three cars and a battery of consumer durables with a resident of a third world country with no vehicle, no electricity and precious little cooking fuel and water.

Energy consumption is a basic measure of lifestyle and dependence on fossil fuels. It varies enormously between countries. If energy consumption is measured in gigajoules per person per annum the resultant values reveal very large inequalities (IUCN, UNEP, WWF, 1991):

Qatar	642	China	22
USA	280	India	8
Netherlands	213	Nigeria	5
Norway	199	Angola	3
UK	150	Bangladesh	2
Japan	110	Cambodia	1
Mexico	50	Nepal	1
Cuba	42		

Paradoxically many of the residents of these third world countries have been practising sustainable economics for several generations and operate at the very margins of survival. The low energy users in the above table have a much clearer title to any 'sustainability' label than do those at US or UK levels of consumption. They have very little, they use very little, they make hardly any contribution to global environmental problems and the damage they do cause (through the search for cooking fuels for example) is very much less than that of our fossil fuel economy. Nevertheless environmental damage on a large scale does take place. Population growth forces more intensive use of land and water resources and encroaches on more marginal environmentally sensitive land. According to Schramm and Warford (1989) 'poverty compels people to extract from the ever shrinking remaining natural resource base, destroying it in the process'. What Schramm and Warford do not point out is the degree to which land and water resources in the third world are exploited in support of the economy of the North and are therefore unavailable for local food and fuel production forcing the landless and the dispossessed to exploit land, water and fuel at a rate which would not occur if they owned their land and/or enjoyed the security of future use of that land. This point has been made in Buchanan (1967).

Poverty in the South is inextricably linked to the consumerist strategy of the North. Hypermobility in the North is neatly matched by chronic underprovision of basic accessibility in the South. The environmental, health, economic and social problems at both ends of the spectrum are linked by a chain of causality which is not challenged by sustainability. Sustainability means adjustments in lifestyles and structures to bring about a reduction in the consumption of the North and an increase in the consumption of the South. Transport is at the core of this process because it defines the spatial and temporal boundaries of production and consumption and has the potential to accelerate resource depletion and environmental degradation as in the Brazilian rainforest or support energy and resource conservation in environmentally nurturing circumstances as in cities geared to walking and cycling. The harnessing of this potential for environmental gain through land use and structural change has to be at the core of a 'post-sustainability' culture where global inequalities are tackled as a fundamental part of the transition to an environmentally and ecologically sound society. Such a society adds to the stock of resources by careful management of its inheritance, eliminates pollutants that damage human and plant health and nurtures communities and habitats to provide life enriching and socially equitable opportunities for all citizens (Berry, 1987).

Transportation in the third world illustrates some significant elements of what sustainability might encompass and what has traditionally been referred to as Alternative or Intermediate technology (Schumacher, 1973). The main element that could be described in these terms is the dependence on walking and cycling. Lowe (1989) has shown how bicycles contribute to sustainability particularly in third world countries.

The world population of bicycles numbers 800 million and outnumbers cars by two to one. Bicycles in Asia alone transport more people than all the world's cars do (Lowe, 1989). Domestic bike sales in China in 1987 reached 35 million which is higher than global car sales. With a global manufacturing output of more than 100 million each year the bicycle has enormous potential to reduce the number of motorised trips; yet it is under attack in China and in third world cities because of its unglamorous, underdeveloped image and its conflict with the car. Sustainable transport policies, especially if they are to cope with global circumstances and large population growths, need to embrace feet and pedals. The pay-off is very large indeed in terms of space requirements, energy requirements, health and pollution levels.

Bicycles and their pedal-powered variants (rickshaws, trishaws etc) can make up two-thirds of rush hour traffic in Asian cities and frequently double as freight carriers. In Bangladesh trishaws alone transport more freight than all motor vehicles combined (Lowe, 1989). In central Madyha Pradesh the city of Sagar is almost entirely supplied with milk by bicycle from an area with a radius of 25 miles around the city. If sustainability is a useful concept then it has to import examples of sustainable societies at work and translate the experience into policies for achieving stated objectives with reduced levels of energy consumption and motorisation. The third world provides many such examples in transport.

2 GLOBAL WARMING

The discussion surrounding global warming and the emission of greenhouse gases undoubtedly figures prominently in the catalogue of global environmental problems. It has all the ingredients which make environmental problems so intractable and yet so important and it has at its core the concept of sustainability. According to IUCN, UNEP, WWF (1991), climate change induced by the addition of greenhouse gases to the atmosphere is one of the greatest threats to sustainability.

Global warming brings its discussants face to face with the uncomfortable reality that there may be physical limits to the extent to which we can continue to consume. In the case of global warming the physical reality is represented by an increase in average global temperatures as a result of greenhouse gas emissions (principally CO_2, CH_4, N_2O, CFC-11, CFC-12 and HCF-22). These emissions originate in a number of different human activities but transport is a significant source if only for the high growth rates implied in car and lorry forecasts over the next twenty-five years.

Global warming as a scientific debate centres on the link between increasing levels of greenhouse gases in the atmosphere and raised average temperatures. Energy from incoming solar radiation reaches the earth but less is radiated into space than is received because of the 'blanket' of greenhouse gases which keep the heat in. The result is rising temperatures and a fierce debate about the correlation between increasingly high concentrations of CO_2 and temperature and the possibility that any observed changes are nothing more than naturally occurring long term variations in climate (Houghton and Woodwell, 1989).

Whilst carbon dioxide contributes over half of the global warming effect the so-called regulated pollutants (nitrogen oxides, hydrocarbons and carbon monoxide) are also implicated. Nitrogen oxides and hydrocarbons react in strong sunlight to form photochemical smog of which ozone is a major constituent. This ground level ozone besides being a serious health hazard also contributes to global warming. Carbon monoxide at high concentrations reduces levels of hydroxyl radicals. The latter oxidise methane molecules in the atmosphere so that high levels of CO lead indirectly to an increase in methane which is a powerful

Table 2.1 Key data: greenhouse gases

	Carbon dioxide	Methane	Nitrous oxide	CFCs 11/12	HCFC 22
Concentration (1750–1800)	280 ppm‡	0.8 ppm‡	288 ppb‡	0	0
Concentration (current)	353 ppm‡	1.72 ppm‡	310 ppb‡	280/484 ppt‡	?
Rate of increase per year	0.5%	0.9%	0.25%	4%	?
Lifetime (100 years)*	50–200	10	150	65/130	25
Global Warming Potential†	1	21	290	3500/7300	1500
% Contribution to Global Warming	55%	15%	6%	17%	?

Notes: * The effects of a gas on climate have to be considered over various timescales – 20, 100 and 500 years – to understand both short term and cumulative effects.
† The concept of Global Warming Potential is a measure of the relative heat-trapping strength (and hence the potential climate effects of equal emissions of each of the gases, compared to carbon dioxide).
‡ ppm = parts per million; ppb = parts per billion; ppt = parts per trillion.
Source: Friends of the Earth (1991a)

greenhouse gas. Some key data on greenhouse gases are presented in table 2.1.

The science of global warming is well explained in a number of different sources (eg IPCC, 1990) but is plagued by a degree of uncertainty (as is all forecasting) and by the unacceptability (particularly to the USA) of the implications of reducing greenhouse gas emissions. Reductions of the magnitude asked for by the Intergovernmental Panel on Climatic Change (IPCC) will involve changes in lifestyle that go far beyond technological solutions. At the international level the debate focuses on competitiveness within the developed world. Is it reasonable for the EC to impose a carbon tax to reduce emissions if this penalises EC industry to the relative advantage of the US and Japan? The debate also highlights North–South differences. Is it reasonable to invite third world countries to reduce their emissions when they are struggling to improve their standards of living? Should third world countries be invited to stop the exploitation of forests to reduce CO_2 emissions when this natural resource is one of the few ways they might have to reduce indebtedness?

The global warming debate is a scientific debate where uncertainty is being exploited to serve sectional interests and where the implications of a 'business as usual' projection are potentially so damaging. The debate also illustrates very clearly that sustainability is seriously compromised given the severity of the result if forecast temperature rises do happen.

It is also a debate where transport issues are brought very sharply into focus. Forecast growth rates for car ownership and use and lorry activity (Group Transport 2000 plus) indicate growth rates of 1000% in Eastern Europe, 500% in Southern Europe and 83–142% in Britain. There is no possibility whatsoever that any targets for stabilising let alone reducing CO_2 emissions can be achieved against these increases in vehicle numbers and activity.

In its turn transport makes the link between the scientific, esoteric nature of the debate and its roots in how we organise daily life, arrange land uses, fund our public transport, encourage people to walk and cycle and create healthy cities which are not dominated by the internal combustion engine. The growth rates which will ensure that no solution is found to global warming are rooted in a conception of spatial organisation and consumption which is greedy for resources, greedy for space and unable to cope with its own waste (ie unsustainable). If the organisational problems which underpin the movement of people and goods in European cities cannot be resolved at low levels of energy use and emissions and high levels of collective transport, walking and cycling then the fundamental problems of global warming cannot be resolved. A solution to global warming is a solution to the problem of hyperconsumption and non-sustainability.

The scientific background

Activity on the subject of global warming is impressive. Much of this has been orchestrated by the Intergovernmental Panel on Climatic Change (IPCC) which was created by the World Meteorological Organisation and the United Nations Environment Programme in 1988. It reported in the summer of 1990 and was followed by the Second World Climate Conference in Switzerland in November 1990. At the national level equally impressive programmes have been mounted most notably that of the Germans in the Bundestag's 'Enquete Kommission'.

The IPCC conclusions are important for the discussion which follows about transport and greenhouse gases. They calculated with certainty that:

1   there is a natural greenhouse effect which already keeps the earth warmer than it would otherwise be;

2 emissions resulting from human activities are substantially increasing the atmospheric concentrations of the greenhouse gases: carbon dioxide, methane, chlorofluorcarbons (CFCs) and nitrous oxide;
3 this will result in average additional warming of the earth's surface. The main greenhouse gas, water vapour, will increase in response to the global warming and enhance it.

The IPCC calculated with confidence that:

1 carbon dioxiode has been responsible for over half the enhanced greenhouse effect in the past and is likely to remain so in the future;
2 the long-lived gases (CO_2, N_2O, CFCs) would require immediate reductions in emissions from human activities of over 60% to stabilise their concentrations at 1991 levels; methane would require a 15–20% reduction.

Based on current models the IPCC predicts:

1 under the IPCC business-as-usual scenario emissions of greenhouse gases a rate of increase of global mean temperature during the next century of about 0.3°C per decade (with an uncertainty range of 0.2 to 0.5°C per decade. This is greater than that seen over the last 10000 years);
2 this will result in a likely increase in global mean temperature of about 1°C above the present value by 2025 and 3°C before the end of the next century.

Global mean surface air temperature has increased by 0.3–0.6°C over the last 100 years with the five global average warmest years being in the 1980s. Global sea levels have risen in the same period by 10–20cm. Schneider (1990) calculates that the rate of global average temperature rise will be around 10–100 times faster than occurred in the glacial–interglacial transition around 10000 years ago. Rises in sea level of between 10–30cm (best guess 20) by the year 2030 and 30–100cm (best guess 65) by the end of the next century seem likely. This increase is 2–6 times more rapid than the historic rise over the last century and will, according to the IPCC, pose serious problems for the low lying nations and coastal zones.

Some of the more serious implications of the sea level changes predicted over the next 100 years are listed by IPCC. Such changes are likely to:

• displace populations
• destroy low lying urban infrastructure

- inundate arable lands
- contaminate fresh water supplies
- bring recession of shorelines and wetlands
- increase tidal ranges
- spread north vector-borne diseases such as malaria, schistosomiasis, leishmaniasis, dengue and Japanese encephalitis.

Impact of climatic change on Europe

The proper context in which to consider Europe is its disproportionately large impact (in terms of its share of world population) on global emissions. This will be dealt with later when emissions from the transport sector are considered in detail. Nevertheless, Europe will be affected by rising temperatures and sea levels with consequent impacts on growing seasons, crops that can be grown and the risks from unstable weather systems (eg storms). Some of these impacts have been mapped by the 'Sustainable Development of the Biosphere' programme (Climate Network Europe, 1991) at the International Institute for Applied Systems Analysis in Vienna and dealt with more fully in a UK report *The Potential Effects of Climate Change in the UK* (Department of the Environment, 1991). For Europe there is a potential for the northern crop boundaries to shift 5–7 degrees in a northerly direction and an associated limitation on crop growth in parts of the Mediterranean with the southern boundary also shifting 3–5 degrees north.

The prospect of vineyards in southern England should not cloud the ecological realities of changes at the pace predicted by the global warming debate. It is not a case of 'winners' and 'losers' as the maps of what crops can be grown where might infer. Huntley (1990) shows that the 'best-guess' predictions of the IPCC herald ecological catastrophe. Before the end of the last ice age, around 10000 years ago, the world's average surface temperature rose by about 5°C, but it did so over several thousand years not the 100 years or less that it will do in the 'business as usual' scenario of IPCC predictions.

Huntley shows that powerful positive feedback mechanisms exist resulting from the release of methane at high latitudes (methane is thirty times more effective as a greenhouse gas than is carbon dioxide). These feedback mechanisms will accelerate global warming and the problem will be exacerbated by the reduced ability of warmer seas to absorb CO_2. Huntley concludes:

> The consequences for ecosystems and organisms of the rates of climatic change forecast for the next 60 years are extremely severe. If we continue down this path then we are almost certain to be unable to stop there, and the whole

biosphere may be threatened when, during the 22nd century, climates unlike anything since the Cretaceous or before (more than 100 million years ago) seem likely to develop.

Huntley is not the only researcher to sound such a clear warning. The scale of the problem illustrates clearly the central relevance of the precautionary principle which is itself just another way of addressing sustainability issues. The precautionary principle invites us to take a rather more serious view of the kind of scenario pictured by Huntley than a 'pure' scientific assessment of the probabilities might suggest. The reason is that the consequences of taking the predictions seriously when they turn out to be wrong are so much less grave than the consequences of ignoring them when they turn out to be right. There are, of course, degrees of right and wrong but to adopt a 'wait and see' policy in such an uncertain situation carries considerable risks.

Exercise of the precautionary principle would produce a set of objectives, and costed measures to help achieve them which could be pursued in the absence of clear scientific proof that temperatures or sea levels would rise or species become extinct.

Adoption of the precautionary principle is recommended by the World Conservation Union (IUCN), the United Nations Environment Programme (UNEP) and the World Wide Fund for Nature (WWF) (IUCN, UNEP, WWF, 1991). The report recommends that all high and medium energy countries commit themselves to a reduction of carbon dioxide emissions by at least 20% from 1990 levels, rising to 70% by 2030.

Global warming: contributory sources and sectoral responsibility

The relative contribution of different gases to global warming can be seen in fig 2.1. It can be seen that carbon dioxide contributes about 50% of the global warming effect. Transport accounts for significant proportions of more than one greenhouse gas. The sectoral contribution to carbon dioxide emissions is shown in fig 2.2. Transport accounts for more than 20% of UK carbon dioxide with the bulk of this coming from road transport. Aircraft at 3.3% is another important contributor and, like road transport, is anticipating a great deal of growth. Air travel in passenger kilometres is expected to increase by nearly 400% during the period 1990 to 2020 (WWF, 1991), adding considerably to the tally of global emissions from transport. In the case of air transport there are several unresolved issues about the scale of the contribution to global warming. The full global warming effect attributable to aircraft has to take account of the high level injection of NO_x into the atmosphere. The global warming potential of high altitude NO_x is estimated to be

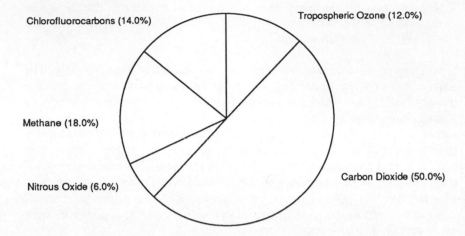

Figure 2.1   Contributions of different gases to global warming
Source: ERR (1989)

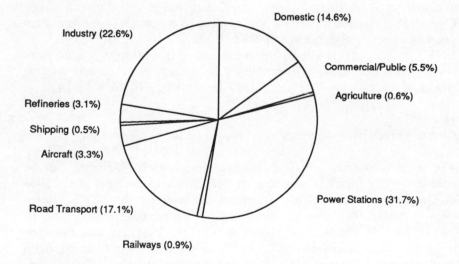

Figure 2.2   Carbon dioxide emissions by source, 1988
Source: ERR (1990)

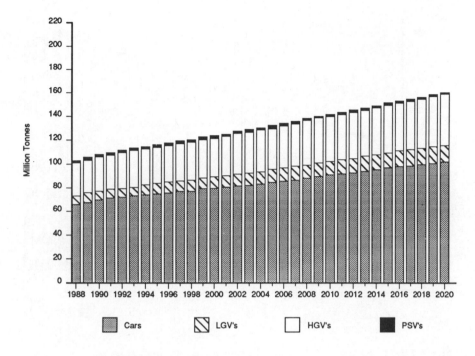

Figure 2.3 Road transport carbon dioxide emissions: low forecast

Source: ERR (1989)

about fifty times that of ground level NO_x (WWF, 1991 quoting Johnson and Henshaw, 1991). When this NO_x factor is added to known emissions of CO_2 then aircraft emissions contribute between 28% over 20 years and 4.5% over 500 years of the total global warming effect. Further uncertainties related to the destruction of ozone at very high altitudes and the effects of water emissions on cloud formation could raise this percentage.

The relative contribution of different modes of transport to total transport emissions is described in ERR (1989). In figs 2.3 and 2.4 road transport carbon dioxide emissions are run forward to 2020 simply on the basis of the national road traffic forecasts (UK). Both the low forecast (fig 2.3) and the high forecast (fig 2.4) show steep increases in CO_2 emissions. These exceed current use by between 60% (low forecast) and 110% (high forecast) and offer no possibility at all of meeting the Toronto conference central target of an initial reduction in overall CO_2 emission rates of 20% by 2005 (World Climate Programme 1988 quoted in ERR, 1990). Total transport carbon dioxide emissions are shown in

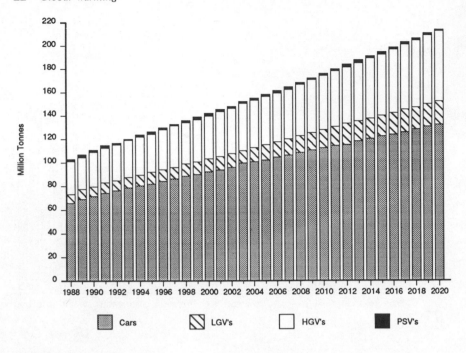

Figure 2.4   Road transport carbon dioxide emissions: high forecast

Source: ERR (1989)

fig 2.5 clearly illustrating the rise in emissions from road transport and the increasing significance of air transport.

The forecasts show that technology in the form of catalytic converters or in improved fuel consumption will not solve the problem. The growth in vehicle numbers, length of journey and number of journeys coupled with the decline in average vehicle occupancy and increases in congestion in urban areas will ensure that emissions continue to rise. This same point applies to many other environmental impacts of transport especially air pollution and its health damaging aspects. These are dealt with in a subsequent chapter.

Global carbon dioxide emissions from cars are shown in fig 2.6. Walsh (1990) predicts a growth in global vehicle population to 1 billion by 2020 or 2025 and sees the possibility of a flattening of the growth in CO_2 under the following conditions:

- lowering growth in vehicle miles travelled
- improving fuel efficiency by 2% pa (not currently achieved) – in fact it is deteriorating according to Walsh (p143))

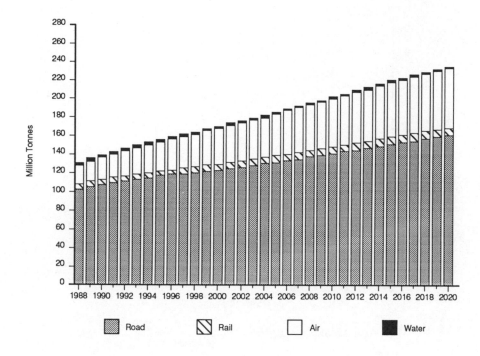

Figure 2.5 All transport carbon dioxide emissions

Source: ERR (1989)

- cutting vehicle population growth rate down to around 2% pa
- having 2% of vehicles go over to fuel cell technology and then to increase this figure by 2% pa.

He does not address the subject of how exactly we might bring about a reduction in vehicle numbers or journey length. He does, however, make the link between reducing CO_2 and reducing other pollutants (CO, NO_x, HC) and thereby makes a fundamental connection between the whole global warming debate and how to create better living environments, sustainable transport policies and a society which conserves finite resources and emphasises social and community objectives more than it does the pursuit of speed, mobility and privatised consumption.

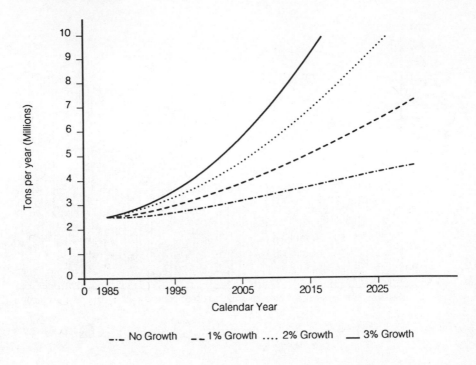

Figure 2.6 Global carbon dioxide emissions from cars under different growth rates

Source: WWF (1990)

How can CO₂ emissions from the transport sector be reduced?

One clear definition of sustainability is the attainment of IPCC recommended goals for reducing carbon dioxide emissions. Clearly this is an international and a multi-sectoral problem but progress in the transport sector is the most urgent priority because of the large growth potential of carbon dioxide emissions from that sector. Cuts in CO_2 emissions of over 60% would be necessary to stabilise 1992 concentrations in the atmosphere at pre-industrial levels. The conclusion of an ERR (1990) report on measures to reduce CO_2 emissions was that UK emissions could be reduced by 20% of the 1988 level by 2005 by a combination of measures, but even reductions of this magnitude would be insufficient to counteract the growth in fuel use by commercial vehicles. Britain, therefore cannot meet the target set by the Toronto conference of a 20% reduction in overall CO_2 rates by 2005.

Contributions to a reduction in carbon dioxide emissions can come from several sources though there is a preference in most discussions for technological solutions rather than for lifestyle/behavioural changes (including more intensive use of transport modes with low or zero CO_2 emissions) or land use solutions. The main sources are:

- fuel economy
- alternative fuels including diesel
- reduced engine size and power
- electric vehicles
- transferring journeys to a mode which produces less CO_2
- land use and other changes to shorten journey length
- substitution measures to allow journeys to be foregone
- speed limitation
- traffic management and traffic calming
- 'civilising' the lorry and transferring freight from road to combined transport.

There is a clear distinction here between the technical fix solutions and those solutions which tackle the problem more fundamentally. In this chapter only the technical solutions are reviewed and implicit in this approach is that they will leave a massive deficit which has to be picked up elsewhere, ie in the land use/alternative mode dimension. This is also the conclusion of Hughes (1992) for passenger transport in the UK.

Technical solutions have very little to offer when faced with a doubling of traffic volumes over the next twenty years. The most promising areas for intervention are land use changes to reduce the demand for travel itself and a switch to walking, cycling and collective modes of transport. A realistic target for modal split for journeys of up to 10km in length is 50% by bike/collective and walk (BCW) and 50% by car. Fiscal and economic incentives are also important in the achievement of these goals and these are discussed in chapter 7.

Fuel consumption

Fuel consumption is closely related to engine size. A two litre petrol engine typically uses nearly 50% more fuel than a one litre one. Fleet composition, therefore, is going to exert a direct influence on CO_2 emissions. Fiscal and structural factors such as the UK company car system or travel expense claims which reward owners of bigger engined cars will lead to more CO_2 production. Figure 2.7 shows the relationship between fuel consumption and engine capacity.

Average fuel consumption of petrol vehicles has fallen over the last twenty years. In 1970 10.84 litres were needed to drive 100km and in

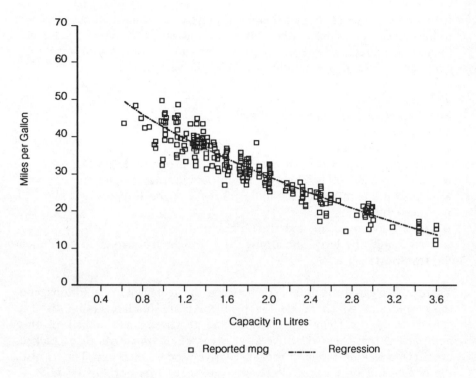

Figure 2.7   Average car fuel consumption against engine capacity

Source: ERR (1990)

1988 9.49 litres for the same distance (Waters, 1990, p21). In the case of heavy goods vehicles fuel consumption has deteriorated. In 1970 26.4 litres were needed for a journey of 100km and in 1988, 35.6 litres. Per vehicle fuel consumption increased by 15% between 1981 and 1986 (ibid, p24). The deterioration is not quite so marked when tonne-km are used as the metric instead of distance alone.

Engine size can be influenced by taxation as already happens in Denmark, Germany and The Netherlands though improvements through smaller engined vehicles can easily be swamped by other market trends such as the preference for pick-up trucks, commercial all-terrain vehicles and their domestic equivalents. Renner (1988) quotes the example of the rising popularity of light trucks as a reason for the limited potential of future efficiency gains. They remain one-third less fuel-efficient than new US passenger cars.

Speed is an important determinant of emissions of all kinds as can be seen in figure 2.8. Speed is easily influenced by both regulation and

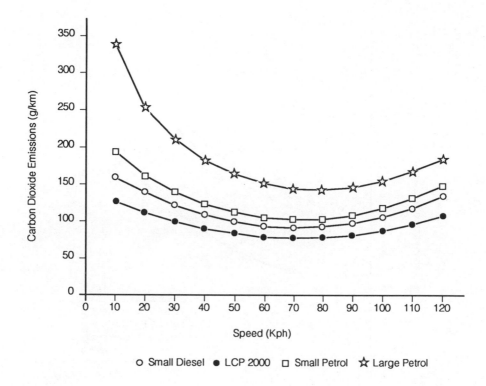

Figure 2.8 Carbon dioxide emission characteristics of a range of car types
Source: ERR (1990)

enforcement on the road and by design in the manufacturing process. The fact that speed limits are routinely broken and some cars manufactured with speed capabilities more appropriate to racing tracks than to the roads typically used is an indication of the lack of commitment to finding solutions to global warming (and other problems). ERR (1990) sum up the design issue thus: 'In all car classes there has been a tendency in recent years to use new technology, which could have been used to improve fuel consumption, to increase the power output and hence performance characteristics of new vehicles.'

Diesel versus petrol

Diesel engines have many advantages over petrol engines in terms of fuel consumption and hence CO_2 emissions. These are illustrated in fig 2.9.

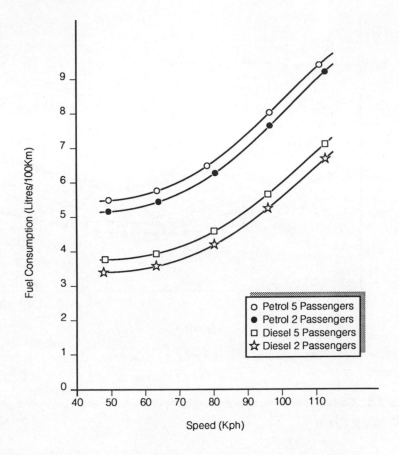

Figure 2.9   Diesel and petrol-engined cars and fuel consumption
Source: Waters (1990)

The diesel engine performs better when running at less than maximum power output and thus is better suited to normal traffic conditions. In a Transport and Road Research Laboratory (TRRL) test over the same distance and conditions of a petrol and a diesel VW Golf car the diesel car saved at least 24% of fuel by volume under all conditions and in densely trafficked areas the saving was 40% (Waters, 1990, p28). This conclusion appears valid even taking into account the comments in ERR (1990) about the higher energy content of diesel fuels per unit of volume.

A switch to diesel engines would seem to offer some benefits for reducing emissions of CO_2 but these would have to be set against what is known about carcinogenic emissions of particulates from diesel engines and the sulphur dioxide they produce. A further point made by Waters is that changes in refinery practice would have to take place if the diesel fleet rose to about 30% (in 1988 diesel cars were about 2% of the fleet). These changes would cancel out some of the gains as would the continued rise in vehicle numbers whether diesel or petrol.

Changes in fuel consumption by either a switch to diesel or downward pressure on engine size would seem to have the effect of buying time. Neither is in fact a solution if all other developments in society continue to reinforce the need to use the car for daily trips and to travel over distances which grow longer each year. A more sensible strategy might well be to use such windows of opportunity to buy time whilst putting in motion longer term strategies to tackle modal split and the propensity to travel.

A number of other issues of relevance to reduced fuel consumption and CO_2 emissions are discussed in the technical literature (eg Waters. 1990). These are not discussed in any detail here but include:

- mass/weight of vehicles and new materials to reduce weight
- rolling resistance/tyre design
- aerodynamic drag (including the effects of crosswinds)
- matching of engine and transmission for economy
- improved engine tuning.

Alternative fuels

Alternative fuels have an attraction which goes beyond global warming issues. Military and security concerns figure significantly as they have done in South Africa for many years and these interests are closely inter-related with the desire to dampen down the price increases of oil suppliers. South Africa's interest in producing transport fuels from coal deposits is a response to perceived threats from the global community but is not too dissimilar from the interest shown in other countries in alternative fuels. An interest in alcohol fuels is particularly evident in the United States and well tested in Brazil. In the US corporate fuel economy standards are relaxed for dual-use vehicles or those which can use 85% ethanol or methanol. Several US states have included alternative fuel programmes in their efforts to reduce carbon monoxide pollution and meet Clean Air Act standards. California has taken the lead on pure methanol and hopes to replace 30% of gasoline consumption with methanol in areas violating federal air pollution standards (Renner, 1988). The South Coast Air Quality Management District covering Los Angeles is in the process of establishing a regulation that requires businesses with passenger, medium-duty and light-duty vehicle fleets to

Table 2.2   Specific heat output and carbon dioxide emissions at point of use: various fuels

Fuel	Chemical formula	Gross cal. value MJ/kg	CO_2 (kg/kg)	CO_2 (kg/MJ)
Coal	70% $CH_{0.5}$	24	2.50	0.104
Petrol/derv	$CH_{1.8}$	43	3.19	0.074
Ethanol	C_2H_5OH	27	1.91	0.071
Methanol	CH_3OH	20	1.38	0.069
Propane (LPG)	C_3H_8	48	3.00	0.063
Natural gas	CH_4	53	2.75	0.052
Hydrogen	H_2	135	0.00	0.000

Source: Waters (1990)

switch from fossil fuels to clean fuels such as methanol, compressed natural gas, reformulated gasoline, electricity or fuel cells (Lents, 1990).

The Los Angeles programme detailed by Lents does not tackle global warming directly and is aimed at improving air quality. Attempts to reduce commuting by setting vehicle occupancy standards (ten vehicles to carry fifteen people to work) will help as will compressing the working week into four ten-hour days and telecommuting; but these are currently of very minor significance. Table 2.2 shows the CO_2 producing capabilities of different fuels.

A clear hierarchy exists in terms of CO_2 production at point of use. The table does not reflect what happens at the refinery. Interestingly in the context of California the results for ethanol, methanol and propane do not have such a great advantage over petrol that the case for using them is strong enough to justify the switch.

It is possible to summarise the potential for reducing CO_2 emissions from road transport (see Table 2.3). The data in this table need careful interpretation. The consequences of switching agricultural output over to bio-fuels could be very grave indeed for food production, especially for the poor, and a 'petrol instead of food' campaign to support high levels of car ownership would not engender social harmony in those areas affected. Similarly hydrogen fuels or electricity for vehicles from non-fossil fuel sources will not be problem free. Either it will excite another wave of nuclear power station construction with all the risks involved in following that route or it will stimulate a new industry with new chemicals and new processes each with their own associated hazards.

A major problem with the search for new fuels is the enormous enthusiasm with which the holy grail of the ultimate answer is sought.

Table 2.3 Potential for reducing carbon dioxide emissions from road transport

Action	Resulting reduced emissions per vehicle	
Diesel for petrol	up to 30%	
Gas for all vehicles	up to 45%	
Bio-alcohol for cars	100%	If electricity from non-fossil sources
Hydrogen for all vehicles	100%	
Electric vehicles	100%	

Source: Waters (1990)

Alcohol fuels produce their own carcinogenic compounds and are not a solution to the space hungry, community destructive impacts of hyper-motorisation. Most alternative fuels will eventually involve the recalculation of both health risks and environmental impacts arising from the rare metals used in the manufacture of the next generation of photo-voltaic cells or their attributable share of caesium, polonium or other radio-nuclides in the environment which will be generated by the commuter journey in a 'clean' car. Such recalculations are already underway for the catalytic converter (Nieper, 1991) and there are problems.

Holy grails can be elusive and may involve a search fraught with dangers and surprises. The catalytic converter offers impressive reductions in CO and NO_x (up to 90%) but produces an increase in CO_2 emissions. This increase is acknowledged by Kuck (1990) and is quantified by ERR (1990). The introduction of catalytic converters brings with it a fuel consumption penalty of 9% which can be converted exactly into an extra 9% production of carbon dioxide. Taken together with the other problems of catalytic converters some caution is advisable with this technology. These other problems include low efficiency at low temperatures (ie on short journeys characteristic of urban areas), uncertainty about efficient operation over the life of the vehicle, disposal of the used product and health effects of the rare metals in the catalyst itself. Nieper (1991) estimates that every car fitted with a catalytic converter emits 5×10^{13} atoms of platinum per mile. These become dangerous free radicals on inhalation.

Electric vehicles

The technology for switching vehicles from diesel and petrol to electric (battery) sources is available and is fully described in Albrecht and Huss (1990). The case for electric cars depends on producing the electricity without fossil fuels and the points made earlier concerning hazards associated with the nuclear fuel cycle need careful consideration. It is possible to make a case for solving local air pollution problems (eg in Los Angeles) by switching the emissions to the place where the electricity is generated but this case cannot be made for reducing carbon dioxide emissions which will add to the global inventory regardless of where they are released. A full balance sheet of all aspects of energy consumption and emissions of electric vehicle technology has not yet been drawn up and it is unlikely that battery powered vehicles can help reduce carbon dioxide emissions.

MacKenzie and Walsh (1990) argue that if electric vehicles are charged by electricity from the expected mix of coal, oil, gas, nuclear and hydro plant in the year 2000, greenhouse gas emissions per mile driven would fall by 25%. In the longer term, they claim, emissions could be reduced to zero by recharging the batteries using either renewable electricity sources or nuclear power plants. No figures are produced to support the 25% reduction claim.

The Los Angeles Department of Water and Power along with Southern California Edison have ordered 10000 hybrid electric vehicles to be on the road by 1995. These vehicles will be battery powered (range sixty miles) and will have petrol engines to charge the batteries for longer trips. This plan will provide much needed operational experience of this technology. The California Air Resources Board has also adopted regulations that will require 10% of all new vehicles to have zero emissions by 2003. This condition can only be met by electric vehicles though the question of carbon dioxide emissions has not been addressed.

What then is the answer to the problem of carbon dioxide emissions from the transport sector? The California experience described by Lents (1990) and by MacKenzie and Walsh (1990) shows that in spite of widespread dissemination of environmentally sound technology the air quality in California has declined over the last twenty years and now fails to meet federal quality standards. New technologies will not solve the problems created by the rising demand for movement over longer distances in space and resource consuming vehicles. If this is the case for CO and NO_x the situation for greenhouse gases is even more intractable.

ERR (1990) have estimated CO_2 reductions from a variety of different measures (see fig 2.10):

• Lower speed limits will produce reductions in fuel use and hence in CO_2; eg a strictly enforced limit of 70mph will reduce total car fuel consumption by 2.4%; 60mph by 4.4% and 50mph by 5.8%.

• Removal of artificial incentives to the ownership and use of company cars which encourage larger engines and extra distance travelled will save 8.5% of annual emissions from cars and taxis.

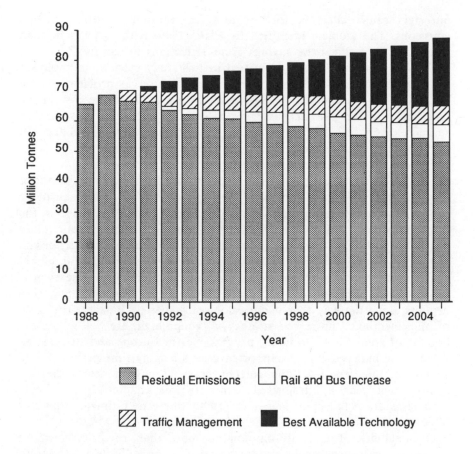

Figure 2.10 Projected carbon dioxide emission reductions from passenger cars
Source: ERR (1990)

- Vehicle efficiency improvements could yield an emission reduction of 25%.
- Traffic management in cities could produce a reduction of 2.5% of national emissions from cars.
- Improvements in public transport to bring about a modal shift could yield a 15% reduction in total car emissions.

The combined effect of all the measures is to reduce UK emissions of carbon dioxide from car travel to 52 million tonnes in 2005 which would be a 20% reduction from 1988 levels. This is based on the low forecast of increased travel by car but whilst a step in the right direction, does not significantly alter the total picture for transport's carbon dioxide emissions. The problem identified by ERR (1990) is the growth in road freight which swamps the savings from reductions in car traffic.

The full range of savings identified in this study even when based on the low traffic forecast do not solve the greenhouse gas problem for the UK. The low forecast may well be exceeded as has been the case in the past and the increase in passenger kilometres occasioned by further spatial changes to extend distances between the things we travel for will also produce increases in fuel use and CO_2.

There is no sign of sustainability in the transport sector even when all the possibilities associated with technology and improvements in public transport are taken into account. The gap between savings that can be produced in a very crude status quo situation and what is needed in the transport sector (ie a 60% saving) is just too big. Clearly sustainability has to be pushed in other directions to yield the necessary reductions in CO_2. This means invoking the 'no regret' principle of eliminating global warming whereby we set out to get the emissions down because even if the predicted disasters do not come about there are so many other benefits along the way that it does not really matter. Further, the costs of implementing a 'no regret' strategy, although high, are well within the bounds of comparable spending programmes in Europe and the US (eg the defence budget), can be supported over a lengthy time period (10–50 years) and are less than the current costs of environmental damage caused each year by motorised transport (see chapter 7). The cost arguments are detailed in Schneider (1990) where he estimates that $10 billion pa is sufficient.

Sustainability, if it is to amount to more than rhetoric, must be associated with clear goals and measures that have some potential to achieve those goals. This is not the case with the European Commission (EC) pronouncements on sustainability (EC, 1992a). The EC has invoked the rhetoric of sustainability at the same time as advocating the construction of 12500km of new motorway standard roads (costed at 130 billion ECUs) in Europe (EC, 1992b) and without any evaluation of alternative strategies to solve transport problems. The publication of road plans in advance of a major White Paper on transport policy (EC, 1992c) is further evidence of a clear disregard for environmental issues and the transformation of sustainability into an argument to support traditional policies.

If sustainability is to have any meaning it must operate as a filter in the policy making processes of national and supra-national agencies. If a policy or set of activities increases land take, emissions or the demand for transport it is not sustainable. Sustainability as an operational target is likely to emerge from a programme of activities across every aspect of daily life that recasts those activities in a low/zero polluting and energy use context.

Operational sustainability will require a fast track evolution of organisational and decision making structures so that they can respond to concerns about finite resources, pollution and social harmony. Transport's traditional links with economic development arguments, mobility and the need to connect peripheral regions with the core and fill 'missing gaps' represents a culture of non-sustainability that is not challenged by simply using the word as in the EC's policy statement on sustainable mobility (EC, 1992a).

In transport the main challenge is to move to lower levels of dependence on motorised transport through changes in the land use planning system and a shortening of journey lengths. Technological solutions are still based on the assumption that mobility is sustainable and the rise in vehicle use is sustainable as long as fuel efficiency is improved. This is a fundamental misunderstanding of the total impact of motorisation on society. Greenhouse gas emissions show this very clearly. The technology is not addressing the problem.

Sustainable solutions will involve the redesign of cities so that walking and cycling are feasible and enjoyable and where high quality public transport satisfies the bulk of journey purposes not carried out by bicycle or on foot. Sustainability has the capacity to deliver high quality urban environments at the same time as meeting the most stringent international targets on greenhouse gas reductions. Current policies with a sustainability tinge do not have this capacity. Passenger transport that can out-perform the car and deliver a good environment is achievable. Freight problems have to be tackled by steering the processes which produce more tonne-km in the reverse direction and utilising those modes which perform best on energy, land use, accident, pollution and CO_2 criteria. This means less space for roads and more for rail and combined transport and it means that the rampant use of space and resources to feed an exploding European industrial-distribution system will have to be made very costly indeed.

3 AIR POLLUTION

Air pollution from motor vehicle exhaust emissions is a major health hazard and in combination with other environmental problems an important policy issue for cities in Europe. The World Health Organisation (WHO) considers that vehicle emissions are responsible for a substantial proportion of air pollution, particularly near busy city streets (WHO, 1990).

The toxic materials listed by WHO are carbon monoxide, nitrous oxides, lead, formaldehyde, benzene, pyrene and soot. The levels at which these pollutants are found in cities frequently exceed EC or WHO guidelines. A survey of nitrogen dioxide carried out in Edinburgh (Edinburgh District Council, 1991) found levels that exceeded EC guideline values at thirteen of the fourteen sites where measurements were made. Three of these thirteen 'failures' exceeded the mandatory limit value of $200\mu g/m^{-3}$ (see below for discussion of limit and guideline values). This remarkable finding confirms the severity of the air pollution problem in European cities and the role of motorised transport in elevating levels of pollution. It is only the lack of monitoring effort of the kind mounted by the city of Edinburgh that has encouraged a lack of interest on the part of public health bodies and a pursuit of transport policies that have brought larger numbers of vehicles into city centres. Transport policies in Reading and Lancaster (both in the UK) have been based on support for new roads in or near the centre of those cities. This pattern is reproduced throughout Europe.

It is quite clear that air pollution related to motor vehicles is increasing at a time when that from other sources, particularly domestic coal fires and industry, is declining. It is possible to make estimates of the share of total pollution which is attributable to transport. The information in table 3.1 shows that transport is a major pollutant. The contribution of the transport sector to total emissions of air pollutants is higher than in the past and high compared with the contribution from other sectors (OECD, 1991).

The percentages quoted in table 3.1 are averages over large geographical areas; local levels of air pollution from vehicles may be higher still. Transport emissions also include a number of less well known

Table 3.1 Transport's share of total pollution (%)

	France	UK	Germany	OECD Europe
NO_x	76	49	65	60
CO	71	86	74	78
HC	60	32	53	50
SO_x	10	2	6	4

Source: OECD (1991), p217

pollutants including heavy metals, asbestos and benzene, and ozone should also properly be regarded as a pollutant largely resulting from motor vehicle exhaust emissions. The transport sector accounts for 80% of all benzene emissions (OECD, 1991, p207) and benzene is a recognised carcinogen.

Both the WHO (1990, p122) and the OECD (1991, p219) recognise that the scale of air pollution from motor vehicles is unacceptably high. The OECD statement is couched in terms of sustainability and the WHO statement in terms of public health standards. The present arrangement is not sustainable and will only become so if transport and environmental policies are better integrated. This means (OECD, 1991, p219):

- some containment of the growth of traffic demand particularly for road transport
- adjustments in sectoral structures (increasing the share of the more environmentally friendly modes and adapting fiscal charges on vehicles, fuels, and the use of vehicles)
- technological progress in the short and long term to achieve quiet, clean and energy efficient vehicles
- developing a sound economic approach based on the polluter pays principle, reducing overall subsidies and eliminating charges and taxes inconsistent with environmental and economic efficiency
- rigorous implementation of the legislation and measures adopted.

The implication of the WHO statement is that the current pattern of transport organisation is not delivering adequate health safeguards to those alive now, let alone future generations. Whilst the health issues are very difficult to translate into sustainability objectives (see chapter 6) it is clear that air pollution is of such serious proportions that it threatens existing populations whereas sustainability debates normally concern the rights of future generations to enjoy those things which we currently enjoy.

The juxtaposition of forecasts of future vehicle numbers, existing failures to meet (not very demanding) EC guideline values for air pollutants, studies relating measures of poor health to rising traffic numbers (see chapter 6) and the advisability of reducing traffic volumes for a large number of other reasons (noise, global warming, children's freedom etc) indicate a very serious state of non-sustainability and an urgent need to steer the transportation system towards a more environmentally sound structure.

At the very least the achievement of sustainability in air pollution involves three things:

1   carbon dioxide reductions of 60% as detailed in chapter 2;
2   achievement of the WHO objective (Target 21: Control of Air Pollution) which states that all people of the region (Europe) should be effectively protected against recognised health risks from air pollution;
3   the adoption of the OECD package, especially containment of growth and adjustments in sectoral structures (ie a shift to less polluting modes).

It is necessary to be more specific about the characteristics of different pollutants before we can go on to examine the potential for reducing levels of air pollution by switching demand to less polluting modes. This is potentially an enormous task as the number of chemicals present in vehicle exhausts is very large indeed. Appendix 1 (p163) lists the compounds emitted by petrol and diesel vehicles and from petrol vapour. Some of their health consequences (including carcinogenicity) will be returned to in chapter 6. Information on the major air pollutants is gathered together as a series of fact sheets covering CO, NO_x, particulates, SO_2, benzene, PAHs, VOCs, lead, O_3 and PAN and cadmium. These are reproduced in Appendix 2 (p174).

Air quality standards and guidelines

Both the WHO and EC set air quality standards primarily for public health reasons. In the case of the EC (but not the WHO) they are standards and mandatory. In practice both sets of information are based on the same technical information on the extent to which health outcomes vary with different levels of exposure to the pollutant (dose–response relationship).

WHO guidelines for Europe have been published as *Air Quality Guidelines for Europe*, WHO Regional Office for Europe, Copenhagen, 1987. EC air quality standards are defined in directive 80/779/EEC, *Official Journal of the European Community*, L229 30 August 1980. EC

Table 3.2 EC directives relevant to air quality and vehicles

1   70/220/EEC (OJ L76 6.4.70)
    Proposed 1969 COM(69) 939
    Directive on air pollution from petrol engines (amended on several occasions
    including 83/351/EEC OJ L197 20.7.83, COM(82) 170)

2   72/306/EEC (OJ L190 20.8.72)
    Proposed 1971 COM(71) 1484
    Directive on the emission of pollutants from diesel engines

3   75/716/EEC (OJ L307 27.11.75)
    Proposed 11.2.74 COM(74) 158
    Directive on the approximation of the laws of the member states relating to
    the sulphur content of certain liquid fuels

4   80/779/EEC (OJ L229 30.8.80)
    Proposed 25.2.76 COM(76) 48
    Directive on air quality limit values and guide values for sulphur dioxide and
    suspended particulates

5   85/203/EEC (OJ L87 27.3.85)
    Proposed 7.9.83 COM(83) 498
    Directive on air quality standards for nitrogen dioxide

6   82/884/EEC (OJ L378 31.12.82)
    Proposed 16.4.75 COM(75) 166
    Directive on a limit value for lead in the air

7   85/210/EEC (OJ L96 3.4.85)
    Proposed 6.6.84 COM(84) 226
    Directive on the approximation of the laws of member states concerning the
    lead content of petrol

8   There are a number of COM documents containing further information on
    emissions from petrol and diesel-engined vehicles. These include COM(86)
    261 on particulates from diesel-engined vehicles, COM(86) 273 on emissions
    from diesel-engined commercial vehicles, COM(89) 662 amending directive
    70/220/EEC on measures to be taken against air pollution by emissions from
    motor vehicles and COM(92) 64 proposal for a council directive relating to
    measures to be taken against air pollution by emissions from motor vehicles

Note: OJ refers to the Official Journal of the European Communities and this
together with COM documents can be found in any European Documentation
Centre

regulatory activity in the field of air quality is substantial and a fuller discussion of this can be found in Haigh (1991). Table 3.2 identifies the main areas of regulation.

Nitrogen dioxide

The EC directive has a limit value and a guideline value. Only the former is mandatory. The limit value is $200\mu g/m^{-3}$ and the guide value is $135\mu g/m^{-3}$. Details on their calculation and precise definition can be found in Ball, Brimblecombe and Nicholas (1991).

Reference Period

Limit value   One year (98 percentile of 1-hour means): $200\mu g/m^{-3}$

Guide value   One year (50 percentile of 1-hour means): $50\mu g/m^{-3}$
One year (98 percentile of 1-hour means): $135\mu g/m^{-3}$

The WHO has set guideline values of $400\mu g/m^{-3}$ for a 1-hour reference period and $150\mu g/m^{-3}$ for a 24-hour period.

Carbon monoxide

The WHO has made recommendations for exposure limits for CO. It has proposed a maximum permitted exposure of $100\ mg/m^{-3}$ for periods not exceeding 15 minutes and a time weighted exposure as follows:

$60\ mg/m^{-3}$ (50 ppm) for 30 minutes
$30\ mg/m^{-3}$ (25 ppm) for 1 hour
$10\ mg/m^{-3}$ (10 ppm) for 8 hours.

Sulphur dioxide

The WHO has produced guidelines for SO_2 expressed in terms of recommended maximum concentrations for different time periods:

10 minutes – $500\mu g/m^{-3}$
1 hour – $350\mu g/m^{-3}$
24 hours – $125\mu g/m^{-3}$
1 year – $50\mu g/m^{-3}$

The EC has also set air quality standards for sulphur dioxide and smoke which are linked as follows:

	Reference period	Smoke $\mu g/m^{-3}$	Sulphur dioxide $\mu g/m^{-3}$
Limit values	One year (median of daily values)	80	120 if smoke <40 80 if smoke >40
	Winter (median of daily values)	130	180 if smoke <60 130 if smoke >60
	Year, peak (98 percentile of daily values)	250	350 if smoke <150 250 if smoke >150
Guide values	24 hour mean		100–150
	One year mean		40–60

Ozone

The WHO has set guidelines for two reference periods as follows:

1 hour – 150–200$\mu g/m^{-3}$
8 hour – 100–120$\mu g/m^{-3}$

In addition to air quality standards based on epidemiological data the WHO has set guidelines relating to ecological effects ie based on the known effects of different pollutants on plants.

WHO guidelines relating to ecological effects

Reference period	Sulphur dioxide $\mu g/m^{-3}$	Nitrogen dioxide $\mu g/m^{-3}$	Ozone $\mu g/m^{-3}$
1 year growing season, 100 days	30	30	60
24 hours	100	–	65
4 hours	–	95	–
1 hour	–	–	200

Lead

The EC has specified an air quality limit value of 2$\mu g/m^{-3}$ (annual mean) not to be exceeded. The WHO guideline value is 0.5–1.0$\mu g/m^{-3}$, also a long-term mean.

Particulates

The WHO has set guideline values for particulates in conjunction with sulphur dioxide. For a discussion of the relationships between sulphur dioxide levels and particulate levels see Holman (1989). WHO particulate guide values are:

Particulates

Reference period	Black smoke $\mu g/m^{-3}$	Total suspended particulates $\mu g/m^{-3}$	Thoracic particulates $\mu g/m^{-3}$
24 hours	125	120	70
1 year	50	–	–

The EC has set limit and guide values for particulates. The limit value (ie one which must not be exceeded) is $80\mu g/m^{-3}$ and the guide value is $40–60\mu g/m^{-3}$.

Problems with air quality guidelines

The existence of air quality guidelines is helpful in giving focus to environmental objectives which are very poorly developed in transport. Such objectives represent the first stirrings of progress towards sustainability. They are also of direct relevance to the quality of life of individuals and describe the outcomes of environmental and transport policies. Unlike emission regulations which give the impression that environmental problems are being solved because technology is bringing down the emissions of individual vehicles, air quality measurements are strongly influenced by increases in vehicle numbers and structural changes, eg lengthening of journeys and increasing frequencies of journeys. One of the effects of the French high speed train (see chapter 5) has been to increase the frequency of trips made by business users (ECMT, 1991). These increased numbers are associated with increased use of private cars adding to a raised level of pollution from sources which at the individual level are improving in their environmental performance.

There are unresolved problems with air quality guidelines. They are muddled in the sense that they are not linked to clear policies for improving air quality over specified time scales. In particular there is no direct link in the EC institutions or in national governments between transport policies and urban air quality (with some notable exceptions such as the Dutch 'National Environmental Policy Plan Plus'). The guidelines and limit values are undoubtedly very conservative in that they still give plenty of scope to the polluter and are not based on long term epidemiological work which would establish the degree of damage to health from living and working in polluted urban environments. They represent the best that can be produced from available data but nevertheless are crude estimates which should probably be revised downwards to gave a substantial safety margin for those with long term exposure to poor quality air and those in vulnerable groups, eg children, asthmatics and pregnant women.

The air quality guidelines do not carry with them the obligation to make detailed measurements. The Edinburgh survey quoted above shows what can be found when one looks but such high quality data are rare. The lack of a dense system of monitoring stations at street level, in homes and workplaces and on individuals is a major obstacle to progress in improving air quality. Closely linked to the problem of lack of data is the lack of enforcement. Europe has nothing in place to compare to the responsibilities and resources of the South Coast Air Quality Management District in Los Angeles (Lents, 1990). This agency has a budget, an inspectorate and the legal basis for implementing measures to reduce air pollution over an area that covers 13350 square miles and 12 million people. Air quality guidelines or limits are not of much value without the intensity of monitoring and action to improve the situation.

Models of transport planning which can cope with environmental objectives, especially air quality, do exist in Europe. The Dutch 'Travelling Clean' report does this (Netherlands Agency for Energy and the Environment, 1989) and the German transport planning framework 'Verkehrsentwicklungsplanung' explicitly builds in an 'ecological scenario'. The 'Gesamtverkehrsplan' for North Rhine–Westphalia compares an ecological scenario with a business as usual scenario to show that reductions in carbon dioxide and other pollutants can be achieved by a strategy of altering the modal split in favour of less polluting modes (Just, 1992).

A further problem with air quality guidelines is that they take only a partial view of the problem of urban air pollution. Many pollutants do not have guideline or limit values, eg the volatile organic compounds (VOCs) and formaldehyde. Many of the VOCs are carcinogenic and hence not readily converted into levels which are 'safe'. Fig 3.1 shows UK road source emissions for a number of potentially hazardous compounds. The vertical axis shows the quantity of emissions and the horizontal shows toxicity. The lower the value on the horizontal axis (ie towards the left) the more toxic a compound is. Apart from those elements discussed above (CO, NO_x, SO_2 and lead) none of these elements has guideline or limit values.

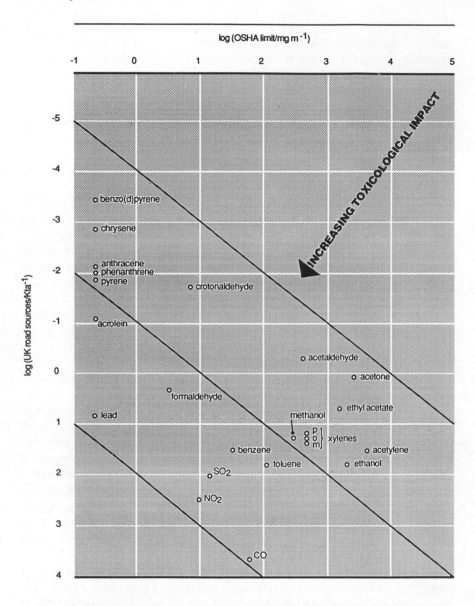

Figure 3.1 Relationship between OSHA workplace limits and UK road source
emissions for a number of potentiallly hazardous compounds

Note: OSHA refers to standards promulgated under s6 of the US Occupational
Safety and Health Act, 1970

Source: Ball, Brindlecombe and Nicholas (1991)

Of particular note in Figure 3.1 are benzene and toluene, both very toxic (of similar toxicological significance to CO, NO_x and SO_2) and both unregulated. Of total toluene pollution, 42% is from the transport sector.

A further problem is a definitional one. Whilst gaseous, evaporative and particulate emissions from engines, exhausts and fuel systems are normally identified, those particulate emissions which are not fuel derived are not. These particulates, many of which will be of respirable size, largely arise from tyre abrasion and from braking systems (Reutter, 1989). These particulates include asbestos, chrome, nickel, copper, zinc, cadmium, cobalt and aluminium. Table 3.3 gives some results from the tyre abrasion alone.

Table 3.3 Emissions from tyre abrasion on a variety of road types

Road type	Total emissions kg/ha/a*	Lead	Chrome	Copper	Zinc
		g/km/a*			
Residential	68	84	14	19	47
Distributor	153	241	40	55	135
Main roads	242	506	84	115	284
Motorway	657	1145	241	329	810

* Total emissions are expressed in kg per hectare per annum and for individual elements in gramms per kilometre per annum

Source: Reutter (1989)

Quite clearly large amounts of chemical elements are being deposited in the environment where people live and no attempt is being made to regulate the amount or to estimate (apart from lead) the cumulative impact of these motor vehicle products when added to doses from other sources. In an urban environment it is likely that cumulative doses will trip thresholds relevant to carcinogenesis and other health problems while potential synergistic effects are so numerous and unknown that we cannot begin to estimate the impact of different pollutants at different levels in the presence or absence of other pollutants.

The routine exposure of well over 200 million Europeans in urban areas to such large numbers of pollutants in such large quantities when epidemiological information is so sparse, especially on synergistic effects, is one of the most damaging manifestations of a car-oriented society and one which will not go away with the widespread adoption of new fuels, electrically powered vehicles and catalytic converters. Indeed many of the new fuels and new technologies introduce new chemical compounds into the atmosphere. Catalytic converters, for example, remove much of the NO_x and CO but introduce platinum and other rare metals which previously did not figure in the inventory of pollutants from motor vehicles (Nieper, 1991). This draws attention to a fundamental problem associated with environmental control and technology and that is our inability to produce 'failsafe' solutions to environmental problems and the likelihood that we simply move the problem around, exchanging old problems for new ones but retaining the built-in inadequacies of a system designed to expand and resistant to solutions that involve structural and/or behavioural change, eg travelling less, over smaller distances and by less polluting modes. As technological advance gathers momentum we are even unable to conduct basic epidemiological, toxicological and long-term ecological assessments of the new technologies. Thus we store up larger problems for the future and damage the possibility that transport might evolve in the direction of sustainability.

To what extent are the limited number of guidelines/limit values actually met? Systematic information on this topic is sparse. Appendix 2 (p174) which contains pollutant fact sheets summarises the range of variability to be found in measurements of air quality. This is expanded on here.

Nitrogen dioxide

Some UK data is reproduced in table 3.4. The Edinburgh study referred to above provides more detailed information of the extent to which guidelines are not met. Three measurements were above $200\mu g/m^{-3}$ and ten above $135\mu g/m^{-3}$. Average mean nitrogen dioxide concentrations in urban areas throughout the world are generally in the range of 20–$90\mu g/m^{-3}$ (Holman, 1989). Levels vary enormously and Holman refers to a London measurement in 1982 of over $3000\mu g/m^{-3}$, measurements in Amsterdam, Brussels and Munich of over $700\mu g/m^{-3}$ and Rotterdam of over $600\mu g/m^{-3}$.

Carbon monoxide

Natural background levels of CO range between 0.01 and 0.2 ppm (WHO, 1987). Typical urban values range from 3–15 ppm though the roadside atmosphere affecting cyclists and pedestrians particularly can show much higher concentrations (Ball, Brindlecombe and Nicholas, 1991). The London Air Pollution Monitoring Network has measured CO at four sites and these are reproduced in table 3.5.

Carbon monoxide is particularly important in urban areas where 90%

Table 3.4   Hourly concentrations of nitogen dioxide (ppb) at selected UK sites during 1987

	Arithmetic mean	50th percentile	98th percentile	Maximum
Central London	39	36	85	239
West London	35	32	84	271
Glasgow	31	30	69	215
Manchester	29	27	65	230
Walsall	30	29	62	104
Billingham	23	19	63	182

Source: Ball, Brindlecombe and Nicholas (1991)

Table 3.5   Carbon monoxide concentrations (mg/m^3) at four London sites in 1988

Site	Annual mean	Max. 8h any time	Above WHO-8h[c]
West London	2.4	19.8	5
Central London[a]	1.5	11.2	1
Central London[b]	4.5	16.2	24
East London	2.9	13.1	2

Notes: *a*: background; *b*: roadside; *c*: number of days between 1 October and 31 December 1988 where an 8 hour period exceeded the WHO $10mg/m^3$ guideline

Source: Ball, Brindlecombe and Nicholas (1991)

of the total pollution is from motor vehicles (Holman, 1989). Eight hour mean concentrations in urban areas are typically less than $20\mu g/m^{-3}$ but levels of up to $60\mu g/m^{-3}$ have been recorded (Holman, 1989). Peak concentrations correlate with rush hours. Worldwide maximum 8-hour averages range from $2-50\mu g/m^{-3}$ with Paris being particularly polluted (Holman, 1989). All Paris monitoring stations exceeded the WHO guideline for the years 1980–84.

Sulphur dioxide

Sulphur dioxide was not considered to be very important by Ball, Brindlecombe and Nicholas (1991). Urban emissions have reduced in recent years and large cities such as London have concentrations in the range $20-60\mu g/m^{-3}$ which are well below EC limit values and close to or within WHO guide values. There is evidence that emissions are increasing in Southern Europe (Holman, 1989). Annual mean sulphur dioxide levels in major European cities have decreased from within the range $100-200\mu g/m^{-3}$ a decade ago to mainly below $100\mu g/m^{-3}$ (ibid). Some European cities continue to experience high annual mean concentrations. Milan is the only city in the developed world to be found in the worlds top ten most polluted cities (ibid).

Of the European urban areas participating in the Global Environmental Monitoring System (GEMS) of the WHO and the United Nations Environment Programme (UNEP), sites within Brussels, Gourdon (France), Frankfurt, Milan, Warsaw, Wroclaw, Madrid, London and Zagreb exceeded the level considered safe by the WHO (guideline value of $150\mu g/m^{-3}$).

Ozone

Ozone is described in Appendix 2 (p174). It is formed as a result of chemical reactions between other pollutants and is not emitted directly into the atmosphere. The major source of ozone precursors is motor vehicles which produce the nitrogen dioxide and hydrocarbons needed to 'generate' it. This is the main source of photochemical smog (of the type found in Los Angeles, for instance). Natural background daily average levels of ozone are usually in the range $40-60\mu g/m^{-3}$ (Holman, 1989). In polluted air in Europe maximum 1 hour ozone levels may exceed $500\mu g/m^{-3}$ in rural areas and $350\mu g/m^{-3}$ in urban areas. The highest 30 minute value in Europe recorded in the former West Germany was $664\mu g/m^{-3}$ (ibid). Typical concentrations of atmospheric pollutants associated with transport are shown in table 3.6.

Forecasting of air pollution

The forecasting of air pollution is essential to give a clear indication of the consequences of continuing present arrangements in transport. It also serves a useful purpose in making assumptions explicit and allowing these assumptions to be varied to reflect policy options. The problems underlying a forecast in this area are enormous especially as pollution from motor vehicles is so obviously a function of the number of vehicles in use and their emission characteristics. Forecasts of vehicle numbers, passenger kilometres and tonne-km are the basis of any forecast of NO_x, CO, SO_2 etc from transport. These forecasts have not proved very reliable in the past (they were underestimates) and the likelihood is that passenger-km by car and tonne-km by lorry will continue to grow at a rate which is faster than official forecasts indicate.

Table 3.6 Typical urban concentrations of atmospheric pollutants associated with transport

Pollutant	Concentration	Measurement
Nitrogen dioxide	$400\mu g/m^{-3}$	Daily maximum
Carbon monoxide	$20mg/m^{-3}$	8 hour maximum
Sulphur dioxide	$250-500\mu g/m^{-3}$	Daily maximum
Ozone	$50-350\mu g/m^{-3}$	Hourly maximum
Lead	$0.5-3\mu g/m^{-3}$	Annual mean
Particulates	$200-400\mu g/m^{-3}$	Daily maximum
Benzene	$3-16\mu g/m^{-3}$	Hourly mean
Formaldehyde	$5-10\mu g/m^{-3}$	Annual mean
Benzo-α-pyrene	$1-5ng/m^{-3}$	Annual mean

Source: ERL (1991c)

The penetration of catalytic converters to the whole European, petrol-driven vehicle fleet will ensure reductions of NO_x, for example, to 10% of the 1989 level by the year 2006 (ERR, 1989). After that date emissions increase once again in line with the growth in vehicle use. This forecast draws our attention to an important issue in forecasting air pollution which cannot easily be resolved. Whilst it is possible to improve individual vehicle performance from an emissions point of view it is not possible (with current transport and environment policies) to counteract the tendency for such gains to be swamped by increased vehicle numbers, vehicle use or both. The point at which gains are overtaken by growth in the size of the fleet will depend on many factors including land use policies, congestion policies and road construction. If space is liberated in cities by new roads or road pricing then it will be filled again by more vehicles and ensure that the tipping point (when gains are cancelled out) will be sooner rather than later.

Emissions also depend on speed, the decline of public transport in the face of deteriorating conditions for public transport vehicles, reductions in walking and cycling because conditions are so poor in heavily trafficked environments and the continuing high level of investment and fiscal discrimination in favour of private motorised transport.

Forecasts at a European level have been made but these do not build in the level of detail which is necessary to understand the contribution of different segments of the transport sector to total transport emissions and to relate these to the impact of catalytic converters and to the underlying growth rate in vehicle numbers and use.

The European Commission (EC, 1991) has made a forecast under five different scenarios of fuel consumption and emissions to the year 2000 using 1985 as the base year. Emissions forecasted include NO_x, CO, VOCs, CO_2, lead, smoke and SO_2. The results are less useful than they might have been because of unrealistic assumptions about distances travelled (ie too short) and the absence of a thorough 'ecological scenario' that would describe the possibilities of achieving lower levels of vehicle use, distances travelled etc. This represents a missed opportunity to give some substance to the discussion of sustainability.

For a detailed understanding of the factors at work and the extent to which air pollution presents some formidable obstacles in the drive towards sustainability it will be necessary to focus on one country. Earth Resources Research (ERR) in the UK has produced a particularly good example of the level of detail necessary. The ERR (1989) study of atmospheric emissions shows that road emissions dominate all transport emissions even though there is cause for concern with the continuing expansion of the air industry. For nitrogen dioxide ERR predicts that emissions from cars will fall to less than 10% of current (1989) levels by 2006 when all cars will be fitted with catalytic converters. From that time emissions begin to increase once more in line with the growth in vehicle use. Total vehicle emissions are predicted to fall to a minimum of about 70% of current levels with lorries making an increasingly important contribution. The projections do not suggest that a dramatic reduction in nitrogen dioxide emissions from road transport can be anticipated. Indeed, according to ERR, emissions of nitrogen dioxide from road vehicles may be higher in 2020 than in 1992.

For carbon monoxide ERR predicts a significant reduction from cars by 2006 and as the major source of CO is petrol engines a comparable reduction is predicted for road transport as a whole. By the year 2020 CO emissions are projected to be 50–63% of 1989 levels. Of relevance to the sustainability debate in cities ERR does not expect this reduction to make any difference to urban air quality as that is where catalytic converters will be least effective and where most stop/start conditions will apply. Total hydrocarbons (see Appendix 1) are predicted to be 56–74% of 1989 levels by the year 2006.

Figures 3.2 and 3.3 show the NO_x forecast (low and high respectively) broken down between cars, light goods vehicles, heavy goods vehicles and public service vehicles (mainly buses). Both figures show the actual split in 1988 in terms of contribution from different transport sources to total transport NO_x. The diagrams show the increasing significance of lorries in NO_x pollution to such an extent that at the end of the forecast period they will contribute three-quarters of the total from road transport. The problem of lorries is central to the transport and sustainability debate and is returned to in chapter 8. Lorry activity measured in tonne-km will increase by over 100% by the year 2005 (Whitelegg, 1990a) giving rise to levels of NO_x pollution in excess of those predicted by ERR from the heavy goods vehicle group.

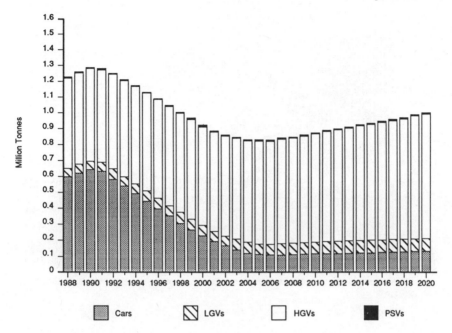

Figure 3.2   Road transport NO$_x$ emissions: low forecast
Source: ERR (1989)

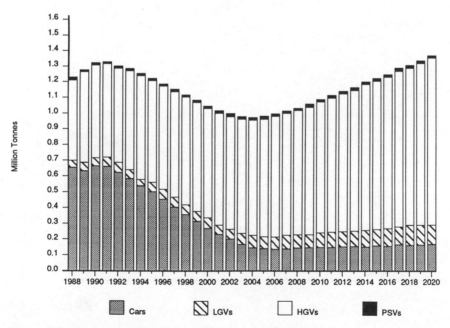

Figure 3.3   Road transport NO$_x$ emissions: high forecast
Source: ERR (1989)

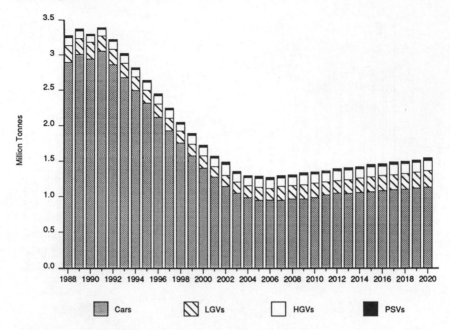

Figure 3.4   Road transport CO emissions: low forecast
Source: ERR (1989)

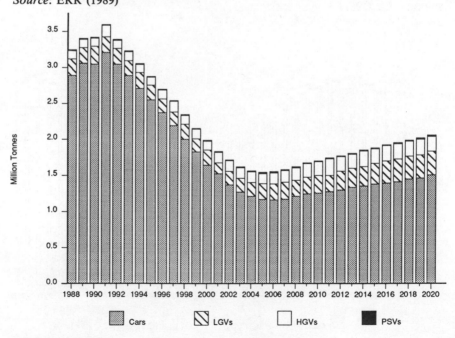

Figure 3.5   Road transport CO emissions: high forecast
Source: ERR (1989)

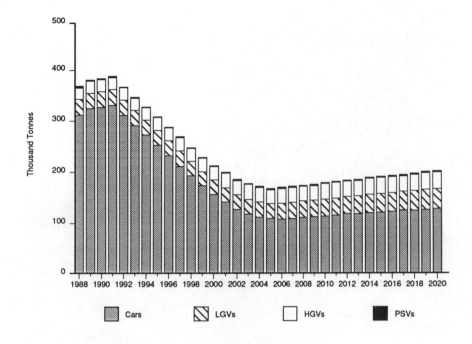

Figure 3.6   Road transport HC emissions: low forecast

Source: ERR (1989)

Figures 3.4 and 3.5 show the ERR carbon monoxide forecasts (low and high respectively reflecting low and high traffic forecasts). The introduction of catalytic converters produces a significant reduction in carbon monoxide emissions from cars by 2006. On the low demand growth predictions total emissions from road transport are predicted to fall to a little below 40% of 1989 levels by 2006, rising again to 48% by 2020. As in the case of NO_x the driving conditions to be found in cities will ensure that gains from catalytic converters will not benefit those living there.

Figures 3.6 and 3.7 show the ERR hydrocarbon forecasts (low and high). Currently cars contribute 85% of these emissions and like CO emissions can only be influenced significantly by policies aimed at the motor car. A reduction to 45% of 1989 levels is forecast on the low growth model and to 55% on the high growth model. In both cases levels rise again after 2005.

Figures 3.8, 3.9 and 3.10 show emissions from the transport sector as a whole (low forecast to the year 2020) and clearly identify the

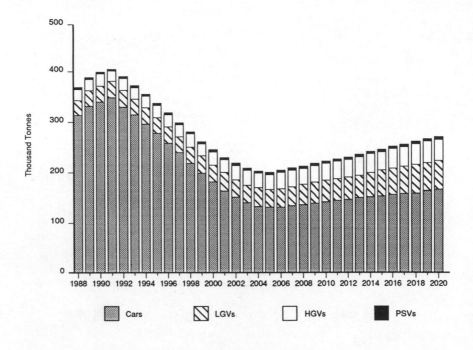

Figure 3.7   Road transport HC emissions: high forecast
Source: ERR (1989)

significance of road as the dominant sector. Road is so important for
NO_x (figure 3.8), CO (figure 3.9) and HC (figure 3.10) that for most
practical purposes the other sectors can be ignored in terms of deriving
strategies for reducing emissions in the transport sector from these three
pollutants. The converse is, of course, the case for those modes which
have a major role to play in taking on board some of the burden of the
freight and passengers currently carried on roads. Reductions in pollution
can only be achieved by bringing about a switch to less polluting modes.

The general conclusion to be drawn from all the forecasts made by
ERR is that technology in the form of catalytic converters is not going
to solve the problem and that road transport is firmly set to continue a
growth trajectory in emissions after a temporary downturn. The size of
the downturn predicted by ERR may well prove to be over optimistic
simply as a result of the high forecast of vehicle use itself being an
underestimate. Further there is nothing in these forecasts to suggest that
air quality in cities will improve. The objective of an environmental
transport policy has to relate very closely to quality of life variables

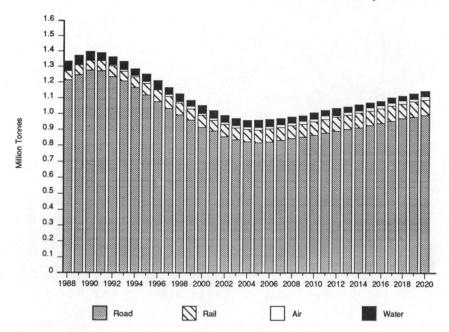

Figure 3.8 All transport NO$_x$ emissions: low forecast
Source: ERR (1989)

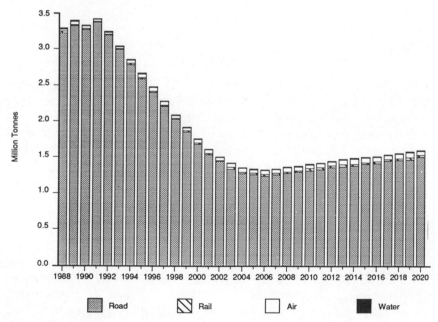

Figure 3.9 All transport CO emissions: low forecast
Source: ERR (1989)

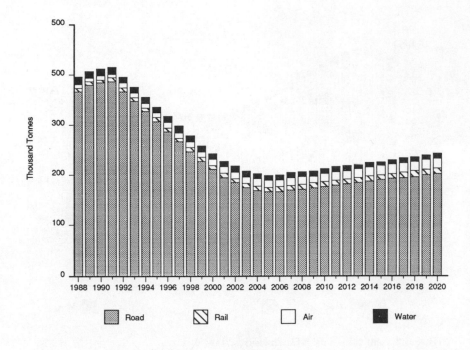

Figure 3.10   All transport HC emissions: low forecast

Source: ERR (1989)

precisely in those areas where population is concentrated. Even reductions of the scale forecast by ERR to 2005/2006 will deliver very little
improvement in air quality in cities. Moreover the ERR forecast has
correctly identified the lorry as a major problem for the future. If emissions of lorries are linked to their noise, vibration, road traffic accident,
road damage and space demand characteristics then something of the
magnitude of the problem can be perceived.

Polluting characteristics of different modes

It is quite clear that different modes have different polluting
characteristics. When these are expressed in some unit of work done, eg
passenger-km for people movement and tonne-km for freight movement,
a wide range of values is revealed which in all cases identifies road
transport as the most polluting land-based mode. This is important information. If the objective is to ensure that individuals can move around

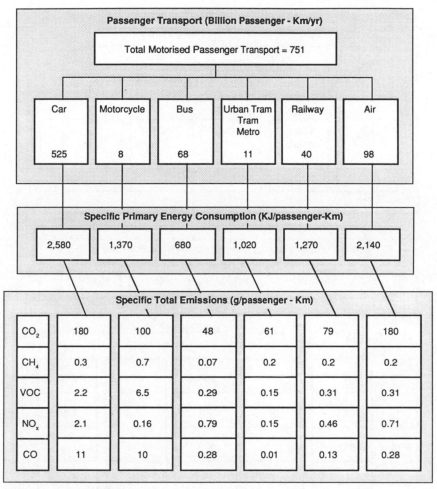

Figure 3.11 Different modes of passenger transport in terms of energy use and pollution

in order to satisfy basic wants and needs and that these wants and needs in their turn generate the movement of freight then a balance can be struck among competing modes that reflects the best mixture of satisfying wants and needs at the lowest possible environmental cost. This will provide an eminently workable definition of sustainability.

Figures 3.11 and 3.12 show the performance of different modes of

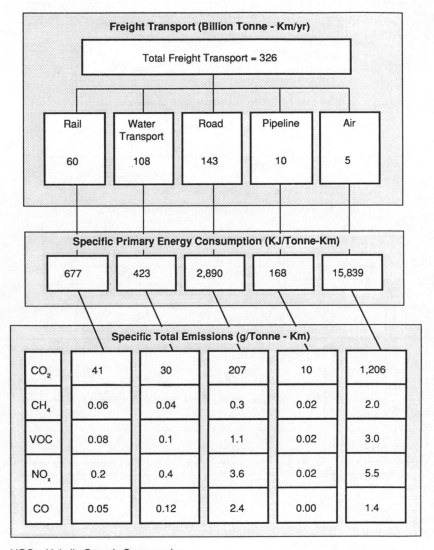

Figure 3.12   Different modes of freight transport in terms of energy use and pollution

transport in terms of energy use and pollution. The data are German and from 1987 but they show very clearly the comparative impact of different modes. In the case of passenger transport (figure 3.11) the bus is the most energy efficient mode with corresponding benefits for emission reduction. Walking and cycling are excluded from this figure though they would produce energy consumption figures and emission levels that are very small indeed. It is very clear from this figure that movement opportunities can be provided at a high or a low energy and pollution cost. Sustainable transport policies need to embrace this kind of information to produce a low-impact result.

In the case of freight transport (figure 3.12) data from the same country and the same year as the passenger information shows that the lorry (of the land-based modes) is a highly undesirable method of moving freight in terms of energy intensity and emission characteristics. Air freight is a particularly intensive user of energy and produces emissions far in excess of the other modes.

Sustainable transport policies in the freight arena can only be derived by utilising those modes which have relatively small emissions per tonne kilometre. It is a source of concern that the road mode is gaining rapidly at the expense of the rail mode (Group Transport 2000 Plus, 1990) at the same time as EC policies proclaim the necessity of yet more road construction (EC, 1992b).

4 NOISE

Noise is more than an irritant even though it commands much less attention than air pollution or other environmental problems. Noise is damaging to health (see chapter 6) and is a major reason why walking or cycling in or near busy roads is avoided. It acts, therefore, as a deterrent to the more environmentally friendly modes of transport and as a reason why it is sometimes preferable to travel by car. The device that produces the noise very conveniently insulates the human occupant from the aural consequences of that trip. Indeed noise insulation and the substitution of pleasing noises (high quality in-car sound systems) are important selling points for car purchasers.

Noise suffers from some complexities of measurement which can obscure the severity of the problem. Should there be any doubt about the intensity of the disturbance produced by noise and the unpleasantness of a noisy environment then a walk along rue de Belliard which houses the European Parliament in Brussels or rue de la Loi which runs parallel to it and houses the European Commission will provide more than enough evidence for a heightened appreciation of the nuisance. There is some poetic irony in the chairman of the environment committee of the European Parliament sheltering behind quadruple glazing to protect him from the noise at street level outside his office.

Noise at street level is continually increasing. Quiet vehicle programmes are useless against the rising tide of vehicle ownership and use and city administrations like Brussels and Düsseldorf which provide up to six lanes of high quality road in city centres and build tunnels to increase motor vehicle accessibility and allow even larger numbers of vehicles to penetrate the heart of the city.

The most important source of noise is road traffic though locally other sources can be more significant. Airports and aircraft flight paths produce serious noise problems as do military aircraft in rural areas. Noise is normally measured in decibels on a logarithmic scale referred to in abbreviated form as the dB(A) scale. As noise varies in its intensity it is necessary to define the time over which the noise is measured and the noise readings are then averaged over that period. This is referred to as the Leq measurement (OECD, 1991, p157). Figure 4.1 shows a range

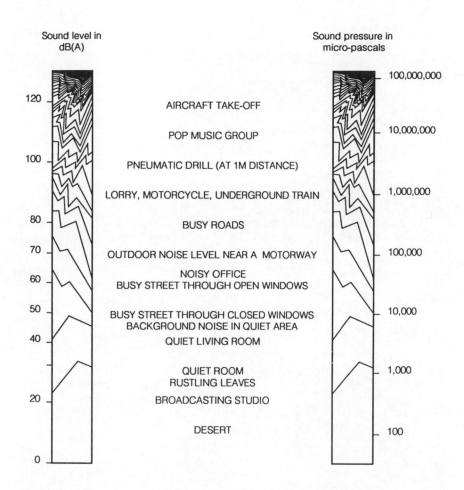

Sound level in dB(A)

Sound pressure in micro-pascals

AIRCRAFT TAKE-OFF

POP MUSIC GROUP

PNEUMATIC DRILL (AT 1M DISTANCE)

LORRY, MOTORCYCLE, UNDERGROUND TRAIN

BUSY ROADS

OUTDOOR NOISE LEVEL NEAR A MOTORWAY

NOISY OFFICE
BUSY STREET THROUGH OPEN WINDOWS

BUSY STREET THROUGH CLOSED WINDOWS
BACKGROUND NOISE IN QUIET AREA

QUIET LIVING ROOM

QUIET ROOM
RUSTLING LEAVES

BROADCASTING STUDIO

DESERT

Figure 4.1 Examples of noise levels

Source: OECD (1988)

of noise readings for different activities. A daily Leq of greater than 65dB(A) is normally taken as an absolute upper acceptable limit and is used in regulations concerning sound insulation compensation (Nelson, 1989).

OECD (1991, p160) estimate that about 130 million people in OECD countries are exposed to unacceptable noise levels (>65dB(A) daytime Leq); 400 million are exposed to levels over 55dB(A). Noise levels have increased over the last twenty years and the major cause of the increase has been the growth in transport. The proportion of the population

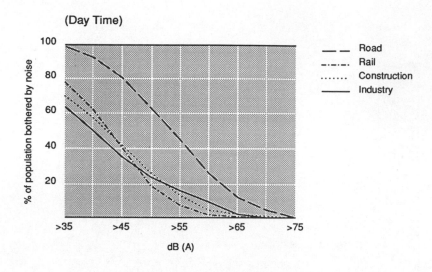

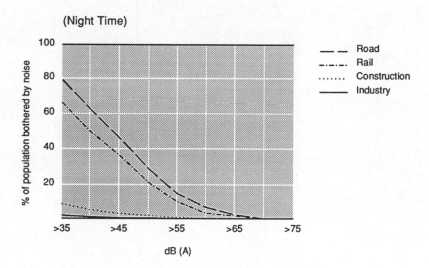

Figure 4.2   Noise impact from different sources in West Germany, 1985
Source: UBA (1988)

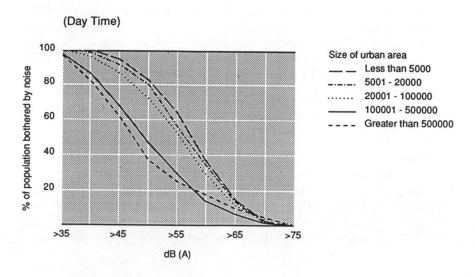

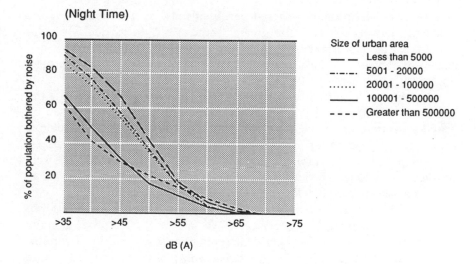

Figure 4.3 Noise impact by size of urban area in West Germany, 1985

Source: UBA (1988)

exposed to more than 65dB(A) can vary from 5% in the 'quiet' countries (eg parts of Scandinavia) to 30% in the 'noisy' countries. The proportion of the population that enjoys a satisfactory outdoor noise environment (less than 55dB(A), daytime Leq) varies from less than 20% in some countries to over 60% in Scandinavia.

The population affected by aircraft noise is between three and fifty times smaller than that affected by the noise of surface transport (depending on the country). Figure 4.2 shows the effect of different modes of transport on the population of Germany for both day and night times. Road transport is by far the most significant source of noise nuisance with rail (in the case of night time noise) following second. Germany is rather a special case in this respect as such a large proportion of freight is moved by rail in comparison with other European countries.

Figure 4.3 shows the concentration of the noise problem in larger cities reflecting the contribution of traffic to overall noise levels.

Speed and vehicle mix as determinants of noise

Different vehicles produce different levels of noise as illustrated in figure 4.4. The lorry with engine size greater than 150kW is particularly noisy but so is the motorbike. Measures to reduce or eliminate these two classes of vehicles will have a greater effect on noise levels than measures not specifically targeted.

Speed is also important and is illustrated for the case of cars in cities in figure 4.5. Figure 4.5 is particularly interesting because it is based on actual measurements in the field and indicates exactly how many vehicles in particular speed bands are related to specific noise values. The streets were subjected to standard noise measurement and 53545 vehicles were counted to produce this diagram. The central line represents a mean value and the upper and lower lines two standard deviations.

Speed and vehicle type in combination also influence noise levels (see fig 4.6). The ranking is quite clear. The largest lorries produce more noise at all speeds than the other vehicles but speed is the critical variable in each case. Speed reduction alone has enormous potential to reduce noise levels in cities.

Noise abatement

It is quite clear from the above that reducing speeds and eliminating noisy vehicles by, for example, transferring freight from road to rail, provides an answer to traffic noise problems. As usual transport policy is directed at areas which are of peripheral relevance but have the

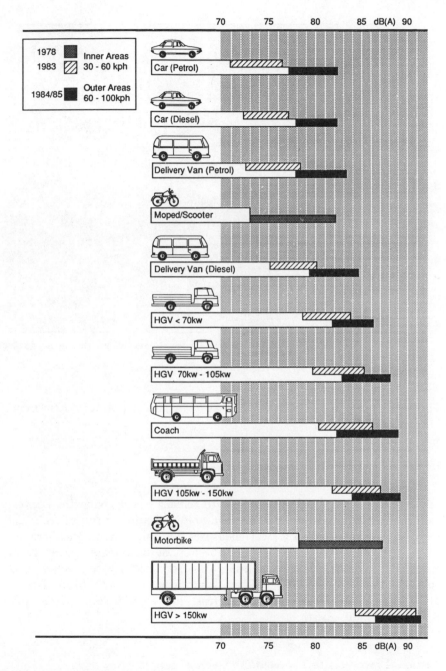

Figure 4.4 Noise levels recorded for different vehicles under differing speed conditions

Source: Steven (nd)

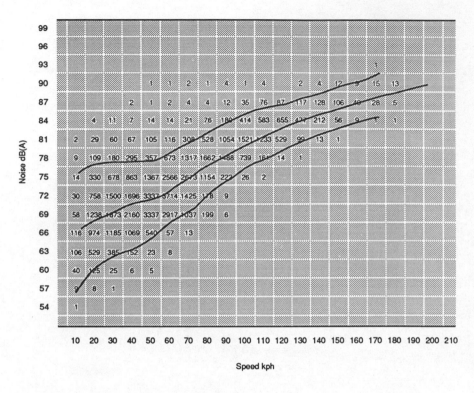

Figure 4.5 Speed and noise in urban areas (noise measured for cars 7.5m from the road)

Source: Steven (nd)

advantage of allowing the status quo to remain whilst giving the impression that something is being done. The noise literature is full of technical discussions about technological measures to limit noise. Nowhere do these same discussions explore the question of how many extra HGVs would be needed to cancel out the gains from better tyres, better road surfaces, muffled exhausts, quieter transmission etc. With forecasts of HGV numbers by 2015 rising by at least 100% (Whitelegg, 1990a) this is the important question.

Technical measures to reduce noise levels at source

These are more than adequately dealt with in Nelson (1989). Sources of noise are identified: engine, air inlet, exhaust and cooling system,

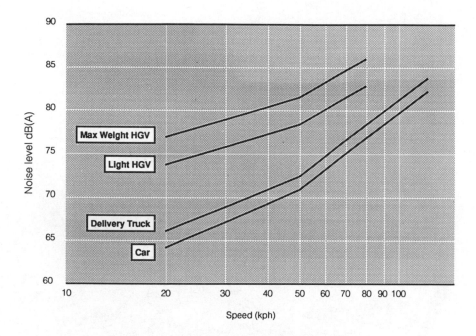

Figure 4.6 Comparison of noise output of different modes of road transport

Source: Steven (nd)

transmission, rolling noise (ie aerodynamic and tyre/road surface), brakes, body rattles and load. In each case there are technical solutions which at varying cost can minimise noise. Measures are aimed either at the vehicle or (in the case of rolling noise) at the road surface.

Considerable experience has been acquired by vehicle engineers through projects such as the UK 'Quiet Heavy Vehicle' project. Further it is possible through driver education and stricter standards on vehicle maintenance to reduce noise which results from bad driving or poor vehicle condition. There are large numbers of uncertainties in this kind of technological approach to what is basically a societal and organisational problem. First there are trade-offs with other policies which may be disadvantageous. Diesel engines offer gains in fuel efficiency and hence reductions in carbon dioxide emissions but they are noisier than petrol engines. How should this be managed when what is needed are reductions in both noise and carbon dioxide? Quieter vehicles still need drivers who are quietly behaved.

The technology exists to control vehicles within acceptable limits of

Figure 4.7   A German view of noise and the citizen (cartoon)

Source: Arbeitskreis Verkehr (1988)

speed, acceleration etc but these are not part of noise reduction technology because they threaten narrow definitions of freedoms and are politically sensitive. Quiet vehicles are heavier as a result of the introduction of new kit. Heavier vehicles consume more fuel which produces more carbon dioxide. Quieter vehicles offer drivers greater levels of insulation from their own noise as well as the environment generally. It is more likely that speeds will rise in very quiet vehicles as opposed to vehicles where the speed is translated into noise. As in all aspects of behaviour in the driving environment, risk compensation (Adams, 1985) will ensure that improvements in noise performance will be 'consumed' in some other way (eg more miles, more speed).

Technology offers a politically acceptable route in potentially controversial areas. It cannot, however, deliver improvements in environmental quality in urban areas. Noise reduces the scope for conversation and discourages use of public space (Appleyard, 1981). It also damages community life and discourages walking and cycling. It actively promotes tendencies which make sustainability difficult to achieve. Journeys to work or school over distances which are walkable and cyclable will not be made by those modes if the streets are noisy, smelly and dangerous. This adds further impetus to the rise of car ownership and use and the pervasiveness of urban traffic congestion.

These problems have been recognised and explicitly incorporated into German urban planning. The concept of *Verkehrsberuhigung* or traffic calming is not a German invention but has been applied enthusiastically in Germany. Just (1992) explains the concept as it is applied in North Rhine–Westphalia in Germany which has now traffic-calmed over 10000 areas. Whitelegg (1990d) discusses the links between traffic-calming and wider objectives for urban transport and the quality of life in cities.

Traffic calming involves a series of physical measures which restrict the width of roads, entrances and exits and slow traffic down by chicanes, humps or imaginative planting of trees. These measures may be used in combination with speed limitation (eg 30kph) but speed limitation can exist without the physical measures. *Arbeitskreis Verkehr*, a German publication on noise reduction through traffic-calming, illustrates the problem with its cover page cartoon opposite.

The results of traffic calming can be seen in many German cities but are particularly well documented in Köln (Cologne). Results are reproduced in table 4.1 for two districts in Köln: Nippes and Agnesviertel. Measurements are expressed as before and after the traffic calming measures were completed. The full results are in Stadt Köln (1989).

Reductions in vehicle numbers and noise levels are associated with reductions in speed which in their turn bring dramatic reductions in accident levels. In Agnesviertel the number of injured persons was reduced by 74% between 1982 and 1986/87, the relevant before and after dates.

Table 4.1 The effects of traffic calming measures on noise levels in Köln

Street	Cars per hour		Noise dB(A)	
	Before	After	Before	After
Nippes				
Turmstr	165	79	64.7	62.8
Mauenheimstr	209	65	65.7	62.5
Kuenstr	206	128	68.9	63.3
Gocherstr	432	309	68.8	61.1
Agnesviertel				
Lupusstr	73	48	64.2	60.4
Neusser Wall	322	234	66.9	62.0
Schillingstr	149	119	64.1	61.5
Weissenburg	109	94	67.0	58.7
Niehler Str	424	462	72.6	70.9

Accident costs were reduced by 58%, from DM650000 to DM270000. In the case of Nippes the number of injured persons was reduced by 84% between 1983/84 and 1987/88 and the costs of accidents by 63%. It is instructive to compare this information with a reputable UK source of information on noise control (Nelson, 1989), where there is only passing mention of speed limits as a policy option for reducing noise and no recognition of the possibility that all the technological improvements may be negated by rising vehicle numbers.

The effects of traffic calming and its associated speed limit of 30kph can be seen over a larger area in figure 4.8. This diagram summarises the results of before and after comparisons at over 100 sites in Baden-Württemberg (Pfundt, Eckstein and Meewes, 1989).

Figure 4.8 shows average speeds before and after traffic calming. The speed measure used is the speed at which at least 85% of the vehicles observed are travelling. The diagram is structured around the two shorter diagonal lines. The upper refers to areas which have only had speed limitation (at 30kph) and the lower speed limitation and associated physical measures to slow traffic. The main diagonal (bottom left to top right) divides the whole diagram into two halves. Those points above this diagonal are areas which have experienced an increase in speed when before and after are compared. Those below the diagonal have experienced a speed reduction. The diagram shows that the greatest speed reductions take place at higher average speeds.

Traffic calming is not without its own problems and these are addressed in Whitelegg (1990b). It is, however, a step on the way to the

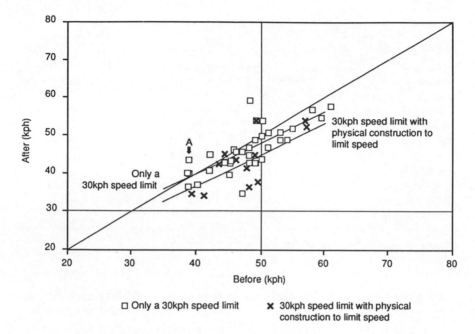

Figure 4.8   Speed measurements before and after the introduction of 30kph
speed limit zones

Source: Pfundt et al (1989)

next level of generalisation which is the car-free city concept now under
active development in Lübeck and in Frankfurt (ILS, 1992).

EC regulation

The development of EC regulation in this area can be seen in table 4.2.
The problem with noise regulation is the same as the problem discussed
for air pollution. Attention on the performance of the vehicle at the time
of manufacture is of very little relevance to its on-street performance
some years later and of even less relevance to the hard-pressed resident
of a street carrying 10000 vehicles per day, 15% of which are lorries. The
effects of noise in traffic 'canyons', its intensity when large numbers
accelerate away from traffic lights or struggle up steep hills and its rising
significance over time cannot be encompassed in the present system of
noise limitation.

Clearly the reductions in values expressed in table 4.2 have not
produced quiet or even quieter streets and the only systematic attempts

Table 4.2 Schedules of directives for vehicle noise limits in the EEC

Vehicle Category	Motor Vehicle Noise Limits dB(A)				Possible Future Noise Limits dB(A)
	70/157/EEC 1970	77/212/EEC 1982	81/334/EEC 1985	84/424/EEC 1989	
Passenger Car	82	80	80	77	75
Small van < 3.5t	84	81	81	78–79	76
Bus < 150kw	89	82	82	80	78
Bus > 150kw	91	85	85	83	80
Lorry < 75kw	89	86	86	81	78
Lorry 75–150kw	89	86	86	83	80
Lorry > 150kw	91	88	88	84	83

Source: Nelson (1989)

to rid the environment of noise are in those areas of Europe where traffic calming measures are being adopted on a large scale. This does not include Britain, France or Italy. The increasingly stringent noise limitation regulations will not provide relief from this problem.

The problem of ambient noise (ie general noise levels in a particular area) is a difficult one. The Netherlands and Switzerland have made a start with regulations and noise zoning to tackle this problem. The approach to noise abatement in these two countries is based on the establishment of noise zones for which quality standards have been set. Such an approach has to involve all sources of noise and is of much wider relevance than traffic alone.

The Netherlands

The aim is to reduce to zero the number of people experiencing serious noise nuisance and reducing by 50% the number experiencing noise nuisance to some extent. The legislation was introduced in 1979 and has been given extra force by the policies adopted as part of the 1990 National Environmental Policy Plus Plan: citizens have a right to 'a good residential and living environment with respect to . . . noise, odour, vibration, external safety, and local air pollution'.

The methods used to achieve noise standards in the Netherlands include source control, zoning, pricing policies and enforcement. A noise levy is imposed and financial incentives are available for the purchase of quiet lorries. Noise zones are required around roads, railways, airports, residential and industrial areas and 'quiet zones'. The Noise Abatement

Act (1979) sets preferred and maximum limits for noise within zones. These range from 40dB(A) at night time in residential zones, through 50dB(A) at the exterior wall of dwellings alongside roads to 70dB(A) maximum permissible load for road traffic noise in the vicinity of existing dwellings. This rather complex system of noise limits under different circumstances, from different sources and in different kinds of rooms is described in Waller (1988).

Germany

Germany has a particularly acute noise problem. Sixty per cent of the population consider themselves to be disturbed by road noise and 25% severely disturbed (DocTer, 1990). Noise levels are specified which may not be exceeded for certain kinds of areas (table 4.3).

Table 4.3 Noise levels for town planning in Germany

Type of area	Day dB(A)	Night dB(A)
Residential and holiday area	50	40
Village area, mixed area	60	55
Core area, trade area	65	55
Special area (depending on use)	45–65	35–65
Cemeteries, allotments and parks	55	55

Germany has invested large amounts in noise barriers to reduce traffic noise in the vicinity of main roads. In 1986 this amounted to DM187 million for walls, embankments, cuttings, tunnels etc. German support of traffic calming and cycling projects (particularly the latter) is likely to have a greater impact on noise abatement than physical barriers that simply mask the noise and divert it upward and outward.

Switzerland

Cantons in Switzerland are required by the Federal Noise Ordinance (1986) to divide their territory into the following zones for which noise quality standards have been set:

Zone 1   Recreational areas
Zone 2   Residential areas
Zone 3   Mixed residential and industrial areas
Zone 4   Industrial areas

For each zone three types of noise standard are set. These are ambient limits, planning limits and alarm limits. These are further sub-divided into day and night and can be seen in table 4.4.

Table 4.4   Noise standards in Switzerland

Zone	Planning Limits dB(A)		Ambient Limits dB(A)		Alarm Limits dB(A)	
	Day	Night	Day	Night	Day	Night
1	50	40	55	45	65	60
2	55	45	60	50	70	65
3	60	50	65	55	70	65
4	65	55	70	60	75	70

Source: ERL (1991b)

The city of Zürich has an integrated environmental traffic management system which aims to reduce ambient noise levels in the city from 70dB(A) to 65dB(A) by 1994. Achievement of this target requires a reduction in traffic of 50% and up to 90% in some areas. The Zürich approach involves measures which will deliver a number of benefits in addition to noise reduction. These include:

- rerouting traffic away from residential areas
- quietening noisy vehicles
- noise barriers and façade insulation
- pedestrian zones
- speed limits of 30kph
- traffic flow control favouring public transport vehicles, bicycles and pedestrians
- use of noise absorbent road surfaces.

The importance of this package of measures from Zürich is that the approach to noise recognises the importance of bringing about changes in behaviour to reduce the demand for the activity which produces noise in the first place. Giving priority to less-noisy modes of transport is both very simple and very effective. Such policies are sustainable policies because they tackle the central issue of rising demand for environmentally damaging modes of transport.

It is not necessary to know the precise limits within which this demand must be managed to emphasise sustainability as a goal. Sustainability is about shifting demand downwards and transferring that demand to less damaging kinds of activities. Sustainability, moreover, will be defined by the size of the benefits obtained compared with the policy introduced. Reducing noise from a diesel engine will not achieve very much for air pollution or making streets pleasant for pedestrians and cyclists. Transferring freight from road to rail and reducing car trips in city centres will deliver air quality benefits, noise quality benefits, safety benefits and enhance the quality of the living environment. The ratio of benefits to costs is very high.

5 TIME POLLUTION

Time is a fundamental metric in transport as in all aspects of human organisation. Hagerstrand's contribution over the last thirty years to the understanding of space–time behaviour is as important as it is neglected in transport planning (Hagerstrand, 1975). His early emphasis on access to facilities identified the importance of making contact with places and people as the central organising feature of human activity. It is this contact rather than either the means or the speed of transport that determines the success of a transportation system. Even more importantly it is this contact that determines the quality of life in cities. Jane Jacobs' account of city life in the USA (Jacobs, 1961) shows just how important diversity and ordinary human contact are to safety, security and feelings of well-being. Societal processes that spread activities over an ever increasing space–time continuum achieve the opposite of well-being: a privatised, socially inert world where neighbourhood counts for little and status depends on the frequency and speed of movement over longer distances.

It is relatively easy to increase the speed at which we move around but quite difficult to ensure that we can carry out a large proportion of our activities with a small time penalty and with considerable spin-offs for neighbourhood, community and attractive city forms. We are good at the former and dreadful at the latter. On these important issues we have very few indicators of performance which can be graphed to reveal how well our transportation systems are performing in the 1990s by comparison (for example) with the 1920s. What is clear is that we must travel further to make contact with work, shops, schools and places of recreation. Since we are able to increase distances between things like hospitals, schools, and shopping centres (and this is the direct result of much public and private decision making), but not increase the number of hours in the day, then we must increase speed. Basically we use technology to permit greater speeds but still work, eat, sleep and play in roughly the same proportions as always. We simply do these things further apart from each other.

The consumption of some technological benefit in terms of increased utilisation of resources is rather important as it defines our capacity to create environmental problems and distribute access to basic things in a way which is socially lopsided. Thus out-of-town shopping centres confer benefits on car owners (we presume) but make life very difficult for traditional retail cores and shops that are within the range of good public transport and walkable distances of residential areas. The consumer Eldorado of the hypermarket with its vast car parks has, therefore, deprived those without cars and those who prefer traditional shopping centres and markets within walking/public transport distances of their choices. At the same time the large traffic generators add their contribution to the air pollution and noise pollution of motorised transport and the reduction of opportunities for walking and cycling.

Such evidence as is available (particularly in oral history from the 1920s and 1930s) shows that over the last fifty years there has been a steady decline in the ease with which the majority of people of all ages and social classes can make contact with basic facilities and walk, cycle or use public transport. Changes in this period are of course very complex and include major economic changes in the pattern and location of manufacturing and services as well as motorisation itself. Nevertheless travelling (without a car) within 5km of a home address would be easier and produce more goods and services in 1930 than it would in 1990.

The conquest of distance by the destruction of time

The history of transport technology and the development of society is a series of distinct steps in our ability to cover a given amount of distance in a given amount of time (Janelle, 1968). The travel range and the range of experiences open to us define a particular culture at a particular time far more clearly than long lists of attributes or characteristics.

Higher speeds extend the spatial domain in any given allocation of time. Thus we can compress distance by conquering time and allocate society's benefits by giving people more time to overcome distance or privileged access to modes of transport with higher speeds. In either case the results are socially skewed. The 'action space' of a poor black resident of Los Angeles or a poor white resident in Montgomery (Alabama), for instance, is no greater than that of an urban resident of 100 years ago. The poor have the time to devote to travel and no money while the rich have the money to buy travel but are more likely to claim time pressures. The more we emphasise time savings the more we skew the whole transport system to serve the needs of a privileged, wealthy, elite.

The ability to buy distance with time savings has other serious consequences. Marchetti (1988) has shown that there is a very rough correspondence in the amount of time each of us devotes to travel regardless of how fast or how far we travel. The significance of this empirical work is that if we save time we use it to consume more distance. We simply make more journeys and contemplate day trips to Brussels, Paris or Stockholm where previously we would have thought the idea to be slightly ridiculous. Thus time savings as promised by high speed trains (HST) and high speed car travel release time for more travel and spur on the consumption of distance to ever higher levels of achievement. The environmental consequences of this accelerating process are as dramatic as they are destructive.

In our home territories we must spend more time in journeys to supermarkets or leisure centres and more time looking for somewhere to park. We add to congestion in cities on our way to airports or HST stations and spend as much time getting to the end point of our HST trip as we do on the trip itself.

Speed and its distance-gobbling effect is a major polluter. It pollutes space, time and the mind. Space has to be consumed in large quantities to provide the infrastructure for high speed travel. The faster the mode of transport the more space it requires (figure 5.1). The space damaging consequences of high speed travel can be seen in the land requirements for new motorways, in the land take for new high speed rail routes in France and Germany and in the enormous amounts of space required for airports, particularly their car parking requirements. Low speeds and non-polluting modes require very little space. Compare the space requirements of a pedestrian in figure 5.1 and the space requirements of a car with one person occupancy. Urban motorway construction and 'relief' road construction provides the ultimate expression of destruction rooted in speed and the destruction of community rooted in the pursuit of mobility for the minority.

The pollution of time is the transformation of useful units of human energy into something which has to be destroyed. Time has to be 'saved' rather than enjoyed and in a subtle reversal of historical priorities anything that 'saves' time is a good thing and anything that 'wastes' it is a bad thing. Time is a valuable resource which should be conserved so that it can produce socially useful products. The urge to save time is fuelled by the belief that the next task is more important than the present task and that speed and crowded diaries correspond to social importance. This is pollution of the mind where no-one has time for a leisurely exchange of views with a friend or colleague or for the kind of social interaction that nurtures community. The production of community needs an investment of time and energy in contact with neighbours and local groups. The opportunities for such contact depend on time available and priorities. The ability to travel longer distances (and save time at higher speeds) means that no time is available for intense interaction with neighbours and groups and so there is little chance of genuine community developing. Time has been saved by a journey at high speed

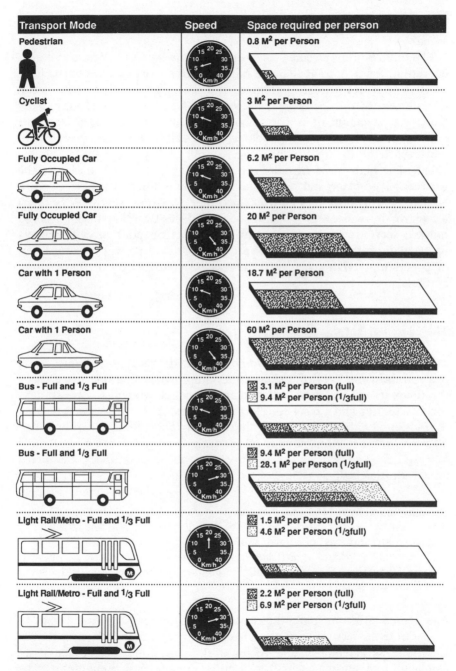

Figure 5.1 Consumption of space by different modes of transport, occupancy and speed

Source: Navarro et al (1985)

on high quality roads or on a HST but what has been done with the time saved?

The three pollutions come together to pollute locality. We are so intent on getting from A to B that the quality of the urban environment in A or B is relegated to the bottom of the list. The quality of the urban environment in Europe is generally very poor and is deteriorating rapidly under the onslaught of traffic. Inappropriate and mismanaged transport policies produce environmental damage and fail to capitalise on the solutions which lie in high quality, local public transport at speeds of 20–40kph. The high speed traveller is making a very real contribution to the destruction of place and the diffusion of environmental problems down high speed corridors to spill over into the next urban centre. New inter-urban roads, widenings of motorways and construction of high speed railways serve to accelerate the conveyor belt effect pouring vast numbers of people into the urban areas already unable to cope with current levels of congestion. High speed travel makes no contribution to the solution of these problems.

The *Momo* effect

Michael Ende's (1984) novel *Momo* described the changes which took place in the daily lives of a small community when time thieves persuade the residents to save time rather than 'waste' it with idle conversation, social activities and caring for elderly relatives. The effect was dramatic. A traditional cafe was converted into a fast-food outlet and people had no time for each other in spite of the time they had saved by becoming more efficient. The village barber took it all very seriously and saved time enthusiastically:

> meanwhile he was becoming increasingly restless and irritable. The odd thing was that, no matter how much time he saved, he never had any to spare; in some mysterious way, it simply vanished. Imperceptibly at first, but then quite unmistakably, his days grew shorter and shorter. Almost before he knew it, another week had gone by, and another month, and another year, and another and another (p66–7).

The *Momo* effect is multi-dimensional. The more effort we devote to saving time the less we have available and the more harassed we feel. The less time we have available for sharing with other people the more damaging the consequences for family, friends and community. The more time we save through our efficiency drives or organisational revolutions the more energy and consumer products we consume, the more space we consume and the more pollution we produce. The destruction

Calculated speeds taking into account the total amount of time spent in transport

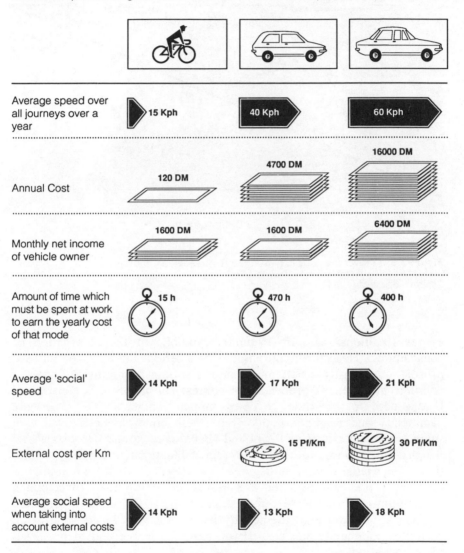

	Bicycle	Car (small)	Car (large)
Average speed over all journeys over a year	15 Kph	40 Kph	60 Kph
Annual Cost	120 DM	4700 DM	16000 DM
Monthly net income of vehicle owner	1600 DM	1600 DM	6400 DM
Amount of time which must be spent at work to earn the yearly cost of that mode	15 h	470 h	400 h
Average 'social' speed	14 Kph	17 Kph	21 Kph
External cost per Km		15 Pf/Km	30 Pf/Km
Average social speed when taking into account external costs	14 Kph	13 Kph	18 Kph

Figure 5.2   Average social speeds of the bicycle and the car

Source: Seifried (1990)

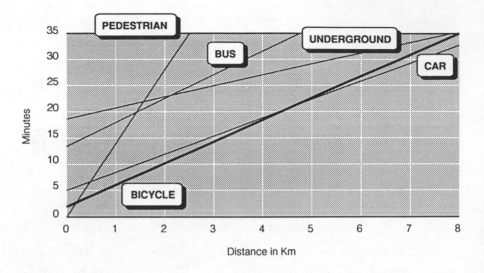

Figure 5.3   Travel times in urban areas from door to door

Source: Bracher (1988)

of the traditional cafe in *Momo* is symbolic of the redefinition of consumption. Henceforth consumption is a serious matter to be pursued in isolation from its social context and is sustained only by the drive to consume more. In its proper social context consumption is constrained by the need to take time, to enjoy human contact and to experience community and neighbourhood. Once these bonds are destroyed consumption breaks out of its social and spatial context and becomes global (tropical hardwoods, tourism) and regional/national (shopping, recreation). The spatial separation demands the allocation of large amounts of time and a premium on speed and moves the act of travel (overcoming the friction of distance) to centre stage. Collectively we have forgotten the central importance of the activity itself (eg a meal in the local cafe), destroyed community and created the basis for higher and higher levels of motorisation.

There is of course a central paradox in the process of transport investment to save time and that lies in the persistence of congestion in cities and the failure of road schemes costing £10 million per mile to move people in their cars costing an average of £20,000 each at speeds not much above 20kph. The speeds at which people actually move in their cars as opposed to the advertised joys of 175kph on roads which rarely see another vehicle represent an extremely adverse energy input to work output ratio. Figure 5.2 shows the interesting concept of 'average social speed' for cars and bicycles to make this point very eloquently. This in its turn is based on an original idea by Ivan Illich who appreciated the links between time, speed and energy conversion over twenty years ago (Illich, 1974).

Bicycles have little difficulty in beating the car on average social speed. Their efficiency from an ergonomic point of view matches their efficiency in coping with urban form where city form still reflects the needs of people rather than those of cars. Their energy efficiency is unbeatable and their health effects of remarkable value to society as a whole (BMA, 1992). Not only does a 'slow' mode of transport reduce the incidence of heart and respiratory disease but it also reduces harmful emissions (see chapter 3) by transferring journeys of 5–10km in length from car to bicycle. Bicycles take up very little space and they perform well over the distances normally represented in city journeys (figure 5.3)

Time and social costs

Transport planners and those responsible for urban design rarely think of the impact of their efforts on women, children, the elderly or the infirm. Similarly they fail to realise that all transport policies and policies which influence location and accessibility will steal time from different groups in society and reallocate it to (usually) richer groups. This is very close to the *Momo* effect. When local shops, clinics, hospitals and schools disappear to be replaced by bigger, better versions at a greater distance from where the demand is located then that spatial and organisational change imposes a time penalty on the users of that service. For those without cars (still about 40% of the UK population), for those without them during the day and for those taking the brunt of the deterioration in public transport services this is a problem. They must spend more time searching for replacement services, waiting for buses which operate in a post-deregulation information famine, waiting for lifts or doing without. The time penalties in making long journeys coupled with the unpleasantness of delays and waiting are a serious burden on those groups. If their time had been valued differently the planning process (public and private) would have produced a different outcome.

For those with cars the large facilities with their even larger car parks are within reach and represent an expenditure of time which is reasonably pleasant even with congestion and frustration. There is no comparison between the depressing search for disorganised public transport in a dark, wet, lonely place and a ride in a car with its heater and quadraphonic stereo. In some places public transport does not even exist. The provision of high quality urban roads, large car parks and

Where pedestrians are left waiting because of cars
How long is the light red for pedestrians?

Where grandmothers have to hurry
This is the speed pedestrians must cross the road when the light is green

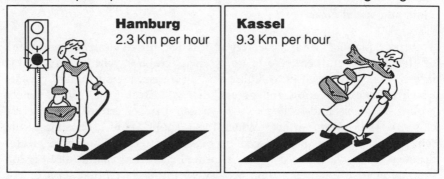

Figure 5.4 Waiting times and crossing speeds at pelican crossings

Source: Seifried (1990)

(soon) in-car navigation represents a high valuation of the time of the car occupant. No charge for use of road space through electronic road pricing (ERP) will ever produce the 'level playing field' in this set of choices. More importantly ERP will not erode the time advantages of a car journey, indeed it is designed to increase these advantages and will inevitably add to the degree of car dependence in society and the spatial decentralisation of facilities. ERP saves time for one group (car users) at the expense of other groups (eg pedestrians) and at the expense of greater levels of space inefficiency. Figure 5.1 shows clearly that in terms of space efficiency the car is an extremely wasteful use of urban space. Paying for that space does not alter this equation.

Pedestrians, cyclists and public transport users are undervalued and underrated throughout the planning process. High speeds with their heightened fatality rates, pollution rates, space sterilisation potential and community disruption effects are valued much more highly than low speeds. There are some particularly clear examples of this discrimination against pedestrians. The delays which are built into pedestrian actuated crossings (pelican crossings) favour the motorised traffic and not the pedestrian. Both in terms of waiting times for a green phase and in the time allowed for the actual crossing the pedestrian is disadvantaged. Waiting times exceed tolerances and pedestrians will consequently behave rationally and cross on the red phase, while crossing times demand athletic performances from the elderly and those in charge of young children, heavy shopping etc (figure 5.4 illustrates this latter problem). All of these situations increase the risks for pedestrians and set out to minimise inconvenience for the road user who is not exposed to the noise, the weather and the danger.

In the case of women travelling alone after dark there are potentially serious consequences arising from waiting at bus stops or for late trains or for using another device designed to maximise vehicle convenience at the expense of pedestrians: the underpass. Women come unstuck in other ways in a car/male dominated urban planning system. They are more likely to be bus users than men, more likely to be in charge of young children in dirty and dangerous pedestrian environments and more likely to be involved with escorting duties arising from the unacceptability of letting children walk unsupervised in environments rendered lethal by traffic. Escorting involves hundreds of thousands of hours of female time spent picking up the pieces of an environment rendered unsafe for children, mainly by men. Estimates of the time involved and of the damage to children's use of time have been made by Hillman, Adams and Whitelegg (1990).

The urge to save time produces serious environmental and safety problems. Roads designed to carry traffic at speeds well in excess of 120kph must take up more land than roads designed for lower speeds. The former cannot tolerate tight radius curves. The same is the case for high speed rail based on new track and new routes. Higher speeds on roads bring more death and injury to pedestrians. In collisions with cars, 15% of pedestrian injuries are fatal or serious at 20kph; 74% at 40kph; and more than 95% at 60kph. This relationship is described graphically in figures 5.5 and 5.6.

The figures show that speed is a critical factor in determining the outcome of personal injury accidents. Figure 5.6 shows for the city of Hamburg the reduction in injuries as a result of introducing 263 zones where speed has been limited to 30kph. Injuries in total are down by 27%, slight injuries down by 26%, serious injuries down by 31% and fatalities down by 90%.

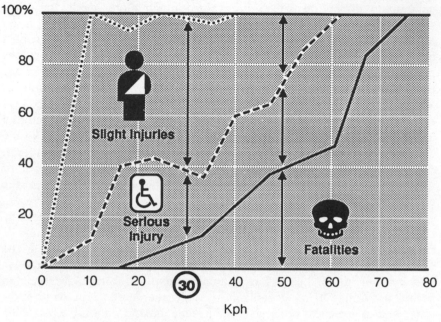

Figure 5.5   The relationship between speed and injury and fatality rates
Source: Seifried (1990)

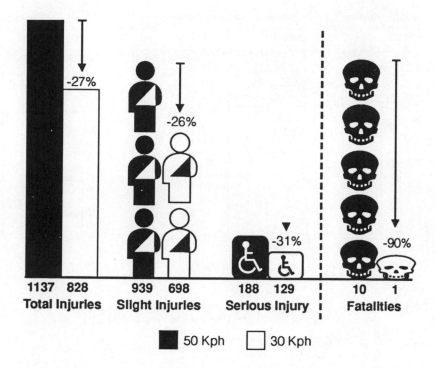

1137 828   939 698   188 129   10   1
Total Injuries   Slight Injuries   Serious Injury   Fatalities

-27%   -26%   -31%   -90%

■ 50 Kph   □ 30 Kph

Figure 5.6 Injuries and fatalities in Hamburg road accidents before and after
the introduction of 30kph speed limit zones

Source: Seifried (1990)

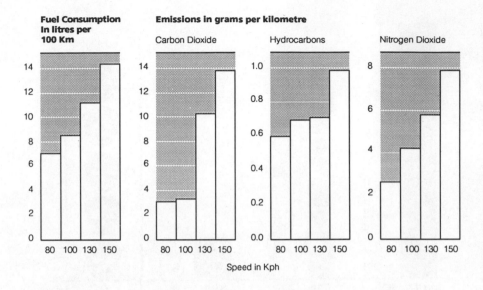

Figure 5.7   Fuel consumption and emissions from petrol-engined cars at
constant speeds (average value for thirty vehicles)

Source: Vahrenholt (1984)

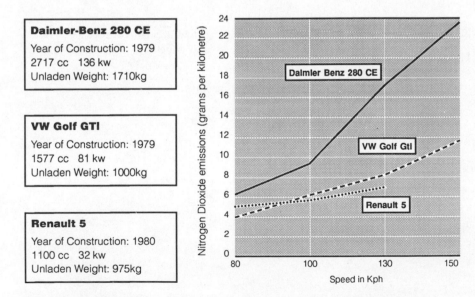

Figure 5.8   Comparison of nitrogen dioxide emissions from cars in identical
driving conditions at different speeds (grams per kilometre)

Source: Vahrenholt (1984)

It is clear that a totally new approach to road safety improvement could be based on speed alone. Not reducing speeds by whatever means possible or arguing for the raising of speed limits is based on a prioritisation of the time of the vehicle occupant. This is higher than the safety of the pedestrian and cyclist in current safety and transport policy.

Speed also figures in pollution. Low speeds are associated with high emissions of certain kinds of exhaust products but these are exceeded at high speeds. Figure 5.7 shows how the emissions of some key pollutants rise as speed increases. Figure 5.8 compares three vehicles of different engine sizes to illustrate the effect of an increase in vehicle size.

Reducing speeds in German cities through traffic calming (Tolley, 1990) has produced dramatic reductions in both injuries and pollution. A simple policy like traffic calming can bring about substantial gains to the environment and improvements for pedestrians and cyclists but only if used as part of a comprehensive attack on overall levels of car use (Whitelegg, 1990b).

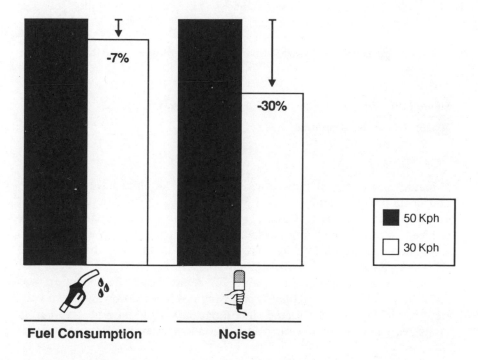

Figure 5.9   Fuel consumption and noise levels under 50kph and 30kph speed limits

Source: Seifried (1990)

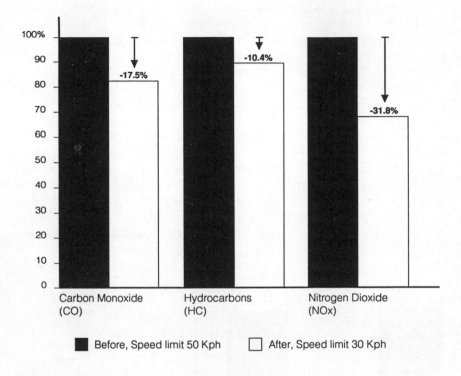

Figure 5.10   Emission levels under 50kph and 30kph speed limits

Source: Umweltbundesamt der BRD (1986)

Figures 5.9 and 5.10 show how 30kph zones in cities have reduced air and noise pollution and 5.11 and 5.12 are based on specific geographical areas in Köln. Figures 5.11 and 5.12 show that the speed reductions have reduced accident and injury levels dramatically but also the costs associated with those injuries. Treating areas in this way has produced financial gains as a result of accident reduction. In Nippes the costs of accidents went down by 63% while in Agnesviertel the reduction was 58%. These are substantial gains and they result from slowing down traffic, something which seems incompatible with current evaluation strategies based on saving time and the monetarisation of those savings.

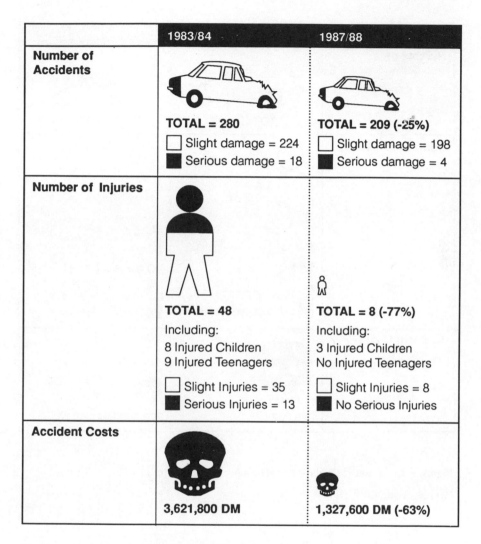

	1983/84	1987/88
Number of Accidents	TOTAL = 280 ☐ Slight damage = 224 ■ Serious damage = 18	TOTAL = 209 (-25%) ☐ Slight damage = 198 ■ Serious damage = 4
Number of Injuries	TOTAL = 48 Including: 8 Injured Children 9 Injured Teenagers ☐ Slight Injuries = 35 ■ Serious Injuries = 13	TOTAL = 8 (-77%) Including: 3 Injured Children No Injured Teenagers ☐ Slight Injuries = 8 ■ No Serious Injuries
Accident Costs	3,621,800 DM	1,327,600 DM (-63%)

Figure 5.11   Accident balance programme: Nippes

Source: Stadt Köln (1989)

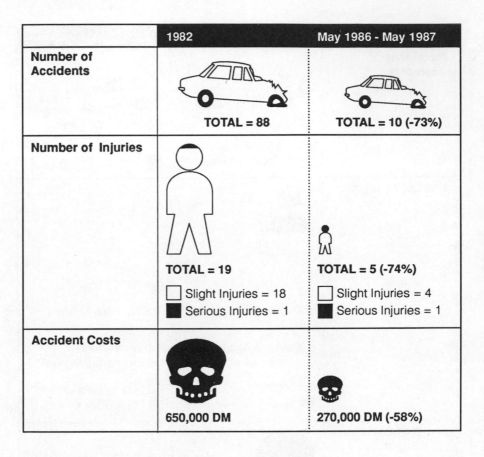

	1982	May 1986 - May 1987
Number of Accidents	TOTAL = 88	TOTAL = 10 (-73%)
Number of Injuries	TOTAL = 19 ☐ Slight Injuries = 18 ■ Serious Injuries = 1	TOTAL = 5 (-74%) ☐ Slight Injuries = 4 ■ Serious Injuries = 1
Accident Costs	650,000 DM	270,000 DM (-58%)

Figure 5.12   Accident balance programme: Agnesviertel

Source: Stadt Köln (1989)

High speed trains

High speed trains (HST) represent a very clear focus of political support and investment for a mode of transport whose primary characteristic is speed. HST developments around the world have been described in Whitelegg, Hulten and Flink (1993) and present serious problems which result from their space expanding, distance consuming role. These effects are described in Whitelegg and Holzapfel (1993). The HST is not the first technology to consume space, energy and resources in an attempt to destroy time. Air travel achieves this much more dramatically than rail travel and the motorway system in its turn has altered the geography of

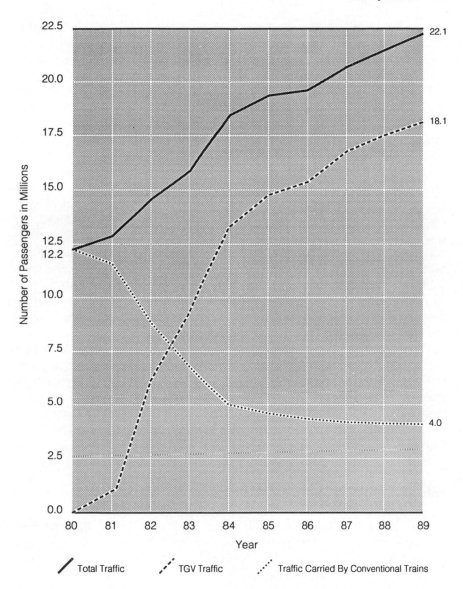

Figure 5.13 Paris – southeast routes: evolution of passenger traffic, 1980–89

Source: Polino (1993)

Britain to permit longer distance trips with the expenditure of smaller amounts of time. This is achieved by increasing the amount of energy consumed and altering the spatial structures of society so that many activities have to be carried out over very long distances.

The advent of the HST is different in that it exploits the environmentally friendly characteristics of rail travel to increase passenger demand, space and energy consumption and the distances that separate activities. High speeds are only useful over longer distances. The HST is not relevant to the vast majority of trips which are less than 10km in length. HST can supplant air travel on distances equivalent to Paris–Lyon, Manchester–London, Paris–London but this is not the same as reducing the demand for air travel. In a crowded sky any air traffic control slots are quickly reallocated to other traffic. The growth in the demand for tourist traffic alone can take up any slack created by HST projects. The net result, then, of a Paris–Lyon type investment in HST is an increase in passenger travel in total (ie all modes) in that corridor (see figure 5.13), an increase in passenger miles in air travel (not necessarily in that corridor) and a change in land uses and locational strategies reacting to the changed accessibility surface which will necessitate more longer-distance traffic.

There are a number of other consequences of HST, not discussed here but relevant to the long term development of sustainable transport policies. These include rail privatisation, noise emission characteristics of HST and the traffic generation characteristics of the HST stations themselves. The nearest analogy to HST is air travel and air terminals need vast amounts of space for car parking. It is unlikely that HST travellers will arrive at their starting point by bus.

Valuation of time as a source of pollution

Sharp (1973) describes an urban road construction and improvement scheme (the Granby Hall project in Leicester) where time savings made up 96.4% of the gross benefits in a cost–benefit evaluation. The average for time savings over several projects was 90% of the value of the benefits. A whole generation of road schemes has been justified on a set of assumptions that boil down to time savings having a monetary value. Where the road might block pedestrian movements and cause delay this amount of time lost has not been offset against the time gained. Nor has any attention been given in the calculations of time saved to the question of how this time might usefully be reallocated in some productive way to justify the inference of monetary values.

One of the many problems with valuing time is the importance which should be attached (if any) to very small time savings, say less than five minutes. A five minute time saving almost certainly falls within the routine variability of any journey and certainly cannot be reallocated to 'useful' time. Its 'monetarisation' is, therefore, a convenient fiction that enables the evaluation routine to come up with the right answer: ie build the road.

In the case of the Leicester example quoted above reducing the value of time saved to 25% of its original value when the time saved is three minutes or less has the effect of cutting the first year rate of return from 20% to 5%. This rate of 5% would be further eroded if the three minute threshold were raised. Even at the 5% rate of return based on the three minute threshold it is unlikely that any urban road scheme would proceed.

The above shows that putting a value on time can act as a powerful push in a particular direction. Putting high values on the time of drivers even down to very short periods pushes the system in the direction of road building with all its harmful consequences. Putting a high value on the time of cyclists and pedestrians would restructure urban transport. Traffic would have to give way to pedestrians so as not to delay them, purpose-built pedestrian and cycle facilities would win new investment and proposals that encouraged pedestrians to linger and make use of space whilst slowing down traffic would gain precedence. This is of course encouraging the waste of time and might infer that time should have a negative value. The theoretical case for time having a negative value is at least as strong as current arguments and would encourage cities to develop as social, productive, enjoyable and secure places (Jacobs, 1961).

It is not difficult to imagine cities restructured so that they serve the needs of people and not cars. This involves the encouragement of walking, cycling, lingering, mutual observation and sociability. A polluted, noisy environment coupled with a retreat into a privatised, defended space is (with some notable exceptions) what is currently on offer. The latter situation results from concepts of time as valuable and its conversion into monetary values or monetarisation; the former would result from concepts of the social use of time. One model uses the language of saving time and the other of time well spent. If it is possible to imagine the kind of city described by Jacobs then it is also possible to map out a route of how to get there and concepts of time are essential to this process.

Time, therefore, is central to notions of sustainability. A sustainable city or a sustainable transport policy or a sustainable economy cannot be founded on economic principles which through their monetarisation of time orientate society towards higher levels of motorisation, faster speeds and greater consumption of space. The fact that these characteristics produce energy intensive societies and pollution is only part of the problem. More importantly these characteristics distort value systems, elevate mobility above accessibility, associate higher speeds with progress and lower speeds with anti-modernism and dislocate communities and social life.

Sustainability involves significant changes in the way markets operate or the ways individuals behave or both. Time valuation is one example of such a fundamental change. Having considered the impact of current methods of valuation it is possible to see why the basic conditions for more travel and more pollution are so persistent and why conditions for cyclists and pedestrians are so poor. It is possible, moreover, to see why 'solutions' such as catalytic converters and ERP and even much improved public transport are so irrelevant. None of these agents will alter significantly the basic trajectory that is now in place.

6 TRANSPORT AND HEALTH

There can be no doubt that transport in its many forms has a significant impact on health. The problem with focusing on this aspect of transport is that the impacts are so many and the state of knowledge in the traditional scientific sense so poor that the subject gets very little attention. There is no example of a public health policy that builds transport impacts into its design and no example of a transport policy that sets out to improve health. There are signs of a growing awareness of the problem particularly amongst environmental groups and health campaigning groups. The issue has also been recognised in a recent article in the *British Medical Journal* (Godlee, 1992).

There is also a growing awareness amongst those groups exposed to traffic hazards and this is manifesting itself in a number of campaigns for car-free/pedestrian friendly cities. Amsterdam adopted a policy of this kind after a referendum in March 1992 and similar policies are in place in Lübeck, Bologna and Aachen.

Table 6.1 Ways in which transport influences health

Type of effect	Results
Health promoting	Enables access to: employment, education, shops, recreation, social support networks, health services, countryside; provides recreation and exercise.
Health damaging	Accidents; pollution: carbon monoxide, nitrogen oxides, hydrocarbons, ozone, carbon dioxide, lead, benzene; noise and vibration; stress and anxiety; danger; loss of land and planning blight; severance of communities by roads.

The Transport and Health Study Group (1991) have produced a useful summary of the ways in which transport influences health. These are divided into health promoting and health damaging groups (table 6.1). The health promoting effects of transport are complex but are well documented. Access to places and facilities is important for the maintenance of health. Access to health care facilities which is often poor for non-car owning groups is an important determinant of health (Whitelegg, 1982). Lack of access because of poor public transport, walking distances that are too long or difficult timetabling problems can lead to lower levels of use of health care facilities (New and Senior, 1991). Improvements to public transport, walking and cycling facilities will improve access and contribute to improved health.

Access to workplaces, recreational opportunities and to friends and relatives also influences health. In the case of work good access is an important precondition for the efficient operation of labour markets especially amongst low income groups. Mortality and morbidity are higher in these groups than in higher income groups and low incomes provide little flexibility for expenditure on travel. The combination of expensive public transport, badly located work opportunities and low pay makes job search and job retention that much more difficult. This ensures that families in poverty are likely to remain there with all the consequences for health, especially child health, noted in Townsend and Davidson (1982).

A system of land uses and transport provision that minimises distances separating activities and maximises the opportunities for walking, cycling and reasonably priced public transport brings with it substantial gains for labour market efficiency, income growth and access to all those facilities that sustain health. This includes shops, schools and recreational facilities so that nutrition, education and exercise with social spin-offs can all be improved. The polar extreme of these opportunities is a characteristic of many urban areas in developed countries. An environment characterised by no local shops, no communal facilities, jobs that are too far away to be affordable to reach and lots of traffic is not a healthy environment.

Social support in communities is very important to maintain health. The Transport and Health Study Group report (1991) draws attention to the work on social networks and psychological well-being. Berkman and Syme (1979) have reviewed the links between social networks and mortality from all causes and Blazer (1982) has examined social support and its relevance for the elderly. Welin et al (1992) go further and show how good social networks provide some improvement in non-cancer mortality rates.

Transport alone cannot deliver rich social networks but it can go a long way to provide the right preconditions. The decline of walking deprives many of the possibility of social interaction and reasons for wanting to be in a car often include feelings of insecurity on the street and the need for private defensible space. Jacobs (1961) describes the preconditions for social interaction very clearly. At the centre of her account of what makes cities vital and attractive places is the street as an arena for social interaction, sustained by a large variety of uses and mixed residential, service, retail, etc premises. On this street there is a continuous movement of people, all supervised informally by other people and a shared responsibility for supervising children. The street depends on the volume of pedestrians and the attractiveness of its uses for its success. The result is a successful neighbourhood, a reduction in crime and an increase in feelings of security and well-being.

This description may represent something which no longer exists but it does identify the elements of a transport policy that would nurture healthy cities and healthy people. The key things are mixed uses, short distances between things, low rents in reused buildings, heavy pedestrian flows and lack of interference from cars.

Cars do obstruct the pursuit of social objectives. They are noisy and intrusive, they carve up neighbourhoods, and they encourage fear and isolation. Fear and isolation have a downward spiral effect. If traffic volumes are so large that the noise and the dirt and the danger are intolerable then people stay away from the streets and use them as little as possible. This reduces trade for businesses and makes residences less desirable so the whole character of the neighbourhood changes. The street that is left is not safe. There is no more community, no more neighbourhood and no more security. Fear also works in other ways and encourages parents to take their children off the streets to protect them producing the spurious result of lowered accident and injury rates and increasing the amount of traffic as children are driven to destinations (eg schools) that formerly would have been reached on foot (Hillman, Adams and Whitelegg, 1990).

Appleyard and Lintell (1969) and Appleyard (1981) have described the effect of traffic volumes on social interaction at the level of the individual street. Their work on the extent to which street traffic annoys and disturbs residents and disrupts social interaction has not been surpassed. Figures 6.1–6.4 summarise their main findings. Figure 6.1 makes the distinctions between light, moderate and heavy traffic in terms of traffic volumes and residents' views. Figure 6.2 shows how noise levels vary and how residents' perceptions of the problem vary. Figure 6.3 demonstrates how these characteristics influence social interaction. The street with heavy traffic has relatively little social interaction and residents have fewer friends and acquaintances. On lightly trafficked streets residents were found to have three times as many local friends and twice as many acquaintances as those on busy streets. Contacts between friends and acquaintances are shown diagrammatically in figure 6.3 making very clear the dense pattern of interaction in 'light' streets in comparison to busy streets.

Appleyard (1981) concludes:

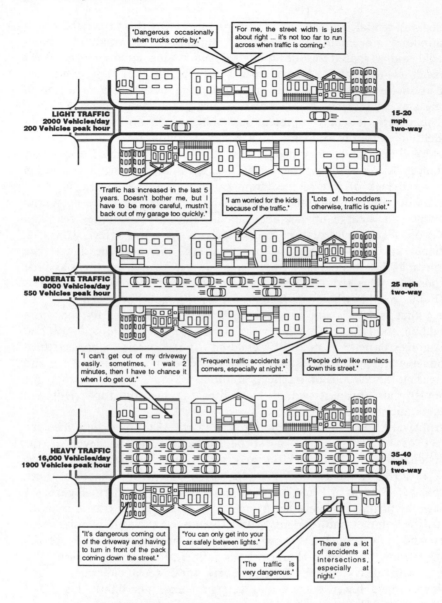

Figure 6.1   San Francisco: traffic hazard on three streets

Source: Appleyard (1981)

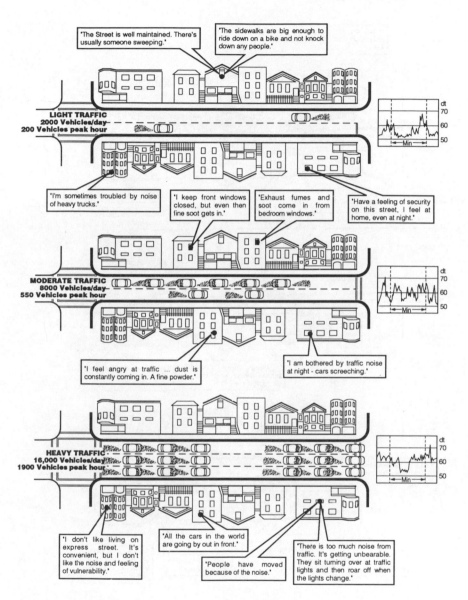

Figure 6.2 San Francisco: noise, stress and pollution on three streets

Source: Appleyard (1981)

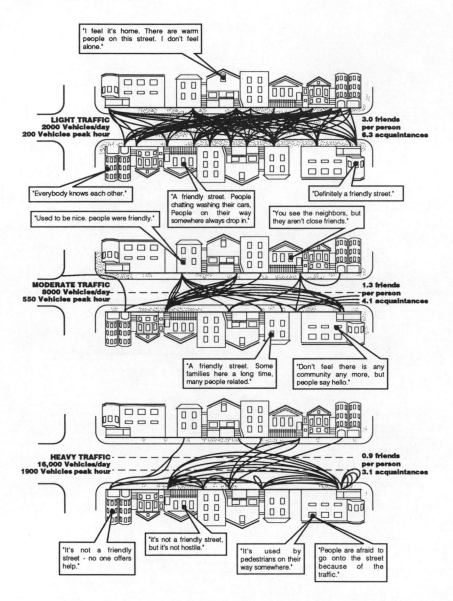

Figure 6.3   San Francisco: social interaction on three streets (*Note*: lines show
where friends or acquaintances live; dots show where people gather)

Source: Appleyard (1981)

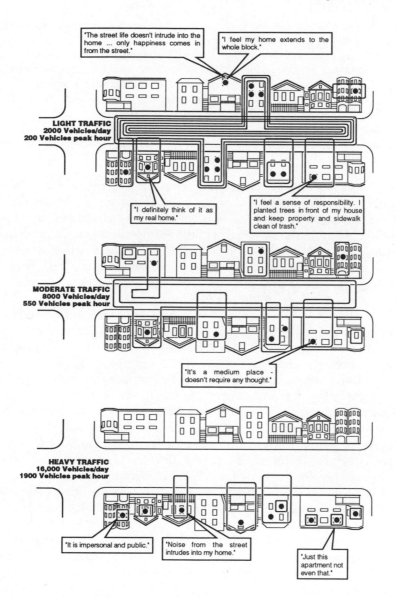

Figure 6.4 San Francisco: home territory on three streets (*Note*: lines show areas people indicated as their 'home territory')

Source: Appleyard (1981)

there was a marked difference in the way these streets were seen and used, especially by the young and the elderly. LIGHT was a closely knit community whose residents made full use of their street. The street had been divided into different use zones by the residents. Front steps were used for sitting and chatting, sidewalks for children playing, and for adults to stand and pass the time of day . . . the street was seen as a whole and no part was out of bounds. HEAVY street, on the other hand, had little or no sidewalk activity and was used solely as a corridor between the sanctuary of individual homes and the outside world. Residents kept very much to themselves. There was no feeling of community at all.

Figure 6.4 shows how residents view their home territory. On heavy-traffic streets they withdraw from public space and street life is very clear indeed and has important implications for their own health and for the health of the neighbourhood. Their withdrawal signals a lack of informal supervision and participation which renders the whole street a more dangerous and sterile space. The opposite is the case on the light street. Appleyard (1981) saw this contrast in territorial expansiveness as one of the more salient findings of the study.

It is very important that a link is made between Appleyard's observations on street life under heavy traffic conditions and the research on social interaction and health. Appleyard shows that traffic damages social interaction. Berkman and Syme (1979) reported that people who lacked social and community ties had higher mortality rates than those with more extensive contacts. The most important 'protective' factors among men were married status and frequent contacts with close friends and relatives. This contact is compromised, at least in the local community, by heavy traffic flows. Traffic is clearly implicated as an important causation factor in raised mortality in urban areas.

The finding that traffic is so intrusive and disruptive to social interaction is very important and points to a major negative impact as well as to a clear way forward to improve neighbourhood, social interaction, territorial expansiveness and security.

Given that the impact of traffic on social interaction is so great it is not surprising that it has had a major effect on the freedom of children to enjoy independent travel and use of the street and on the time demands made on others (especially women) to make up for this deficit through escorting (Hillman, Adams and Whitelegg, 1991). Traffic has brought about a substantial change in the environment in which children grow and develop and a child growing up in the 1990s has far fewer opportunities than ever before to explore a local area, interact with friends and acquaintances in a local territory and come to terms with personal development against that background of a familiar physical and social environment.

The child of the 1990s will probably travel to school by car and have

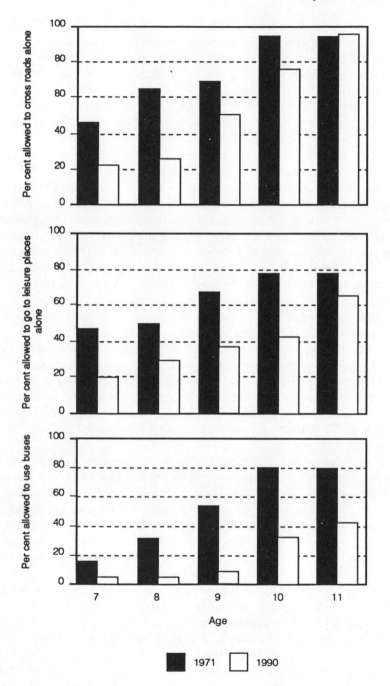

Figure 6.5 Independent mobility of English children by age, 1971 and 1990

Source: Hillman et al (1991)

frequent trips over long distances to holidays and recreational activities; but all closely supervised by an adult and interspersed with bouts of isolation in front of the TV, video and computer. The impact of this pattern on child development is beyond a discussion of transport issues but is not without implications for transport, health and the sociability of cities. Indeed, cities where children have freedom to play on the streets, cross roads to visit friends and explore their developing territorial base could be described as exhibiting a high basic measure of quality of life, hence *Healthy Cities* (Ashton, 1992).

Hillman, Adams and Whitelegg (1991) compared children's independent mobility in 1990 with that of 1971. In 1971 three-quarters of the children were allowed to cross roads on their own. In 1990 the proportion had fallen to a half. Figure 6.5 shows that the younger children were most affected. There was a similar though more marked decline in the proportion of children allowed to go on their own to places other than school: only about half of the 7–10 year olds who were allowed to go to these places on their own in 1971 were allowed to do so in 1990. There was an even more marked decline in the proportion of the juniors allowed to use buses on their own: whereas half were allowed to do so in 1971 only one in seven was allowed to do so in 1990.

The reduction in children's independent mobility is reflected in their changed patterns of travel. Figure 6.6 shows a marked increase in the proportion being driven to school by car and a fall in the proportion going on foot. Nearly four times as many were chauffeured to school in 1990 as in 1971. There is also a steep rise in the proportion of children, especially in the younger age groups, being accompanied on foot by an older person.

Hillman, Adams and Whitelegg (1991) do not present any evidence of a negative health effect but the links between outdoor play, exercise and health are not contrived. Some evidence on exercise is presented later in this chapter in a discussion of policy towards the bicycle. Lifestyles are inextricably linked with health outcomes and a society that deprives children of independent mobility in way that downgrades social experiences is not fostering positive health (Bowling, 1991). Positive health definitions take their cue from the World Health Organisation definition of health as 'a state of complete physical, mental and social well-being and not merely the absence of disease and infirmity' (WHO, 1958). To quote Lamb et al (1988) 'Positive health could be described as the ability to cope with stressful situations, the maintenance of a strong social-support system, integration in the community, high morale and life satisfaction, psychological well-being and even levels of physical fitness as well as physical health.'

It is clear from Appleyard's work and Hillman et al that these conditions are not being achieved and that traffic is the main cause of that

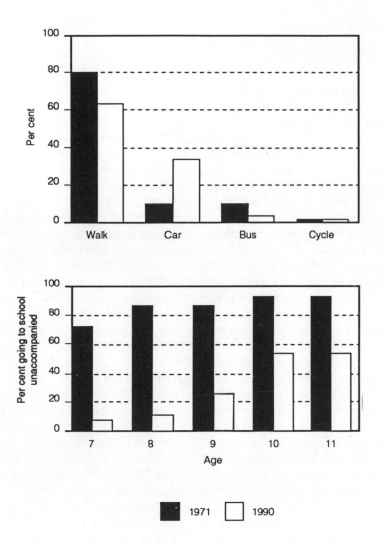

Figure 6.6 Method and supervision of English children's journeys, 1971 and 1990

Source: Hillman et al (1991)

under-achievement. Further growth in traffic volumes and further social disruption can only widen the gap between what is achievable and what has to be endured in the majority of Europe's cities.

Walking and cycling

Walking and cycling are important modes of transport that have a great deal to contribute to the efficient and environmentally friendly movement of people particularly in cities. Both are widely available to most sections of the population, cheap and supportive of local facilities and social networks. Both are ignored as serious modes of transport in most countries with the possible exception of The Netherlands and Denmark and a German programme of cycleway investment. Tolley (1990) has presented a thorough case for the incorporation of these modes into urban and recreational planning and this has been reinforced by Cleary (1992). Walking and cycling clearly have a great deal to offer to the development of healthy cities through a reduction of motorised trips, particularly over short distances, and a commensurate reduction of noise and pollution. Equally these modes have a great deal to offer to individual health as an additional layer of benefit to the social network advantages identified by Appleyard (1981).

The Transport and Health Study Group (1991) have identified exercise from walking and cycling as a factor in reducing the risk of ischaemic heart disease. Quoting the work of Fox and Goldblatt (1982) they show that men who walk or cycle to work have a lower rate of death from ischaemic heart disease than men who travel to work by car. Public transport users fall in between these two groups.

Cycling and walking provide easy and cheap access to physical activity which sustains physical fitness. The reduced rate of coronary disease among those who exercise has been noted by the Coronary Prevention Group (1987) and higher levels of physical fitness 'appear to delay all-cause mortality, primarily due to lowered rates of cardiovascular disease and cancer' (Blair et al, 1989). Physical fitness is an essential condition for good health but the amount of physical exercise taken by most people is not great (Davey Smith and Morris, 1992).

The British Medical Association has produced a report (BMA, 1992) which demonstrates the beneficial health effects of cycling. Cycling reduces the risks from cardiovascular diseases and contributes to lowering blood pressure. It encourages psychological well-being and keeps weight down. There is specific evidence that regular exercise such as cycling can counter depression and improve mental health (Stephens, 1988).

A recent survey of the health and lifestyle of the population of Heysham (Flowerdew, Pooley and Whitelegg, 1992) showed that only 15% of the 30–44 year old group and 8% of the 45–59 age group had any regular exercise that involved some exertion. At a time when the annual economic cost of heart disease in Britain is approximately £2 billion and most lifestyles are sedentary by nature a national policy to encourage walking and cycling has many advantages. The contribution to

individual health through exercise is a major gain as is the encouragement of social networks and the health gains to be had on a city-wide
basis if health damaging vehicle emissions can be reduced by switching
short distance journeys from cars to bicycles.

The British Medical Association study recognised that the health
benefits of cycling might be compromised by the road traffic accident
dangers associated with increased exposure to risks. Indeed this argument
is sometimes used against policies to encourage cycling. This is potentially a very complex issue involving a full audit of all the implications
of low levels of cycling as well as of much increased levels of cycling.
Such 'health audits' do not currently exist but would be very useful in
evaluating alternative policies within transport. In spite of this complex-
ity and against the background of an extremely hostile traffic environment it was possible to demonstrate that the years of life gained from
the exercise involved in cycling exceeded the years of life lost through
accidents. More importantly the risks associated with cycling are very
easily reduced or eliminated through policies that slow down traffic or
eliminate it altogether.

Accidents

In any discussion of transport and health, accidents and injuries come
very high on the list of issues to be resolved. The discussion of road traffic accidents (RTAs) is still dominated by the numbers recorded each
year in official statistics and the self-congratulatory message that in spite
of large increases in vehicle numbers and in vehicle kilometres the situation is improving. There is very little consideration of the much more
plausible interpretation of these declining numbers which is that
pedestrians and cyclists are so frightened to venture out into the streets
that they give up the struggle, stay at home or buy a car (Hillman,
Adams and Whitelegg, 1991). Nor is there very much discussion around
the possibility that much celebrated safety improvements such as seat
belts, helmets, new braking systems, air bags, straightened bends, anti-
skid surfaces etc might actually make things worse by encouraging users
to compensate for this increased personal safety by driving more
'dangerously' (Adams, 1985).

Road safety studies and road safety ideology (Davis, 1993) are locked
into a role which is generally supportive of motorised transport at speeds
that kill children (see chapter 5). It is possible to improve the health of
the nation enormously by ridding cities of cars, slowing down traffic to
speeds that do not kill and making sure that pedestrians and cyclists have
absolute priority on all their trips. As this would necessitate substantial
changes in the way in which society is organised it is not on the agenda.

Society chooses to kill people as a reasonable price to pay for the benefits to be had from a spatially dispersed, mobile and fast moving lifestyle (Whitelegg, 1983). It is not necessary to add to the numbers game by listing RTA data over time, space, by age-group, by gender, by category of injury and type of collision. This is done each year in most countries (eg Department of Transport (1991) and Statistisches Bundesamt (1990)).

None of these publications documents the scale of under-reporting of accidents and injuries which is very large indeed for cyclists (Watkins, 1984). Even for serious and fatal injuries there is a 16% under-reporting (Feanby, 1992) which indicates a serious problem of underestimation for all accidents and injuries. For Britain the health impact is documented in a more digestible form in the report of the Transport and Health Study Group (1991). In this report the concept of years of life lost is used to good effect. In England and Wales in 1986 RTAs were responsible for 146872 years of life lost which was 5.8% of years of life lost from all causes. Years of life lost are calculated by subtracting the age of death in a RTA from the figure for life expectancy. This can then be used to produce a figure for all deaths combined and an estimate of the impact of that cause of death. In the case of RTAs the impact is equivalent to that of cancer of the lung, trachea and bronchus. In 1985 it was estimated that one out of every 250 people alive would die in a road accident (Department of Transport, 1986).

The health impact of RTAs extends beyond the arithmetic of deaths and injuries. It is a major source of concern for parents contributing to stress and anxiety (Hillman, Adams and Whitelegg, 1991) and an important reason why children are deprived of independent travel and play opportunities in their local environment. It is an important source of stress and anxiety for the elderly and the mobility impaired and produces particularly serious problems where access to shops, post offices, community care centres etc is obstructed by fast moving traffic. The noise and the danger represent serious problems for these groups which contribute to social isolation and lack of independence. These are health issues.

Table 6.2   Average costs per casualty and per accident in Great Britain in 1990 (£)

Accident/casualty type	Cost per casualty	Cost per accident
Fatal	644935	742840
Serious	20160	25930
Slight	410	2440
Damage only	–	930

Source: Department of Transport (1991) p20

The valuation of life which goes into cost–benefit analyses of road schemes puts a high value on grief arising from RTA fatalities. The total cost of accidents in 1990 in Britain was £6770 million based on average costs per casualty and per accident listed in table 6.2. The costs associated with these events depend on a methodology which is suspect (Adams, 1981). Nevertheless they convey an impression of a substantial deficit associated with motorised transport, a subject which is returned to in chapter 7. More importantly 341000 people were victims of RTAs in Great Britain in 1990. Such an event is traumatic and traumatic events do affect the health of all those involved whether these events are loss of job, divorce/separation, robbery, rape, assault or RTA. If we take some very conservative estimates of how many friends, relatives and (where appropriate) work colleagues each of us has and multiply this by 341000 we can get an idea of the impact of RTAs on everyday life (and death). Ten 'contacts' of this kind would not be excessive. In 1990, therefore, over three million people were 'contact victims' of RTAs adding a significant dimension to everyday life and its expectations.

In the former West Germany in 1989 there were 1997787 accidents which produced 457392 injured persons (Statistisches Bundesamt, 1990). The total of 'contact victims' is that much larger than in Britain making the RTA a major concern of everyday life of much greater significance than numbers of killed and injured can convey.

The risks associated with road traffic accidents are an important determinant of everyday behaviour. The risk of a pedestrian suffering an accident in his/her own area of residence is rated as 'high' by 56% of the inhabitants of all EC countries (UITP, 1992). This is a staggeringly high percentage providing graphic illustration of the enormous impact of the road traffic environment on Europe's citizens. The variation by country provides some interesting insights into European traffic problems (table 6.3).

In table 6.3 not even The Netherlands and Denmark could be regarded as having a satisfactory environment for walking and cycling though it is much better than the other countries. At the individual level considerable amounts of stress and anxiety are generated by this structural failure to deliver basic security and at the community level social interaction and use of local facilities are hindered by the dangerous environment that has been created.

Life on the streets really is dangerous even when substantial numbers have been deterred from using those streets giving road traffic accident policies a spurious legitimacy. In a comparison of Manchester and Köln (Whitelegg, 1988) a wide range of injury rates was discovered. Road traffic accident data was analysed for a sample of small areas in both cities (wards in the UK and *Bezirken* in Germany) over a two year period (1983 and 1984) and converted into rates where the denominator was the actual

Table 6.3   Risk of accidents to pedestrians and cyclists (percentage of sampled population estimating the risk of an accident as 'high')

Country	Pedestrian	Cyclist
Germany (East)	70	85
Italy	65	73
Luxembourg	60	75
Spain	60	69
Portugal	58	55
Ireland	57	67
UK	55	68
France	55	67
Greece	55	65
Germany (West)	53	72
Belgium	51	71
Netherlands	42	64
Denmark	35	62
EC	56	70

Source: UITP (1992)

population of that area. The data for both cities was for pedestrians, cyclists and motorcyclists and not for car occupants. Only fatal and seriously injured categories are used. The results are summarised in table 6.4.

Road traffic accident statistics are a very imperfect descriptor of the conditions to be found on the streets and do not measure danger. Numbers of those killed or seriously injured are influenced by many factors including both under-reporting and the very rational avoidance behaviour of those put in danger.

The variation within Manchester and Köln in table 6.4 is indicative of the variation in street type, traffic speed, ethnic group composition and social class. As such it shows that road traffic accident policies aimed at particular groups (eg child pedestrians) or at particular types of driving (eg drunken) miss the central point. Accidents and injuries are a function of the total lifestyle and built environment characteristics of an area and traffic itself forms only one component of that mix. Policies to reduce road traffic accidents have to address the problem of getting rid of the traffic which has usurped the space of the child pedestrian and not 'teach' the child pedestrian to 'respect' the car.

The impact of traffic on communities in cities can be illustrated by applying the same methodology used at national level to identify lifetime risk to the local level. As stated earlier, the UK Department of Transport

Table 6.4 Fatal and serious injury rates from RTAs in Manchester and Köln per 10000 of the resident population for a two year period (pedestrians, cyclists and motorcyclists only)

Köln		Manchester	
Agnes	28.2	Ardwick	13.7
Brusseler	28.3	Beswick	19.6
Ehrenfeld	33.3	Bradford	11.6
Humboldt	6.6	Burnage	6.2
Kalk	15.6	Cheetham	7.2
Mulheim	38.1	Didsbury	6.9
Nippes	24.5	Hulme	19.2
Sulz	30.3	Longsight	10.9
Zollstock	17.3	Moss Side	26.5
		Newton	15.8
		Northenden	8.2
		Withington	10.6
		Woodhouse	12.5
Total sample	25.3	Total sample	12.2

(1986) estimated that of the 55 million people alive in 1985 1 in 250 could die in a road traffic accident. Whitelegg (1988) took this methodology and excluded car drivers and occupants from the analysis whilst including deaths and serious injuries. Lifetime risk assessment was then carried out at small area level in Manchester and Köln.

The methodology is based on the calculation of age-specific death and serious injury numbers for every age cohort in every area and subjecting each annual cohort to these statistical losses each year until they run out of life at the national life expectancy figure. Each year, each age group experiences attrition and then goes on to the next year to experience a different set of probabilities. The procedure accumulates these 'losses' for each cohort to give a total for all the losses over the lifetime of the cohort. The procedure simply gives a lifetime view of road traffic accidents rather than the one year snapshot we are all used to.

The results of these lifetime risk calculations provide further insight into the extent of the road traffic accident problem. In Köln 1 in 40 of those alive in 1984 can expect to become a fatal or seriously injured casualty in their lifetime. There are marked variations by area: Humboldt Gremburg at 1 in 200 is the best performer on this measure whilst Mulheim at 1 in 24 is the worst. In Manchester the overall result was 1 in 79 with the best performer (Burnage) at 1 in 225 and the worst (Moss Side) at 1 in 30.

Table 6.5 Summary of the health effects of the major air pollutants

Pollutant	Source	Recognised and suspected health effects
Carbon monoxide (CO)	Incomplete combustion of fuel	Reduces the absorption of oxygen by haemoglobin, impairs perception, thinking, reflexes, induces angina, causes drowsiness; can cause unconsciousness and death; affects fetal growth and tissue development of young children. Has a synergistic action with other pollutants to promote morbidity in people with respiratory or circulatory problems; it is associated with lower worker productivity and general discomfort.
Nitrogen oxides (NO)	Fuel combustion	Increased susceptibility to viral infections; can irritate the lungs, cause oedema, bronchitis, and pneumonia, and result in increased sensitivity to dust and pollen in asthmatics. Most serious health effects are in combination with other air pollutants. Increased occurrence of hay fever.
Sulphur dioxode (SO$_2$)	Sulphur in fuel	A harsh irritant, exacerbates emphysema, asthma and bronchitis; causes coughing and impaired lung functions. Strong irritant to eyes and mucous membranes, a cause of cardiovascular problems at high concentrations. If present with particulates can be carried into lungs and form sulphuric acid.
Hydrocarbons (HC)*	Exhaust emission/ evaporation of fuel	Cause eye irritation, coughing and sneezing, drowsiness and symptoms akin to drunkenness; heavy molecular-weight compounds may have carcinogenic or mutagenic effects. Some hydrocarbons have a close affinity to diesel particulates and may cause lung disease.
Formaldehyde	Fuel combustion	Suspected carcinogen; eye, respiratory and skin irritant causing headaches and nausea.

Pollutant	Source	Recognised and suspected health effects
Asbestos	From transmission/brakes etc	Induces asbestosis, lung cancer and mesothelia although some studies suggest that current ambient levels are too low to be causative.
Diesel particulates	Carbon based diesel emissions	Classified as a probable carcinogen. Irritates respiratory system; fine particles may cause cancer and exacerbate morbidity and mortality from respiratory dysfunctions. Strong correlation exists between suspended particulates and infant mortality in urban areas. Suspended particulates have the ability to adhere to carcinogens.
Lead (Pb)	Anti knocking agent in fuel	Affects circulatory, reproductive, nervous and kidney systems. Suspected of causing hyperactivity and lowered learning ability in children; damage to hearing, the brain and complication of pregnancies.
Ozone[‡]	HC and NO_x	Irritates mucous membranes of respiratory system; can aggravate chronic heart disease, asthma, bronchitis, and emphysema. Causes headaches and physical discomfort; reduces resistance to illness.

Notes: 'Fuel' covers all fossil based power sources; * includes Volatile Organic Compounds (VOCs); ‡ secondary pollutant

Sources: TEST (1991).

The significance of this kind of analysis does not lie in the exact magnitude of the numerical output. It lies in a realisation that road traffic accidents have an enormous impact on daily life and one that paradoxically is downgraded by the one-off annual body count and the apparent satisfaction that can be gained from the knowledge that the number of deaths in any one year is less than at some arbitrary time in the past when the number of vehicles was only a fraction of the current total.

Air pollution

Vehicles are a major source of health damaging air pollutants. Chapter 3 described the gaseous and particulate pollution originating from vehicles and quantified the relative contribution of transport sources. Evidence on the health effects of transport's emissions is widespread though pollution from cars and lorries is not yet perceived as a serious public health hazard. Schmidt, Mampel and Neumann (1987) have reviewed the health damaging effects of traffic air pollutants, Friends of the Earth (1991b) has collated much of the scientific data on air pollution and health and TEST (1991) has summarised health damaging effects of the main pollutants in tabular form (reproduced as table 6.5 and table 6.6). Air pollution from traffic sources is growing with the increase in traffic and poses significant problems for any attempt to work towards sustainability objectives. Air pollution in Britain has risen by 35% in five years with a third of the UK population living in places where EC air quality guidelines are not met for NO_x (Campbell, 1992).

Air pollution is a significant health hazard. It causes a number of basic adverse health effects:

1 aggravates cardiovascular and respiratory illness;
2 adds stress to the cardiovascular system forcing the heart and lungs to work harder;
3 reduces the lungs' ability to exhale air and speeds up the loss of lung capacity;
4 damages both the cells of the airway's respiratory system, and the lungs even after symptoms of minor irritation disappear;
5 it may contribute to the development of diseases including bronchitis, emphysema and cancer.

These health effects are not felt evenly amongst the population and there are a number of groups at a greater risk of suffering adverse health effects for a given level of pollution. A study of populations at risk (Rowell, Holman and Sohi, 1992) identified the following groups: pre-

Table 6.6 Summary of typical atmospheric levels, their quantified health effects and examples of the WHO (1987) air quality guidelines

Pollutant	Common levels	WHO European guidelines	Health effects
Carbon monoxide	Background level of 0.01–0.23mg/m³ In urban areas 8h mean usually <20mg/m³, but levels of 60mg/m³ have been recorded. In and around 30m levels of 41mg/m³ observed.	60mg/m³ for 3 minutes 30mg/m³ for 1 hour 10mg/m³ for 8 hours	Effects measured in COHb blood conc (%): 2.3–4.3% decrease in relation between worktime & exhaustion in exercising healthy young men (HYM); 2.9–4.5% decrease in exercise capacity and increase in length of attacks in angina sufferers; 5.0–5.5% decrease in maximum O_2 uptake & strenuous exercise capacity in HYM; 5.0–7.6% impairment of vigilance tasks; 5.0–17% lessening of visual perception, manual dexterity, learning, and performance.
Nitrogen dioxide	Background levels of 850μg/m³ (30 min value) and 400μg/m³ (24 hour value). In urban areas annual average is 20–90μg/m³. Peaks during rushhours Hourly average near roads can exceed 940μg/m³.	400μg/m³ for 1 hour 150μg/m³ for 24 hours	Exposure for 30 mins at 560μg/m³ to lightly exercising asthmatics – decrease in Fev_1 & partial expiratory flow rates at 60% TLC. Exposure for 1h at 560μg/m³ to normal subjects – small increase in SRaw Exposure for 20 mins at 230μg/m³ and above to exercising normal subjects – increase in SRaw at 460μg/m³, decrease in SRaw at 910

Table 6.6 contd

Pollutant	Common levels	WHO European guidelines	Health effects
Sulphur dioxide	Background levels of $5\mu g/m^3$. In urban area annual levels below $100\mu g/m^3$. Daily mean values $250–500\mu g/m^3$. 1h peaks $1000–2000\mu g/m^3$.	$500\mu g/m^3$ for 10 mins $350\mu g/m^3$ for 1 hour	Exposure for 10 mins to $655–2620\mu g/m^3$ for asthmatics leads to large SRaw increase. At $1310\mu g/m^3$ 43% asthmatics have breathing difficulties. Exposure for 3h at $1310\mu g/m^3$ for resting asthmatics leads to 2.7% fall in MMFR.
Particulate matter	Background levels of $0–10\mu g/m^3$ (rural areas) and $10–40\mu g/m^3$ (urban areas). Levels of $50–150\mu g/m^3$ to $200–400\mu g/m^3$ recorded.	$120\mu g/m^3$ 24h level (in conjunction with (SO_2 guidelines)	Danger to health on its own and with SO_2 at levels of $180\mu g/m^3$.
Formaldehyde	Background level of a few $\mu g/m^3$. Annual average is $0.005–0.01mg/m^3$ (urban). Peak traffic average is $0.05–0.1mg/m^3$.	$<0.1mg/m^3$ (30 min average)	Effects of short-term exposure: $0.01–1.9mg/m^3$ eye irritation; $0.1–3.1mg/m^3$ throat irritation; $2.5–3.7mg/m^3$ biting sensation in nose & eye; $5–6.2mg/m^3$ tolerable for 30 mins; $37.5mg/m^3$ danger to life.
Lead	'Baseline' level $5\times 10^{-5}\mu g/m^3$ Annual means of $0.5\mu g/m^3$ (non-urban), $0.3\mu g/m^3$ (rural areas) and $0.5–3\mu g/m^3$ (urban areas).	$0.5–1.0\mu g/m^3$ annual mean	Effects measured in Pb blood conc ($\mu g/ml$). $0.1–0.2\mu g/ml$ ALAD inhibition, erythrocyte protoporphryin elevation in women & children; CNS electrophysiological changes

Table 6.6 contd

Pollutant	Common levels	WHO European guidelines	Health effects
			0.2–$0.3\mu g/ml$ Erythrocyte protoporphyrin in males. Cognitive CNS deficit in children. Peripheral nerve dysfunction. $>0.4\mu g/ml$ Increased urinary ALA and elevated coproporphyrin. $>0.5\mu g/ml$ Reduced haemoglobin production in adults. Overt subencephalopathic neurological symptoms. 0.7–$0.8\mu g/ml$ frank anaemia. 0.8–$1.2\mu g/ml$ encephalopathic symptoms.
Ozone	Background level of $120\mu g/m^3$ ($24hr$ mean). City $1hr$ means of $350\mu g/m^3$ (Europe) and $400\mu g/m^3$ (USA) recorded. Levels of $240\mu g/m^3$ ($1hr$ mean) may be exceeded for 10 hours or less. Level of $664\mu g/m^3$ ($30min$) recorded in FRG.	150–$200\mu g/m^3$ for 1 hour 100–$120\mu g/m^3$ for 8 hours	Eye irritation and decrease in pulmonary functions at $200\mu g/m^3$. Coughs and headaches at 160–$300\mu g/m^3$. Exposure of heavily exercising people to conc. of $240\mu g/m^3$ for $2.5hrs$ resulted in decreases in pulmonary function. Effects worsen with higher conc.

Table 6.6 contd

Pollutant	Common levels	WHO European guidelines	Health effects
Asbestos	Rural areas 100F/m³, urban areas 100–1000F/m³. Street crossing with heavy traffic 900F/m³, express-way 3300F/m³.	No safe level	Current environmental concentrations are not considered a hazard with risk to asbestosis. A risk of lung cancer and mesothelioma from current levels has yet to be ruled out.

Notes: COHb = Carbohaemoglobin; FEV_1 = Force expiratory volume at 1 second; TLL = Total Lung Capacity; SRaw = Specific Airway Resistance; MMFR = Maximum mid-expiratory flow rate; ALAD = Delta aminolbevuhnic acid dehydrate; ALA = ALAD substrate; CNS = Central Nervous System

Sources: WHO (1987), Holman (1989)

adolescent children; individuals with asthma, pre-existing cardiovascular disease or pre-existing respiratory disease; people over 65; and pregnant women. The study concluded that 18 million people (or 38% of the population of England) were in at-risk groups from air pollution. This includes 2 million asthmatics, 1.1 million of whom are paediatric.

The global threats posed by air pollution (including vehicle sources) have been addressed by the Worldwatch Institute in Washington (French, 1990). Ozone pollution in the United States as a result of the interaction of sunlight with nitrogen oxide emissions is a major health problem. In 1988 the air in New York City violated federal health standards on thirty-four days, two or three times each week through the summer. In Washington DC the same standard was exceeded every third day on average throughout the summer. In Los Angeles in the same year federal standards for ozone were exceeded on 172 days. Altogether 382 counties in the USA are out of compliance with US Environmental Protection Agency standards for ozone (French, 1990).

Vehicle emissions may be responsible for a number of serious diseases including some cancers. The association between exposure to vehicle emissions and cancers is well established though often in an occupational context (Godlee, 1991). Wolff (1992) has examined the hypothesis that leukaemia 'clustering' as well as national leukaemia incidence in the UK is related to non-occupational exposure to benzene formed by petrol consumption and resulting from petrol evaporation. He found a statistically significant association between car ownership and acute myeloid leukaemia, the cancer specifically associated with benzene exposure, as well as between all lymphoproliferative diseases and car ownership. The research methodology based on geographical variation in car ownership and leukaemia data for the same spatial units cannot demonstrate causation. It does, however, indicate a need for further research.

There are important contributions to the cancer debate in community based studies. Savitz and Feingold (1989) observed that rates of leukaemia were higher in areas of higher traffic density in a study of childhood leukaemia incidence in Denver, Colorado. Whilst the authors of this study make a plea for cautious interpretation they conclude that their results indicate an association between traffic density near the home occupied at the time of diagnosis and childhood cancer even when confounding variables are taken into account. Evidence of increasing risk with increasing traffic densities was found for the total number of cancers and leukaemias.

Blumer, Blumer and Scherrer (1989) carried out a statistical comparison of two groups of subjects in Netstal, Switzerland. One group lived in the vicinity of a heavily trafficked road and the other 400m away from the main road with no through traffic. At the end of 1958 in the houses located within 25m of the main road 25 persons of the 232 adults in the group has died of malignant tumours (11%). In the control area three persons of the 259 residents had died of cancer (1.2%). The study linked the higher mortality on the heavily trafficked street to higher concentrations of particulates (*Teerstaub*), mainly heavy polycyclic hydrocarbons.

In an epidemiological study carried out in Hamburg, Ippen, Fehr and Krasemann (1989) observed a 12% increase in cancer incidence for men on 'heavily trafficked' streets when compared with lightly trafficked streets. Heavy traffic was defined as over 30000 vehicles per day. Taking their data from the Hamburg cancer registry they calculated rates for heavily trafficked areas and compared them with Hamburg-wide rates. Lung cancer rates in the heavily trafficked areas were 34% higher than expected and colon cancer 68% higher. There was no attempt to control for cigarette smoking or dietary factors.

In a more wide ranging study, Siemiatycki et al (1988) identified associations between several types of cancer and ten types of exhaust and combustion products. This study carried out interviews with 3726 men aged 35–70 in Montreal, Canada, who had been diagnosed as suffering from cancer. The most important results were the associations between squamous-cell lung cancer and both petrol and diesel exhaust. Petrol exhaust was also associated with rectal cancer and diesel exhaust with colon cancer.

There is a relative dearth of community based studies of air pollution and human health. A notable exception is the study by Ackermann et al (1987) in the cantons of Basel and Zürich in Switzerland. This study targeted 0–5 year olds and demonstrated a relationship between the severity of respiratory symptoms and air quality. The South Coast Air Quality Management plan (American Lung Association, 1990) covering the urban areas of Los Angeles, Orange, Riverside and San Bernadino counties in California is based on a highly sophisticated model which determines the total population exposed to air pollution both before and after pollution controls. The 'Regional Human Exposure Model' (REHEX) calculates the daily exposure to air pollution by each member of nine demographic groups living in 32 pollution 'exposure districts'. The demographic groups were distinguished by age, working status and whether or not they worked indoors, outdoors or predominantly in a car. The model translates concentrations of ozone and particulate air pollution recorded at monitoring stations into actual amounts of pollution inhaled by each of the demographic groups using 1000 time-activity patterns and six exercise states. The conclusion reached through the application of the REHEX model was that nearly everyone living in the South Coast area is exposed to concentrations of ozone or particulate pollution that exceed federal or Californian public health standards.

School age children, college students and adults working outdoors were judged to experience the highest ozone exposure per capita.

The South Coast study identified nearly 1000 health effect studies with which to identify pollutants of interest and their effects on health. The report focused on morbidity effects from ozone and on mortality and morbidity effects from particulate matter. Five morbidity effects were analysed for exposure to ozone pollution: mild cough, eye irritation, sore throat, headaches and chest discomfort. Using dose-response coefficients from the scientific literature and the results of the REHEX analysis the study predicted that reducing ozone pollution to meet the federal public health standard would eliminate annually 121.7 million occurrences of mild cough, 191.6 million eye irritations, 179.0 million sore throats, 107.4 million headaches and 64.5 million cases of chest discomfort. The South Coast plan then translates these health benefits into monetary values as part of the argument for paying the very large bill associated with cleaning up California's air (see chapter 7 for a discussion of monetary values and the environment). The plan is aimed at all sources of air pollution though in the Californian context pollution from its 16 million vehicles is a top priority and the main reason why zero emission (electric) vehicles are the favoured option for reducing pollution from mobile sources.

The American Lung Association (1990) estimated that in the United States as a whole 'an upper bound of about 120000 excess deaths attributable to air pollution in 1985 is reasonable and that a lower bound of approximately equal likelihood is about 50000'. Vehicles produced 40.5% of the total discharges of the pollutants examined but the authors concluded conservatively that vehicles were responsible for 15–25% of the total health costs from air pollution. They were in effect concluding that vehicle emissions prematurely killed between 10000 and 24000 people each year. This assumes a 20% apportionment of air pollution to vehicles which is very conservative indeed when in the USA car exhausts contribute 66% of the nation's total carbon monoxide pollution, 43% of the nitrogen oxide pollution and 34% of the reactive hydrocarbon pollution (American Lung Association, 1990).

More recent work on air pollution in urban areas has enabled a detailed picture of air quality at street level to be built up (Senatsverwaltung für Stadtentwicklung und Umweltschutz, 1992). This is essential for community-based epidemiological studies which are designed to establish relationships between health and sources of pollution. Whilst some progress has been made with point sources of pollution (Bhopal et al, 1992) studies of traffic and health are not yet fully developed especially to the point where they can control for factors such as smoking and social class.

Lead

Lead is a serious neurotoxin that has been deliberately introduced into the environment because of its role as an additive to petrol. The health effects of lead are detailed in Appendix 2 and in tables 6.5 and 6.6. A regulatory impact analysis (RIA) in the US considered the main health effects of lead to be high blood pressure, kidney and liver damage, interference with blood creation and basic cellular processes and retardation in cognitive development in children (American Lung Association, 1990). A study of children living in an area polluted by a lead smelter in Greece (Benetou-Marantidou, Nakou and Micheloyannis, 1988) showed that children living near the smelter demonstrated retardation of motor maturation and poorer school performance when compared with a control group from an unpolluted area. Age, sex, social class and family size were controlled for. Lead has also been implicated as a cancer causing agent, possibly in conjunction with benzopyrene (Blumer and Reich, 1980). Effects of lead in humans can be seen even at the lowest blood lead levels. It poses a health risk at any level of exposure (Goyer, 1990).

Lead is considered here because it is an example of the deliberate introduction into the environment of a known toxic element for the convenience of the internal combustion engine user. Three-quarters of children in the USA under the age of eighteen had blood lead levels exceeding the 10 micrograms per decilitre of blood threshold concentration linked to adverse biological effects (American Lung Association, 1990). There is no doubt that lead causes serious health problems and yet its application as a petrol additive in the 1920s and its extensive use until very recently took place in the absence of public health checks. This continued for approximately sixty years in spite of the growth in vehicle numbers and petrol sales between the 1920s and 1985.

Lead poisoning in children was recognised in Queensland, Australia, in 1892 and lead paint was identified as the source in 1904. Childhood encephalopathy produced by lead was recognised in the 1930s and 1940s and the neuropsychologic effect of lead was recognised in 1943 and yet lead was introduced into city streets and allowed to rise in volume as the car population rose until 1985.

In the UK the legally permitted maximum concentration of lead in petrol was reduced from 0.4 to 0.15 g/l in 1985, ten years after a similar reduction in the former West Germany. This reduction represented a decrease of 60–65% given that lead content was a little below the permitted maximum at 0.35–0.38 g/l before the change was implemented (Jensen and Laxen, 1987). The actual reduction in lead-in-air concentrations was less than expected, lying between 34 and 55%. This is explained by the presence of lead from other countries, UK industrial sources and possibly the re-suspension of lead containing dusts (ibid). The problem with lead, therefore, is that it is still in the environment available for redeposition when circumstances permit, eg when new roads are built or old roads and their immediate surroundings are remodelled. It is also available in combination with other sources, eg lead in drinking water, as an additional burden for those groups of unknown size who are exposed to both traffic (present or former) and drinking water sources.

Prior to the reduction in lead content of petrol at least 90% of the air lead in the urban environment was from petrol (Fergusson, 1986). This proportion was confirmed experimentally in Turin when a decision was taken to use the city as an experiment by replacing the lead in its petrol with lead from another source with a known ratio between two isotopes. The new lead came from Broken Hill in Australia with a ratio of Pb206:Pb207 of 1.04. The experiment ran from 1974 to 1980 and the lead in the air in Turin adjusted to the new ratio between two lead isotopes (Fergusson, 1986). The original source of lead in petrol was reinstated in 1980 and the lead in the air once again moved into line with the lead in the petrol. The Turin study estimated that one third of blood lead came from petrol lead.

Conclusion

Transport's health damaging effects and health damaging potential are very great indeed. Our level of knowledge of the full impact of all psychological pressures, all air quality consequences and all noise quality consequences is barely adequate; yet the number of vehicles and production of pollution continues apace. Sustainability is normally taken to imply some measure of consumption in the present which does not damage the prospects of future generations. Many of the health impacts referred to in this chapter specifically target children and will continue to do so even if a zero emission vehicle does come to dominate the market. Through the impact of traffic on health it is obvious that a society organised around hypermobility, distance consumption, speed and motorised domination of space cannot deliver sustainability. Up to 10% of the child population of the UK are asthmatic. The number of hospital admissions for childhood asthma increased fivefold between 1979 and 1989 (Holgate, 1992) and whilst there is still no clear cause and effect we do know that urban air quality is deteriorating and that most of the pollutants responsible for this deterioration are from motorised transport.

Improvements in child health on which is based the health of future generations requires a major shift in behaviour towards less consumption of distance, space and energy. It is in this direction that the real significance of sustainability lies. Health studies show that catalytic converters or electric vehicles will not solve the problems generated by early twentieth-century technology bolted onto late twentieth-century consumption patterns. Catalytic converters shift the hazard to possible impacts of rare metals used in their manufacture (Nieper, 1991) whilst new fuels are not without health risks and still contribute to global warming. Electric vehicles are being designed to emulate the urban speeds of conventional petrol vehicles (and therefore the accident risks) and will still deprive children and the elderly of space and freedom. It is possible to design a transport system that will nurture health, nurture community, scale down demands on finite resources and deliver equitable solutions where we now have division and exploitation. This is what sustainability means and child health will be the acid test of whether it will be realised or whether it will remain as a convenient label to describe technical fixes and assuage the occasional pricking conscience.

7 THE COST OF TRANSPORT

Transport is a costly activity. The provision of transport infrastructure for road, rail, air, inland waterways and shipping is a major item of public and private expenditure in all countries. The maintenance, repair and renewal of that infrastructure is a feature of most annual budgets and personal and corporate expenditure on vehicle purchase, vehicle maintenance, fuels and taxation is a significant part of consumer expenditure.

These items are all direct expenditures and should be distinguished from the costs which those activities impose on third parties or on society as a whole. It is assumed that these indirect costs or externalities are unintended by-products of the transport activity itself and are costs which have to be met at some time in the future. Some of the costs, eg road traffic accidents, injuries and fatalities, have to be paid almost immediately in the form of medical costs whilst other impositions might be deferred. The costs associated with carbon dioxide emissions and the greenhouse effect could be evaded in the short to medium term but only at the expense of potentially enormous costs when uncertainty about climate change and biodiversity becomes certainty. At that point it is theoretically possible that the costs are infinite.

Most of the debate about costs in transport concerns this category of externalities, particularly the costs associated with emissions, noise, damage to human health, damage to habitat and road traffic accidents. It is possible to measure the costs implied by these by-products of transport but the important issues are not those of monetary valuation but those of political decisions about priorities and tricky distributional issues about who gains and who loses in market transactions based around the incorporation of environmental values into cost benefit analyses or investment appraisal decisions.

An example will help to illustrate the central problem. Let us assume that there are no technical problems in putting monetary values on human life, time, nice views, peace and quiet and lively neighbourhoods full of intense social interaction. How does this help to make decisions about whether or not to have a bypass or whether or not to introduce road pricing in cities? The bypass might be justified on the logic that peace and quiet coupled with road safety gains would be 'purchased' in the bypassed community by the new road. The problem is that the bypass itself shortens journey times and encourages more use of the road by car and lorry thus adding to emissions, global warming and damage to health. It also damages the alternatives by conferring on roads competitive advantages when compared with rail. It also shifts the whole of society a little bit further along the curve to higher levels of car ownership and use, higher levels of lorry dependence and more energy-greedy land use arrangements that discriminate against pedestrians and cyclists.

The neat logic of monetary valuation around a bypass cannot cope with these larger strategic issues even if it can 'monetarise' peace and quiet in the bypassed settlement and show that this is 'worth more' than the loss sustained by damage to landscape attractiveness along the route of the bypass. More importantly, perhaps, the bypass would always come out as a preferable option because of time savings and the values given to that time (see chapter 5). In effect the outcome is 'rigged' because of a cultural commitment to time saving and a wide discretion about how to value time. Neither the environment nor sustainability can emerge as a high priority in such a system.

In a densely populated urban area where congestion is a serious problem, road pricing is perceived as a solution. The congestion would be seen by environmental economists (Pearce et al, 1989) as a market failure which would be rectified by increasing the price for the road space which is in short supply. Road space could then be allocated (by the market) to those users who most need it at that time and in that place. It is quite possible to work out the costs of all the noise, emissions, accidents and injuries and loss of time associated with congestion and to use this information to set a price for the use of that road space. The problem is that all the technical sophistication of this approach misses the basic issues.

If local residents are experiencing the health damaging consequences of the noise, stress and air pollution from congested traffic then how does some additional payment from that traffic help them? If congested traffic can be turned into free moving traffic then there will be some diminution of air pollution but only as long as the volume of traffic remains static. Moreover, free moving traffic implies higher speeds which brings with it greater risks of serious injury and more noise. The monetarisation of environmental factors does not resolve important political and distributional issues. It is quite likely, if not certain, that local residents will still suffer health damage and usurped road space which should be social space after a complex process of pseudo-market rationality.

Estimating the costs of transport in the sense of putting monetary values on environmental disbenefits needs to be treated with a great deal of caution. It cannot be a substitute for clear decisions emerging from the political process about the kind of cities or environment that we wish to have into the next century. To regard current environmental and transport problems as market failures is to misunderstand a complex social and political process. To try and correct market failures by putting monetary values on environmental factors will not solve the problems that currently make cities unpleasant places in which to live and work. Nor will they produce strategic decision making about transport of the kind that will put walking and cycling within a supportive system of land use arrangements at the top of political priorities.

The same point can be put in a different way. The cities of Lübeck and Aachen in Germany have implemented car-free city concepts. A large part of their central areas are now virtually free of traffic noise and pollution and the environment, particularly for children and the elderly (groups with very little bargaining power in a market situation) is now much more congenial. It is very difficult to imagine how this might be brought about through an elaborate economic analysis based on correcting market failures.

The problem, then, with the discussion of costs of transport is that it actually involves a number of separate issues. The technical issue of valuing environmental factors is not challenged here. It is assumed that it is possible and that it may be useful. What is not accepted here is the closely related notion that building these costs into decision making will fundamentally alter the present situation. It may even make things worse as it assumes that no other kind of state action is needed to produce sustainability other than actions related to prices, taxes and charges. Further it is not accepted that the translation of these valuations into prices or taxes will produce the necessary changes in human behaviour or socially just outcomes.

Some of these issues are dealt with in Bowers (1990) where much of the Pearce logic is questioned because of flaws in the way it deals with distributional issues between nations and flaws in the ways it deals with contemporary distributional issues. This critique is particularly relevant to transport issues where there is no evidence that the Pearce approach would benefit those groups disenfranchised by current transport policies. A transport policy to restore urban space to children, protect the respiratory health of children, guarantee local facilities for the elderly, guarantee clean air for inner city residents and guarantee safe cycling routes for commuters does not square with the logic of rectifying market failures.

What then is the point of valuing the environment in the sense of putting monetary values on environmental factors? It is very tempting to reply 'none' especially after reading the first page of Jean-Philippe Barde and David Pearce's introduction to the subject (Barde and Pearce, 1991).

The first issue they raise as an example of the problem of valuation is the M3 motorway and its environmental damage. The problem is immediately perceived by these authors as one of a tunnel versus non-tunnel option in a particular location with no sense of questioning about wider strategies, rail versus road options, the consequences of not building the motorway at all or the crudeness of a road building programme which generates conflicts of this kind because it is so manifestly out of line with any set of environmental objectives at national or local level. Under these conditions the problem of valuation is simply the problem of carrying on a business-as-usual road construction programme with the addition of some environmental street credibility.

There is, nevertheless, some justification for putting monetary values on the consequences of current transport policies:

1   There is a political debate about transport policy and there is a lot at stake including a £20 billion road construction programme in the UK, a new European high speed rail system and 12000km of new motorway in Europe. Infrastructure investment in transport in the EC up to the year 2010 is estimated to cost 1000–1500 billion ECUs (Transport Europe, 1992). These are enormous sums of money and it is important that the political debate is informed about the wide-ranging and costly consequences of implementing a strategy of this magnitude.

2   National and EC governments do not work in an objective manner, independent of strong pressure groups. Some of the strongest pressure groups are those representing the motor vehicle industry, oil industry, construction industry and motoring organisations. All these groups make intensive use of comparisons between taxation paid by vehicles and public expenditure on roads to show that the motorist and road haulier subsidise general revenue. These claims are based on partial accounting and ignore the costs associated with accidents and injuries, health of those affected by traffic, noise and pollution. It is important that as full an account as possible is presented so that discussions about subsidy and who subsidises whom take place against a background of full information.

3   Public transport operators and railway enterprises operate on a very non-level playing field when investment decisions have to be made and prices set for both passengers and freight. The extent to which investments and/or lower prices will reap wider gains for society as a whole depends very much on our ability to do some thorough accounting of all aspects of transport benefits and disbenefits. This has been the basis of much fare setting and investment in German public transport, eg in Bremen (Bremener Strassenbahn AG, 1990).

4 There is an interest in Europe, particularly in the European Parliament, in fiscal and economic incentives as a means to a cleaner environment (Whitelegg, 1990c). Even though it is not absolutely necessary to produce valuations of environmental factors in order to impose some fiscal burden aimed at reducing environmental damage it is in practice a first stage in the argument. Further along the path of fiscal rectitude are proposals such as 'ecological taxation reform' (Whitelegg, 1992d) and they too are more easily discussed against a background of reasonably accurate assessments of the amount of damage currently caused by the consumption of transport.

Valuing the environment: the case of transport

Some of the most detailed estimates of the costs of transport's impact have been carried out in the former West Germany. Wicke (1987) calculated that the sum of all environmental damage in West Germany for one year was DM103.5 billion or 6% of GDP in 1985. Schulz (1989) has calculated what proportion of this total can be assigned to cars and this is shown in table 7.1

Table 7.1 An environmental damage balance sheet (costs in billion DM per year)

Pollution type	Total costs of damage	Damage by motorised traffic
Atmospheric	48.0	12.0
Noise	>32.7	30.0
Water	>17.6	?
Ground	>5.2	?
Totals	>103.5	>42.0

Source: Schulz (1989)

Schulz adds to this the cost of road traffic accidents which in 1985 amounted to DM35 billion. Teufel et al (1988) and Teufel (1989) have compared the total costs imposed by cars and lorries with the totals of taxation of all kinds which they pay. In both cases the comparison reveals a substantial deficit. Cars and lorries cost far more to support than they remit in taxation. In the case of lorries (table 7.2) taxation amounts to about 15% of the costs they impose and in the case of cars (table 7.3) the figure lies between 26 and 29%. This conclusion is

Table 7.2   Total costs and taxation income for lorries in West Germany, 1987
(middle estimates; all figures in million DM)

Income (all taxes)	6724
Costs	
Road expenditure	8730
Accident costs	5030
Distress related to accidents	2600
Air pollution	6350
Noise costs (private dwellings)	9850
Other noise costs	2500
Congestion	2000
Water pollution (from dangerous goods)	3800
Water pollution (from road salting)	2800
Health damage to lorry drivers	1100
Other	1200
Total costs	45960
Total costs not covered by tax income	39236

Source: Teufel (1989)

Table 7.3   Total costs and taxation income for cars in West Germany, 1987 (all
figures in billion DM)

	1960–1986 (cumulated)	1986 (one year)
Total income from taxes	441	31.4
Costs		
Expenditure on roads	551	29
Accident costs not covered	456–710	27–35
Air pollution	265	18
Noise	625	35
Total costs	1897–2151	109–117
Deficit	1456–1710	78–86

Source: Teufel et al (1988)

Table 7.4 Social costs in relation to transport modalities (by percentage)

Social costs	Air	Rail	Inland waterways	Road	Total
Air pollution	2	4	3	91	100
Noise pollution	26	10	0	64	100
Land coverage	1	7	1	91	100
Construction/ maintenance	2	37	5	56	100
Accidents/ casualties	1	1	0	98	100
Total in billion DM/year	2	14	2	68–77	86–95

Source: Group Transport 2000 plus

reinforced by the information in table 7.4 which shows that road transport accounts for the bulk of costs in transport as a whole arising from environmental damage. Road transport accounts for 91% of the costs associated with air pollution and 98% of the costs associated with accidents and injuries. Figure 7.1 shows in graphic form the extent of the disparity between road and rail for passenger transport.

Figure 7.2 shows how these unmet social costs translate into an additional amount which could be levied on every litre of fuel purchased. This amounts to a DM2 increase on the price per litre of petrol (which was approximately DM1 in 1989). If this price increase were implemented then it would produce an 'ecological bonus' equivalent to DM1800 per annum for every inhabitant of Germany, a sum of money which could be returned to individuals or invested in public transport.

Detailed costings for both passenger and freight transport for all modes and for six categories of environmental impact and presented in a standard format using pfennigs per passenger-km/tonne-km are available in Planco (1990). Total external costs for the private car are 7.46 pfennigs per passenger-km compared with 1.74 for rail and 1.51 for bus. In the case of freight transport (per tonne-km), road transport costs 5.01 pfennigs and rail 1.15 compared with internal waterways' 0.35.

Similar calculations have been carried out by the International Union of Railways (1987) demonstrating that in transport at least it is possible to achieve reliable estimates of the external costs imposed by different modes of transport.

All this information at an aggregate level shows quite clearly that present levels of motorisation and dependence on cars and lorries is very

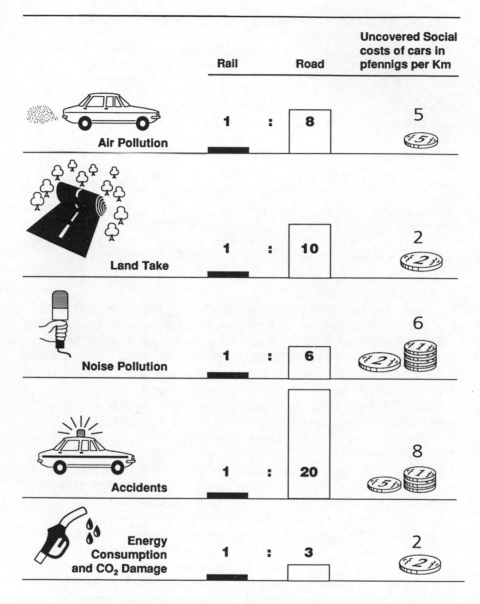

Figure 7.1   Environmental damage and costs of different modes of transport
Source: Seifried (1990)

Petrol Price

Production   Taxation   Uncovered social costs
Costs

Petrol price which covers all these costs

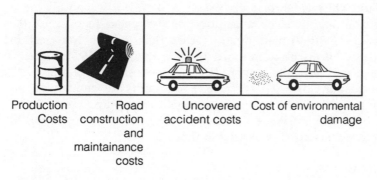

Production   ·Road   Uncovered   Cost of environmental
Costs   construction   accident costs   damage
and
maintainance
costs

Öko - Bonus
The result of redistributing the product of
a 2DM per litre increase in petrol at 1989 prices

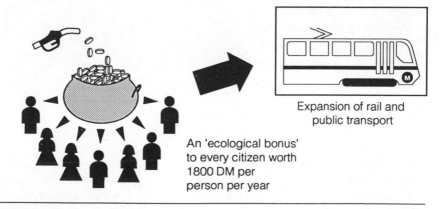

Expansion of rail and
public transport

An 'ecological bonus'
to every citizen worth
1800 DM per
person per year

Figure 7.2   The inadequacy of present fuel taxation levels

Source: Seifried (1990)

expensive indeed. As numbers of vehicles increase then these costs will also increase adding to the fiscal problems of those countries and regions carrying the costs. More importantly in the age of the Single European Market is the prospect of these costs being exported as is already the case with non-German lorries travelling on toll-free German motorways.

Calculating the costs of private motorised transport can be very useful at the level of individual cities as a context within which public transport strategies can be determined. Apel (1988) has made such a calculation for (West) Berlin. He concluded that the car imposes a cost on that city of DM4.47 billion which is DM0.64 per passenger-km. This can be compared with public transport on the same basis. Public transport cost DM1.48 billion which is DM0.38 per passenger-km. It is financially much more prudent as well as environmentally much sounder to organise the demand for transport around public rather than private transport in Berlin. This study is discussed in more detail in Barde and Pearce (1991).

The Bremen transport undertaking (Bremener Strassenbahn AG, 1990) has used calculations by Gleissner (1987) to identify an annual sum of DM46 million which could be spent on public transport improvements and results from the contribution made by public transport operations to environmental quality in Bremen (table 7.5)

Table 7.5   The contribution of public transport in Bremen to improving the environment (all values in million DM)

Contribution to air quality, water quality and soil quality	29.8
Contribution to noise alleviation	26.7
Contribution to traffic safety	24.8
Reduction demand for road space	7.7
Reduction in energy consumption	19.6
Reduction in congestion	9.4
Sub-total	118.0
Deduct contribution to public transport operator	72.0
Net social benefit	46.0

Both the Bremen and the Berlin costings are based on car to public transport comparisons. If the costings were done on a walking/cycling to car comparison then these non-motorised modes would appear a very attractive bargain indeed.

The German research is not well developed for the costs associated with health damage. US research summarised by the American Lung Association (1990) has made estimates of the costs of damage to health from car-produced air pollution. This was put at between $4.43 billion and $93.49 billion and is available on a state by state basis. Thus California's annual health costs from motor vehicle pollution are in the range $0.5–$10.7 billion. The range reflects differences in the valuation of human life. Estimates of savings in health costs as a result of enforcing stricter air quality standards are a routine feature of regulatory impact analyses (RIAs) in the USA. Comprehensive estimates exist for lead, particulate emissions and sulphur dioxide. Similarly health cost assessments have been made for specific areas where attempts have been made to enforce federal air quality standards. In the Denver area annual health costs of $104 million could be avoided if air quality complied with the federal particulate standard. Nearly 90% of this would result from reduced mortality, the remainder coming from avoided emergency room (casualty) visits and the elimination of days of restricted activity.

The Denver study placed a value of $21 on each restricted activity day due to respiratory discomfort. Asthma attacks were assumed to involve a more serious disruption in activity and a $43 value was assigned to each attack. Eye irritations were valued at $9.

It should be clear from these attempts to quantify health costs that a major component of any rigorous attempt to include environmental valuations in decision making is likely to founder on arguments about the appropriateness of any numbers that are used. This is not a new phenomenon. Most cost–benefit analyses that have been attempted in the transport field have struggled to come up with numbers for the monetary value of noise, time or life. As long as these valuations do not seriously challenge the road building programme or increases in airport capacity then they will be incorporated into decision making. If they do challenge the prevailing ideology surrounding car ownership, use of cars or doubling of airline passengers every ten years then all the uncertainties and flaws in the methodology will be identified as reasons why they should be ignored.

A major unresolved difficulty with environmental valuation is where to draw the boundaries around any impact and who makes that decision. The boundary problem is both spatial and temporal. The impact of motorised transport on the environment must involve some assessment of life cycle impacts of vehicles. In other words the environmental impact of all the mining and smelting for the metal components of vehicles should figure in the calculations. Similarly all the impacts associated with the sand, gravel and aggregate industries which supply road building materials including the transportation of those materials should go into the calculations. All the activities which go into oil exploration, drilling, extraction and transportation should be added, including the disasters associated with oil spills and the geopolitical disasters like military intervention in Kuwait. The use of oil feedstocks to make plastics and

Individual costs
1. Ownership costs
2. Operating costs

Direct costs
1. Highway and road expenditures
2. Interest on provincial debt due to previous highway spending
3. Government spending on the environment (ie pollution control and clean up)
4. Road safety
5. Health care
6. Policing
7. Court costs
8. Subsidies to companies

Hidden costs
1. Destruction of farmland, urban green space and habitats
2. Excessive energy costs from making and using the car, especially in areas of urban sprawl
3. Damage to air and water from mining
4. Air and soil pollution and contamination from smelting
5. Air and water pollution from drilling and processing petroleum
6. Water pollution from the production of petroleum-based chemicals
7. Damage from the transport of petroleum on land and water
8. Acidification of land and water from car emissions and auto industry smokestacks
9. Damage to plant and crop growth from elevated levels of ozone

10. The growing environmental and health costs of global warming
11. Damage to water and vegetation from the use of salt and historic use of oil as a dust suppressant
12. Damage to air, land and water from the disposal of cars and their component parts
13. Damage to human health from regular discharge of toxic waste into lakes and rivers by auto industry
14. Respiratory damage from elevated levels of SO_x
15. Respiratory damage from elevated levels of ozone
16. Impaired co-ordination and heart damage from CO
17. Neurological damage from elevated levels of lead
18. Damage to skin and eyes from ozone depletion
19. Loss of time due to overcrowded highways
20. Stress and decline of quality of life
21. Unique costs to transportation-disadvantaged
22. Financial costs due to lost productivity
23. Emotional damage to victims and families

Opportunity costs of car dependence
1. Lack of R&D for rural and public transit and alternative fuels
2. Growing inflexibility of the economy

Figure 7.3   Inventory of costs associated with car ownership

Source: Pollution Probe (1991)

rubber for vehicles and the use of CFCs to make foams and keep air conditioning systems working also need to be included.

At the disposal end of the life cycle something has to be done with the vehicle. The landfill problem in most developed societies is now acute and groundwater pollution from dumped vehicles is another impact to be quantified. Before the final exit the vehicle makes its contribution to mountains of tyres, lead acid batteries, contaminated exhaust systems and, increasingly, contaminated catalytic converters.

During its brief life as a moving object the vehicle will produce hundreds of litres of waste oil, brake fluids, particulate pollutants from tyres and braking systems and contaminated water from car washes. All these activities in their turn have land use sterilisation and health impacts and so it goes on. The reduction of complex issues of this kind to some arbitrary set of valuations surrounding noise and air pollution is logically incorrect and methodologically invalid. A discussion about a new road around Winchester, through Oxleas Wood or through the Ruhr area of Germany has to be informed by information about its proportionate responsibility for all the impacts at every stage of the life cycle of the vehicle and the life cycle of the road. The degree to which this may be regarded as excessive or ridiculous is inversely related to the importance we attach to the environmental impact of transport.

Many of the issues associated with life cycle analysis of motor vehicles have been addressed in Pollution Probe (1991) and monetary valuations are produced for the state of Ontario, Canada. In addition they have produced an inventory of costs associated with the car. This is reproduced as figure 7.3. Ontario generates 7–8 million scrap tyres each year, 60% of which end up in landfill sites and 10% in tyre piles. It was one such pile at Hagersville, Ontario, that caught fire causing a serious health hazard with benzene emissions and oil runoff. The total cost of this fire was approximately $50 million.

In 1988–89 Ontario's seven petroleum refineries discharged 261kg of benzene, 3766kg of chromium and 34kg of phenol. Uniroyal, the tyre manufacturer, discharged nitrosamine into Elmira's water supply and Goodyear's engine belt plant discharged PCBs into Owen Sound. A programme of environmental auditing and environmental systems management would in theory be capable of identifying every environmental impact at every stage in the production, consumption and disposal cycle for every supplier of every product no matter how remote from the 'final' product in the form of a car or a road. Environmental economists are silent about total life cycle health and environmental impact analysis.

Many of these impacts are spatially very dispersed and represent complex flows of materials and energy in space and time. Some are dominated by the temporal dimension in that their important impacts are in the future and therefore subject to varying degrees of uncertainty.

This is particularly the case with greenhouse gases and global warming and ozone layer depletion. Current activities contribute to environmental damage which is possibly catastrophic but is in the future. It is, therefore, uncertain and lack of certainty is a powerful argument for inaction.

Taxation

Given that the environment is suffering from the depredations of traffic, and given that this threatens the health of both present as well as future generations, action to curb emissions, protect landscape and habitat and minimise energy and land consumption seems a reasonably logical course of action. Life, however, is not so simple. Economic growth is still of the highest importance. Governments worry a great deal about their own economic activities and international competitiveness which might be damaged if unilateral action were taken on energy prices through a carbon tax for example. Further worries exist about inflation and social equity.

Owens, Anderson and Brunskill (1990) make the case for some kind of environmental taxation:

> The price of many products fails to reflect the full environmental costs of their production and consumption . . . prices could be adjusted through the taxation system to encourage producers and consumers to act in an environmentally friendly manner.

They argue for some short term changes rather than more fundamental taxation reforms and they argue for the continuation of a regulatory framework to control environmental damage. At the core of their suggestion is a very modest proposal for extending the present arrangement whereby leaded petrol attracts a greater tax element than unleaded petrol. In other words they are advocating tax differentiation to stimulate the consumption of environmentally friendly products and reduce the demand for the opposite. In transport they propose that 'clean' cars (ie with catalytic converters) should be zero rated for VAT purposes and large cars should be discouraged through higher rates of VAT on purchase as well as through fuel tax and differential rates of vehicle excise duty (VED).

These tax differentiation measures fall far short of any attempt to make the polluter pay by recouping the costs of environmental damage and they fail to identify the real environmentally friendly alternatives which in the case of transport are other modes and land use changes. In effect they leave the status quo substantially intact with as much dependence as ever on motorised transport.

Slightly more effective as a way of containing growth in fossil fuel consumption and hence to put the brakes on global warming are various forms of carbon tax. The European Commission proposed a carbon tax/energy tax of 2.81 ECUs per tonne of carbon dioxide produced by combustion and 0.21 ECUs per gigajoule of energy, to be applied from 1 January 1993. The tax has a large number of exemptions attached to it which may well nullify its usefulness. It is the policy of the EC that the tax should be neutral, ie there should be reductions in other forms of taxation to the equivalent value to avoid inflation. Like the differential taxation proposals of Owens et al the carbon tax proposal falls short of any rigorous application of the polluter pays principle.

The economics of a carbon tax is discussed in detail in Barrett (1991). He makes the point that a major difficulty is the determination of the actual amount of the tax. Estimates already exist in the range $3-$107 per ton of carbon. Three countries already have a carbon tax: The Netherlands ($1.30), Finland ($6.10) and Sweden ($40). However, on the positive side a carbon tax would bring many other gains in the form of reductions in other pollutants eg sulphur dioxide. Indeed it could bring about a transfer of trips from car to public transport if the tax were high enough to deter short journeys in cities and if public transport were improved sufficiently to attract defectors. This in its turn would benefit the city in other ways, eg through reductions in road traffic accidents and injuries and improvements in noise levels and social interaction.

There are problems with carbon taxes. Loske (1991) maintains that carbon taxes are 'substitution strategies' that will shift energy consumption from oil and coal to natural gas and nuclear sources when what is really required is conservation or a reduction in energy consumption per se. This is a further indication that most taxes under discussion are still ineffectual and are not steering the economy and its use of finite resources in the direction of sustainability. Loske's concluding remark is very relevant to transport's use of energy: 'a general increase in energy prices could help create energy awareness. For what is needed is not just a degree of switching between coal and gas or nuclear energy, but a more fundamental transformation: leaving the fossil–nuclear age behind us and approaching the solar age.'

What is needed in transport is not a switch to 'clean' fuels or a rash of catalytic converters but a switch to a low-energy/high social output system where all the damaging consequences of motorised transport are eradicated by the gradual increase of public or non-motorised modes of transport within a land use system that reduces the 'need' to travel. Ecological taxation reform offers this possibility. Ecological taxation reform has been developed in several papers by Von Weizsacker (1988 and 1990) and summarised by Whitelegg (1992c) and Von Weizsacker and Jesinghaus (1992).

Cost recovery versus ecological taxation reform

The differential between costs imposed on society and income received from taxation is a clear price signal to car users and lorry operators to continue to base their planning and their spatial decision making on that assumption. The result is more pollution, more health damage and more community disruption. As distances to work, shop and school continue to increase and firms embrace logistics and long distance sourcing of inputs so transport work done goes up, environment suffers and infrastructure demands rise. Europe is currently awash with proposals for new roads, bridges and tunnels all on the basis of a space economy and organisational system arranged around large subsidies to movement. This is a massive misallocation of resources.

One solution to this misallocation is to charge via the taxation system (on fuel) the rate which will bring income into line with costs. This is the cost recovery route. It would bring in substantial extra revenues and would exert a substantial dampening effect on car use and fuel purchases (Teufel et al, 1988). This approach has much in common with ideas to introduce a carbon tax as a means of bringing about a reduction in fossil fuel burning and its associated greenhouse gas emissions.

Large increases in taxation even if introduced progressively over a number of years can be problematic. They can add substantially to production costs, to public and private expenditures and to inflationary pressures. They can, if introduced in one country only, put that economy at a disadvantage in comparison with countries without this kind of tax. More fundamentally they do not necessarily tackle the root problem by using the price mechanism to send the right signals to every level of the economy and every public and private producer and consumer. To be successful such taxes should have an explicit set of objectives related to steering the economy towards a genuinely sustainable level of activity.

If environmental problems are to be tackled by use of fiscal and economic instruments (EC, 1990b) then they need to be embedded in a comprehensive strategy which tackles all sectors (waste, energy, water, agriculture, transport etc), do this on a European level and do it in a way which does not increase overall levels of taxation or cause distortions between different sectors of the economy. A set of proposals to achieve these objectives has been outlined by von Weizsäcker (1988 and 1990) and compared with other solutions in Bleijenberg and Sips (1989). These are referred to as ecological taxation reform (ETR).

The objectives of ETR are to steer the whole economy in the direction of greater environmental and ecological efficiency and to establish 'frame' conditions and avoid detailed regulation of the 'command and control' kind which has not produced the environmental gains that might have been expected.

What is ecological taxation reform?

Ecological taxation is based on the principle that taxes should fall most heavily on those activities and materials that produce pollution and/or environmental damage. Such taxes would replace taxes on labour and capital, would be phased in over thirty years and would exert a steering effect on the economy so that environmentally damaging activities (eg freight carried by lorries) would gradually be replaced by environmentally friendly alternatives (eg rail). The total taxation burden in Europe would remain constant. ETR is not an additional tax; it is a replacement tax.

By the end of the transition period the space economy itself would evolve to produce a pattern which could be serviced for lower inputs of energy and lower outputs of waste and pollution. It would make much more efficient use of space as a resource and by emphasising shorter distances would make the conditions for walking, cycling and public transport much more favourable than at present. This is the fundamental answer to congestion.

Specific taxes have been suggested by Von Weizsäcker to bring about this change (all at 1988 prices):

- Energy: 10 ECUs per gigajoule of fossil and nuclear energy;
- ground coverage: 100 ECUs per sq metre of ground newly covered by buildings, concrete or macadam and 2 ECUs for re-using ground;
- water: 10 ECUs per cubic metre of polluted waste water and 3 ECUs per cubic metre of water used;
- waste: 50 ECUs per tonne of unsorted waste and 500 ECUs per tonne of hazardous waste;
- air: 1000 ECUs per tonne of SO_2, NO_x, CO or hydro-chlorocarbons and 50 ECUs per tonne of CO_2.

Results of implementing ETR

Bleijenberg and Sips (1989) have assessed the implications of ETR. It would bring about a shift away from investment in polluting activities towards energy conservation, environmental technology and public transport. It would make these activities more profitable than at present and exercise the steering effect suggested by von Weizsäcker. Clean products become cheaper and the cost of products manufactured with a relatively large proportion of energy use and pollution will rise.

Unemployment will decline as an environmentally oriented economic policy will generate jobs (600000 in The Netherlands). Some detailed environmental regulations will become redundant and the problems of enforcement will become fewer. It is already very difficult indeed to enforce existing regulations in waste disposal, water pollution and transport of toxic wastes. Incentives to avoid/evade taxes on labour will diminish and labour intensive operations become more economically viable eg more staff on buses and at train/underground stations.

The impact of ETR on lower income groups can be minimised. In any case they consume fewer of the environmentally damaging (and higher priced under ETR) goods than higher socio-economic groups. More public transport together with better facilities for walking and cycling and denser local facilities can only enhance environmental quality where it is often the poorest, ie where poor people live. A shift of taxation away from income taxes also helps all those groups in low pay jobs and for whom conventional employment was not possible because of income tax burdens. Bleijenberg and Sips (1989) show how the poor can be protected against high energy taxes by the introduction of thresholds.

Conclusion

Current levels of traffic are supported by a system of subsidy which is built into the supply of public infrastructure and into the minds of car users and lorry operators. The price signals clearly indicate that it is correct to consume more passenger kilometres and more tonne kilometres and for society to continue its development along a space greedy and energy greedy trajectory. This is not a sustainable situation and congestion represents one, and only one, manifestation of the malfunctioning of our land use and transportation systems. Indeed higher transport costs in a system that ensures social equity has the potential to harness the land use system fully in the interests of reducing the demand for transport by encouraging the development of facilities at high densities near to where people live and work.

Motorised transport is so deeply embedded in our societies that a little traffic calming together with slightly improved public transport and a little more tax on fuel will not alter anything. Nor will technology rush to the rescue. Road pricing, like in-car navigation systems, is only a device for squeezing more capacity out of the system and/or allocating road space to those willing to pay (with someone else's money). Such measures may help to give the impression of some relief somewhere but society will not be deflected from its car orientation and the cars will pop up somewhere else to carry the pollution and danger and road construction to another quarter. In the case of in-car navigation we have nothing more than pre-programmed, commercial, rat-running.

A more fundamental solution is required and that lies in sending the right price signals so that every public and private decision involving expenditure is a choice between a cheap, clean, energy efficient and pollution free option and an expensive, dirty, damaging option. This is possible and feasible and the idea of ecological taxation reform is well suited to the task (see also EC (1990b), Bleijenberg and Sips (1989) and Whitelegg (1990b).

8 TRANSPORT AND EUROPE

Changes at the European level, particularly the Single European Market (SEM) add a major new dimension to processes of social, economic and spatial change that underpin the consumption of distance and resources in transport. When production and consumption are bounded by clearly defined national frontiers the potential for major plant rationalisation, increase in length of haul for road freight and repeated cross haulage of products at various stages of the manufacturing cycle is necessarily limited. If the artificial constraints of the nation-state are removed and replaced by common regulations, access, currency and opportunity over a much larger area then the rules of the game are dramatically altered. If there are substantial disparities in wage rates, infrastructure provision and incentives to firms to adjust their locational structures then major changes can be expected in the location of production and distribution functions.

The SEM is not quite the United States of Europe feared by those who prefer the nation-state concept to anything that implies a dilution of sovereignty but it is well on the way and in terms of the organisation of production and consumption it is almost there. It is, moreover, exactly what the term implies and makes it considerably easier for firms to exploit whatever economies of scale are available in their sector.

The goal of European integration expressed in the SEM and the Maastricht Treaty is inextricably linked to the desire on the part of all European states to create an economic power to rival that of Japan and the United States. The debate about the SEM has been couched primarily in economic terms (EC, 1988b) and the vast majority of directives concerned with the implementation of the SEM are economic. The many problems surrounding the rather uncritical acceptance of conventional economic growth models and theories have been reviewed by Ekins et al (1992). The SEM, rooted in a traditional economic growth framework, presents a number of difficulties for the improvement of environmental quality in Europe. These have been identified in publications of the EC itself notably those of the task force on the internal market (Task Force, nd), the green paper on the urban environment (EC, 1991) and the Green Paper on sustainable mobility (EC, 1992a). Transport is a major component of this environmental problem.

For European policy making and the credibility of European institutions the growth in transport demand associated with the SEM is a problem. The EC has a clear environmental policy and in the person of Carlo Ripa di Meana, Environment Commissioner until 1992, pursued an aggressively interventionist policy on the environmental impact of roads. It is quite clear, however, that the EC's commitment to economic growth, deregulation and road construction is the primary source of environmental threats in sensitive areas of Europe. The growth in traffic which is a direct consequence of these processes is a major source of environmental degradation. The EC has unleashed a process which threatens urban quality of life through its support of lower car prices and the delivery of large amounts of new traffic at the end of the inter-urban road conveyor belt. EC policy on road construction (EC, 1992b) threatens a large number of sensitive corridors such as the A5 route through the Snowdonia national park and routes across the Pyrenees through the implicit bias towards road freight and road infrastructure. This will become clearer through an examination of the SEM process and its road freight implications.

EC environmental policy has clearly taken second place to single market policies. The publication of grandiose road construction plans and associated funding mechanisms in 1992 before the publication of the transport policy White Paper (EC, 1992c) demonstrates the primacy of transport infrastructure arguments and the relative insignificance of both environmental arguments and a balanced transport policy. Quite clearly 'sustainable mobility' does not encompass any diminution of road building nor any weakening of economic growth imperatives.

The single market, structural change and freight generation

Completing the internal market is a process of removing internal barriers within the Community to produce economic gains. These gains have been quantified by EC (1988b): a one-off inflation-free increase of GDP in the range 4.5–7%, a lowering of consumer prices in the range of 4.5–6% and an increase in employment of between 2 and 5 million. The single market and its expected economic effects are summarised in a number of commission documents (EC, 1988a, 1988b).

The barriers to be removed are physical, technical and fiscal. Physical barriers are delays and costs associated with border controls. Technical barriers are standards and specifications which exclude the products of one nation from the domestic market of another and fiscal barriers are the differences between rates of VAT and consumption taxes in member states.

An important element in the single market strategy is the liberalisation of road haulage. This means that after 1992 it will be possible for non-resident hauliers to collect and deliver loads within the boundaries of another member state. This access to other domestic markets is normally referred to as 'cabotage'. A liberalised regime for international haulage would exert considerable pressure on domestic haulage with the result that rates would fall, quantitative restrictions on the numbers of operators would become meaningless and tariff regulations would be unworkable (Whitelegg, 1990a).

Completing the internal market embraces both static and dynamic effects. The static effects are those changes which will reduce costs to industry, stimulate trade and improve competitive efficiency. The dynamic effects are those changes which will result from this different operating environment. We can expect more innovation, greater and greater levels of efficiency and productivity and substantial changes in the location and organisation of manufacturing and service industries. These changes will have clear spatial effects with a reduction in numbers of plants as industries achieve economies of scale and a large increase in international flows as a European scale of organisation becomes the norm. A quote from an EC document (Task Force, nd) will clarify this point:

> Completion of the internal market is likely to stimulate growth in the transport sector, which would in turn give rise to environmental impacts in the form of the air pollution caused by motor vehicle emissions, and in the form of land use impacts, both directly resulting from transport infrastructure development, and also associated with changes in industrial location and in the pattern of population. Increased urbanization and concentration of population – along route corridors and at transport nodes – can have visual impacts . . . and strain the capacity of infrastructure.

Put quite simply we can expect a substantial increase in road traffic, particularly road freight, from the combination of removal of barriers, liberalisation of road haulage, economic growth and achievement of economies of scale. The effect on vehicle-km and tonne-km will be exaggerated by the increase of longer distance movements as the single market increases the interdependence among member states (EC, 1988a).

The effects of removing technical barriers are difficult to quantify particularly as they are so closely associated with price reductions and liberalisation of road haulage. Nevertheless policies which will open previously protected trades as in public purchases and the food and drink industry will increase exchanges between countries and the amount of tonne-km. In the foodstuffs industry consultants working for the EC have identified over 200 barriers to free trade (EC, 1988b). These barriers have acted as mechanisms to restrict import penetration and the spatial range of the good traded. Whatever the merits of wider consumer choice and free trade there is an impact of their removal on the size and direction of freight flows.

In the case of Italian pasta the removal of regulations permitting only durum wheat to be used will allow the penetration of soft/durum combinations of 10–20 per cent of total pasta consumption (EC, 1988b). A similar argument exists in the case of German beer. The elimination of restrictions on the definition of beer will increase market penetration. In total one-third of the fifty product markets considered in the foodstuffs study would be 'significantly affected' (EC, 1988b).

The food industry in addition to extending the spatial range of its products is also likely to undergo major rationalisation and reorganisation as it moves from a position where it serves national markets to one where it serves a European market. The emergence of a small number of very large plants with very large transport demands is likely in this industry as long as the rewards from economies of scale in production and achieving brand leadership are greater than the transport costs which will be incurred. Analyses of other industrial sectors, eg pharmaceuticals and telecommunications, show results which are in agreement with the foodstuffs study (EC, 1988b).

Given the lowering of transport costs as a result of 1992 (EC, 1988a), the removal of technical barriers and the reforms to make mergers and the movement of capital much easier, all the conditions necessary for a sustained growth of freight and spatial concentration of production are in place.

Cabotage

Many of the fears in Germany about the single market and its effects relate to the growth of road freight and its associated environmental damage. Cabotage is at the centre of these concerns. Cabotage will open up all national markets to the operators of all other member states. This is a natural corollary of other policies to eliminate barriers and create one community for all trading purposes. It is also viewed by the EC as a means of reducing empty running of vehicles which costs 1.2 billion ECUs and contributes to an environmental problem which could be removed (EC, 1988a). If return and outward journeys are run with empty vehicles because of restrictions which prohibit cabotage then the EC position has some merit. If the empty running is the result of other factors then the EC position falls.

The EC's own study of empty running identifies only 20% of empty running which can be attributed to regulatory restrictions (EC, 1988a). The other 80% is due to lack of knowledge of load availability and imbalances in trade flows. In the case of London, for example, inward flows exceed outward flows by a large margin. This is also the case for Britain as a whole. It would be very difficult to reduce empty running on the outward journeys. Other reasons include specialisation by body type. Tippers, for example, cannot be used for carrying fresh food or hanging garments and considerations of this type account for half of the empty running (Cooper, 1990). Another factor is the development of sophisticated contract services in the haulage industry. Companies such as Exel Logistics and Christian Salveson provide 'tailor-made' services which cannot easily accommodate back-loading.

This strongly indicates that the EC has made an error in its emphasis on cabotage. Cabotage cannot supply a solution to the problem of empty running of lorries. This view is supported by the UK experience where twenty-two years of deregulated road haulage have failed to reduce empty running below 30%. Cooper (1990) concludes that 'empty running has remained at stubbornly high levels'.

Cabotage will deliver lower freight rates and rates which are much lower than the 5% reduction predicted (EC, 1988a). Protected markets like Germany will be put under particularly severe stress from non-national hauliers at both ends of the 'sophistication' spectrum. Germany can expect to lose market share to UK hauliers who are fully experienced in a deregulated market and already buying firms in Germany to use as a base. Germany's labour costs are the highest in the EC which puts the haulage industry at a competitive disadvantage when compared with low wage countries in southern Europe. Greek and Portuguese wage costs are 31% and 19% respectively of those in Germany. As 1992 will bring about the harmonisation of fuel taxes in Europe and possibly the 'variabilisation' of all vehicle taxes on a territorial basis it can be assumed that these differences will cease to be important. Labour cost differences will, however, remain and will provide a strong incentive for southern European road hauliers to break into the north European market. Cabotage makes this possible.

Cabotage without a significant improvement in the pursuit and prosecution of breaches of social regulations is likely to produce an increase in such breaches. The existing situation with respect to breaches of regulations on driving hours and rest periods is already unsatisfactory and represents a 20–25% cost advantage for the road sector (Whitelegg, 1992a). Intense competitive pressures from countries with less stringent technical standards and controls on vehicles and operating a long way from home will make the situation worse. This is both a road safety problem and a problem for the environment and increases in direct proportion with the increase in vehicle-km.

The deregulation experience in other countries

Australia deregulated inter-state road haulage in 1954, Britain in 1968 and the USA in 1980. Whilst comparisons between such different places are fraught with difficulties the experience can help to prepare for the results of 1992. The US experience is quoted by the EC as a justification for its own approach (EC, 1988a). Savings from deregulation amounted to about $26 billion in 1985 compared with total transport costs of $260 billion. Cooper (1989) puts the annual savings at $38 billion and claims that there has been a 25% reduction in charges for full truckloads. In Australia the reduction was 50%.

Cooper (1990) shows that deregulation such as is proposed on a European scale for the SEM produces no perceptible impact on empty running, a significant impact on freight rates (lowered) and a loss of rail freight. A combination of reduced freight charges, more lorry operators competing for traffic and new investment in roads is a powerful cocktail for environmental degradation. The origin of the problem in EC policies must cast serious doubt on the ability of the same institutions to produce environmental gains. Talk of sustainability under these circumstances is, at the very least, logically inconsistent. Investigations at a more detailed sectoral level tell the same story.

Structural changes in retailing and increased road freight activity

Retailing is a significant generator of freight in Europe. Foodstuffs account for 13% of tonnage carried by road and agricultural products 9% (EC, 1989a). This sector has been identified as one which will be significantly affected by the single market. The main change will be in the internationalisation of buying, manufacturing and retailing which is currently dominated by national markets. The EC predicts a shift towards Europe-wide operations with the emergence of clear brand leaders and wide geographical coverage as has happened in the USA (EC, 1988b). The removal of trade barriers will encourage EC food concerns to increase geographical coverage and hence their dependence on the transport function. They will consume a lot more vehicle and tonne-km.

The EC calculates that the single market will create significant benefits for this sector, of the order of 500–1000 million ECUs per annum in the foodstuffs sector alone (EC, 1988b). This will be achieved largely through 'restructuring and consolidation' which means fewer and bigger plants. The EC also refers to a positive correlation between growth in trade and plant size. If this is correct we can expect a period of mergers and rationalisations (ie plant closures) to produce larger plants with larger trade flows.

These findings are corroborated by a UK study of retailing and 1992 (Oxford Institute of Retail Management, 1989). This study predicts lower transport costs and improved pan-European buying for retailers (ie more transport). It also predicts increased concentration in the retailing sector and the greatest growth in consumer expenditure in southern Europe. Italy is expected to be the 'leading' EC economy by 1995. The implications of the internationalisation of retailing, differential growth in the EC and spatial concentration in this sector provide a significant boost to freight transport.

Forecasting the scale of the increase in road freight transport

The EC expects an increase in freight traffic but is very reluctant to put any figures on the increase, perhaps because this would expose the contradiction between the economic motives of the single market and the environmental remit of the EC. The official journal of the European communities announcing the EURET research programme (EC, 1989b) states quite clearly: 'Completion of the internal market is inconceivable without . . . [an] increase in demand, in volume and in qualitative terms for all types of transport'.

The Task Force report (Task Force, nd) also refers to a significant growth in freight traffic but does not attempt to quantify this growth beyond an estimate that cross-border traffic will increase by 30–50%.

Whitelegg (1990a) identified nine different forecasts which had been made for what was then West Germany. These forecasts produced results in the range of a 20–25% increase in tonne-km by the year 2000 using various base years in the 1985–89 period. There are two problems with these forecasts:

1   neither of them makes explicit assumptions about the spatial restructuring effect which will result from the operation of the single market, and
2   all the increases are less than that which would be expected by the application of an average ten-year growth rate to freight volumes.

Working on German data Whitelegg incorporated these factors into a forecast of road freight activity and using 1987 as a base year calculated that a 73% increase in tonne-km of road freight activity was likely by the year 2000. The increase in freight activity arose from a number of different sources and these are listed in table 8.1.

The exact size of the forecast increase in freight tonne-km is not so important. What is more important is that the processes which drive the increase are identified. These increases, which in the case of Germany

Table 8.1   Proportionate contribution to increased road freight activity in
Germany, 1987–2000

Source of growth	% of total growth
Increase in GDP	54.2
Spatial restructuring	26.3
Loss of rail freight	6.9
Impact of logistics	6.9
Impact of cabotage	5.7
Total	100

need to be revised upwards to take account of vigorous east–west freight
flows which were not in the original calculations, produce increased
levels of pollution.

Whitelegg (1990a) used these forecasts for Germany to estimate
increases in air pollution for the main pollutants, noise pollution, road
traffic accidents and the numbers of people affected by these hazards on
main traffic corridors. The results show that EC policies are responsible
for a major additional environmental burden affecting more than 20
million people in this one country.

Sustainability is difficult to define and may be less than useful as a
concept that will help to sharpen perception and assist the design of solutions. What is clear from the European dimension, however, is that
major additional environmental burdens are generated by a set of
economic policies which are not modified by the need to minimise vehicle
exhaust emissions, reduce land take for new transport projects or create
cities which are free of noise, danger and cars. The SEM and its
legislative base has unleashed a process of accelerated traffic growth with
all the consequences noted in earlier chapters. No amount of ex-post
rationalisation and amelioration can alter this basic trajectory. The EC
has not created non-sustainability but in its economic and spatial logic
underpinned by strong notions of deregulation and liberalisation it has
ensured that sustainability cannot be achieved. The EC merely gives
clearer expression to the fundamental logic of a consumer society locked
into growth, incapable of another vision and determined to achieve
higher levels of output, traffic, consumption, road building, air transport
and spatial concentration of production. Sustainability cannot be
achieved under such conditions.

9 CONCLUSION

This book began with a discussion about sustainability. The term is almost impossible to define in an operational sense but it has come to signal a concern for environmental impacts and resource conservation which is based on an understanding of processes as they unfold through time. Meadows, Meadows and Randers (1992, p209) define a sustainable society as one that can persist over generations, one that is far-seeing enough, flexible enough, and wise enough not to undermine its physical or social system of support. This echoes the emphasis in this book on traffic as a serious problem for the social environment of cities and the health of urban residents.

The invention of a process-based understanding coupled with the recognition that there may be critical thresholds beyond which it is simply too late to take remedial action has sharpened the debate and spurred governments into action aimed at reducing environmental impacts. Much of this action is nothing more than rhetoric and is based on playing with technology in the hope that fundamental changes in behaviour can be avoided. Catalytic converters and electric vehicles fall into this category. There is, in consequence, a dark side to the sustainability issue which can be summarised as the commitment to existing patterns of resource consumption whilst installing end-of-pipe technologies to solve any problems that might result from that consumption.

Much of transport at national and EC level is dominated by this end-of-pipe approach. The level of debate surrounding changed land use arrangements or trip 'degeneration' (Roberts, 1992) is minimal whilst vast sums are devoted to the development of new technologies and policies which will continue to stimulate higher levels of traffic demand. The EC itself is energetically pursuing more road construction, support of high speed rail and airport expansion in the full knowledge that the higher levels of mobility that will be created impose demands on air quality, noise quality, health and ecology that destroy urban environments and replicate the Gotthard Pass horrors all over Europe. The Gotthard Pass carries such substantial volumes of traffic (over 500,000 heavy goods vehicles of over 3.5 tonnes per annum) that it clearly illustrates the problem of large volumes of traffic channelled into a small number of corridors (Verkehrs Club der Schweiz, 1991). Investing in new infrastructure to cope with increased traffic volumes is not a sustainable policy and yet the term 'sustainable mobility' is used in EC documentation.

Satisfying the demand for higher levels of mobility or, more accurately, creating that demand, is not sustainable for a number of reasons. On a global scale it cannot be replicated in countries like India and China. The resultant demands on energy and air pollution burdens including greenhouse gases trip the thresholds identified by organisations like IPCC (global warming) and WHO (air pollution). If we accept the accelerating upward trend in vehicle use in developed societies then we must accept it for the remainder of the planet. If we cannot accept the conversion of all third world countries to European levels of consumption as far as vehicles and transport are concerned then we are expressing a commitment to global inequality and exploitation neither of which is compatible with any definition of sustainability. An acceptance of a global vehicle population in excess of 2 billion by the year 2025 (achieved by taking the combined populations of South America, India, China and the Confederation of Independent States and applying a low – by European standards – car ownership rate) compared with the 1992 level of 500 million is not sustainable on any level. If this view causes difficulty then the whole sustainability argument must be discarded as meaningless. Meadows, Meadows and Randers (1992) do not consider traffic and transport but they are clear that current patterns of consumption are non-sustainable.

It is unlikely that sustainability can ever be defined in terms of a specific level of consumption of a specific commodity but if a trajectory can be identified and scaled up to include the effects of opening up motorisation to India, Africa and China, for example, then it is possible to identify the likelihood of such a dramatic change threatening global environment and health. The information presented so far in this book and more than adequately reinforced by TEST (1991) shows that present levels of consumption and burdens imposed by traffic more than surpass what is tolerable and acceptable. Indeed it is important to emphasise tolerability and acceptability in case a wider ranging discussion of what sustainability means should gloss over the very serious problems that afflict urban residents here and now and that require immediate solutions.

Sustainability also glosses over affordability. It is clear from chapter 7 that the present system of state subsidised mobility in Europe is enormously expensive and that for similar or smaller sums we could have a system that guarantees clean air, safe streets, strong communities and a healthy population linked to a strong economy. What is currently on offer is quite simply bad value for money and the lack of widespread acknowledgement of this bad deal is a monument to the success of motoring organisations such as the AA and RAC in Britain and the ADAC in Germany who have lobbied so successfully over the years that they have succeeded in identifying motoring with democratic freedoms. They are, of course, supported by a vast network of like minded bodies (Hamer, 1987) who collectively have engineered a situation where enormous subsidies to roads and vehicles are regarded as good value for money and indeed only partial recompense for motor vehicle taxation whilst bus and rail are regarded as dreadfully inefficient and wasteful of public funds.

Sustainability is a very flexible concept and can be used to justify policies which are definitely not sustainable. California's commitment to zero emission vehicles certainly looks as though it could be described as a contribution to sustainability whereas in reality it is a commitment to displace the unwanted consequences of energy consumption elsewhere (the point of electricity generation) whilst maintaining a system that consumes vast amounts of space and converts cities into parking lots and freeways. The emphasis on zero emission is, once again, instructive. No-one is suggesting a zero space, zero energy, zero speed vehicle (it would be acceptable to substitute 'low' for 'zero'). Such a vehicle would have the advantages of feet and bicycles and also of high quality public transport systems. It would also inject health and community into the urban equation. It would be, in a word, sustainable.

In spite of the heightened level of debate about environmental impacts spurred on by sustainability arguments and the Rio summit in June 1992 most traffic problems continue to worsen and continue to exhibit a peculiar immunity to fairly obvious solutions. It is highly unlikely that an awareness of sustainability has helped to solve traffic problems in those places where daily life is increasingly intolerable because of the depredations of traffic. These depredations were described in some detail in Jacobs (1961) and again by TEST (1991). The intervening thirty years saw a considerable deterioration in air quality, noise quality and urban quality of life, a deterioration that is set to continue at an accelerating pace.

There is clear evidence that policy makers are out of step with those who suffer these depredations. Roberts (1989) quotes from opinion surveys which show that access to cars comes quite low down the list when compared with safe streets, an unpolluted atmosphere and good public transport. Jones (1992) reports the results of a number of opinion polls registering support for traffic restraint and support of public transport. What we get from most governments in Europe and from the EC is support for road construction and that tiny percentage of rail use that is intended to serve distances of over 500km.

If sustainability as a concept is to be put to good use in transport it will need some guiding principles. Those that arise most naturally from the pioneering work of John Roberts and other commentators on contemporary transport policy (Roberts et al, 1992) are:

1   Transport is a vital element in economic and social activities but must serve those activities rather than be an end in itself.
2   The consumption of distance by freight and passengers should be minimised as far as possible whilst maximising the potential for locally based social interaction and locally based economic activity.
3   All transport needs should be met by the means that is least damaging to the environment.
4   There should be a presumption in physical land use planning against those activities which by nature of their size and importance attract car-based users from a large area.
5   All transport investment plans should be subjected to a full health audit notwithstanding the uncertainties surrounding epidemiological proof. Proposals which are potentially health damaging should be rejected.
6   All transport investment plans should have clear objectives designed to cover social, economic and environmental concerns and be evaluated by an independent authority with sufficient expertise to comment on value for money, costs and benefits and the availability of alternative strategies to achieve the same objectives.
7   All transport investments should be monitored over their lifetime to check on the degree to which they meet their stated objectives and their contribution to environmental damage.
8   All transport policy matters should be dealt with in a transport policy directorate that has no direct responsibilities for the management of individual modes. The responsibilities of the directorate are to deliver sharply focused policies that minimise danger, minimise air and noise pollution, maximise social interaction and urban quality of life and oversee the non-policy making executives (for road, rail and air) whose role is to implement the directives of the transport policy directorate.

These principles represent a starting point for a new approach to transport policy. The existing approach in all European countries, given extra weight by EC policies, falls far short of anything that could be called sustainable. Quite simply there is nothing in place that has any chance of modifying the accelerating demand for transport.

At a European level policies are in place (chapter 8) to lengthen the distances that separate economic activities, to reduce the cost of transport (deregulation), to incorporate southern Europe, Mediterranean

Europe and Eastern Europe into a motorway-linked economic system and to reduce the cost of cars. Reductions in the cost of cars is the inevitable result of single market changes to ensure that vehicles made anywhere in the EC can be sold anywhere in the EC satisfying an EC-level technical standard rather than a number of different national technical standards. Variation in the retail price of cars has also been identified as a problem and will not survive the full implementation of the single market. The ending of peculiar retailing practices in the motor vehicle industry will produce a downward pressure on car prices.

Many of the important EC effects are driven by policies which are not transport based. The single market itself is intended to boost economic growth which if successful will add to the demand for cars and travel. The abolition of all barriers to the movement of goods and capital precipitates the changes noted in chapter 8. Most importantly, however, all these changes are to be grafted onto a system which is almost totally dependent on road-based transport and in which road-based transport is given a major boost. The dominance of road based transport is the result of an historical process of fiscal discrimination in favour of road supported by major land use changes which set that dominance in concrete. The problem with EC level changes in the spatial and economic structures of Europe is that they can only be delivered by road-based transport. They lack a transport dimension which offers alternative scenarios for the achievement of EC objectives through the application of principles such as those listed above.

It is for these reasons that much of EC and national environmental policy and attempts to cloak transport policy in green credentials are seriously flawed. It will be possible to modify some impacts at the margin but Europe covered in traffic at levels lower than those predicted by UK forecasters will be a sorry sight when it is perfectly obvious that most cities, most corridors and most people are already suffering a level of discomfort, displeasure and disease that goes beyond the tolerable and hence the sustainable.

On the positive side, there are examples of transport policies in Europe that do have the potential to break through the barrier and establish a new trajectory. Many of these are reviewed in Roberts (1989) but caution is necessary in their interpretation. Traffic calming on an enormous scale in North Rhine–Westphalia in Germany has not dented the dominance of the car or ameliorated the unpleasantness of cities dominated by traffic and of wooded areas whose escape from vehicle noise is virtually impossible.

Public transport investment in many European cities has produced rates of use vastly in excess of Britain with Zürich a much-quoted example. What is clear from those cities with well-funded public transport systems is that local democracy and control is just as important as fiscal ability. The main flaw in Britain's transport policies is the enormous weight of a centralised and dogmatic London-based administrative machine. In the British system there is no room for local democracy as it exists in California, Amsterdam and Zürich. It remains to be seen whether or not the single market and post-Maastricht developments will add to or detract from the possibility of local autonomy. The Maastricht Treaty has produced a great interest in 'subsidiarity', particularly on the part of the UK government. The principle of subsidiarity states that decisions and actions should be taken at the lowest level of policy making consistent with competence and efficiency. The UK support for the principle is paradoxical given the UK government's dislike of allowing local government to act in areas like transport where local autonomy can deliver high quality solutions to traffic congestion and environmental disturbance. Subsidiarity in its pure form would represent an enormous boost to the implementation of innovative solutions to traffic problems but is unlikely in the UK where support for the principle in EC–UK arguments will be as strong as opposition to it in UK government–local authority rows.

Sustainability would be much more promising as a basis for action if it were grafted on to a strong regional based government that recognised local competence and local self-determination. The actions of national governments, like the actions of the EC, are constrained by objectives and structures which are inimical to the concept of sustainability. A national government or the EC has to facilitate a space economy and a supporting transport system that centralises, captures economies of scale and increases the amount of passenger and freight movement. The alternative of a large number of autonomous regions each with their own version of a space economy and productive system would satisfy a higher proportion of its needs and wants locally and hence reduce demand for passenger and freight movement. It would be more dynamic in an entrepreneurial sense and would be a much more appropriate structure to deliver the sustainable society defined in Meadows, Meadows and Randers (1992).

Sustainability is basically a scale problem. At the right spatial scale where social and environmental objectives are genuinely high on the agenda it can be designed and delivered. At higher scales and at the EC level itself it cannot be designed or delivered. The right spatial scale is for wider debate and discussion. A small community knows that it wants safe streets, clean air and a vibrant, friendly neighbourhood. It also knows that it will not get these things from a national government whilst the EC declares its hand with grandiose military style transport planning that routes international highways through local communities with no thought for the consequences and a set of vague notions about linking the periphery or binding the community together. This is the process of downgrading the importance of local environments and local communities that is at the centre of national and EC level planning.

The EC does have the potential to trigger important developments. This is the case with the car-free city concept. Pioneered in Lübeck and Aachen (Germany) and subsequently implemented, at least in part, in Bologna and Florence (Italy) the idea has now been given additional credibility by an EC initiative (Transport Europe, 1992). As a break with traditional cosmetic policies this idea is very significant. In Lübeck the city centre which is defined as larger than a pedestrian precinct or central shopping area was declared car-free and obstacles erected to prevent the passage of vehicles between 10.00 and 16.00, initially on Saturdays only but now extended to the rest of the week. Amsterdam voted in a referendum in 1992 to follow a similar path.

The EC published a document in June 1992 (Transport Europe, 1992b) declaring that a city without cars was a viable proposition and could be up to five times cheaper to run than a city with cars. The research behind the statement showed that the cost of a motor-free city chargeable in full to the public authorities, can be up to five times less than in 'normal' cities where the cost is borne to a great extent by the private sector. The implementation of such a concept would go along with improvements in public transport. An initial group of cities with an interest in this plan included Amsterdam, Aosta, Louvain, Naples and Bath.

The car-free concept is a radical one and perhaps the only example of this genre. It is only likely to be successful if it is implemented as part of a comprehensive set of measures which rearranges all travel priorities in cities in favour of pedestrians and bicycles and then public transport users. This not only demands reductions in car parking in city centres but also private car parking associated with businesses and major investments in park-and-ride facilities outside of cities. It also demands land use policies which can discriminate in favour of those activities which emphasise short distance, non-motorised trips as opposed to activities like out-of-town shopping centres that encourage the opposite. This would have to apply *a fortiori* to leisure, recreation and tourism trips which are major growth areas in travel behaviour. This is likely to be very difficult.

Such a policy also demands the abandonment of traditional thinking about inter-urban roads, ring roads, relief roads etc which are justified on unproven economic development arguments and yet serve as arteries for short distance trips and dump large numbers of car users at overloaded points in the urban road network. There is no clear difference between intra-urban roads and inter-urban roads in the ways in which they are used. The categories are artificial and serve to undermine whatever progress can be made in urban areas as well as undermine railway planning and economics. This is essentially the M25 problem where something that was planned as a bypass and a major strategic route serves as an ordinary local road.

A car-free city concept does not directly address the problem of lorries particularly on major inter-urban corridors and strategic links. The concentration of lorries on Alpine transit routes is a major European transport problem that can only get worse as the economies of southern and northern Europe become more interdependent. The traffic problems associated with the Brenner Pass and other Alpine routes are being replicated all over Europe as high capacity motorways are overwhelmed by the volume of traffic. In Britain the M62 around Manchester is seriously overstretched and all countries have similar examples. Chapter 8 set out to show how this will get much worse, a trend that will be exacerbated each time a 'missing link' is plugged. Thus the new bridge connecting Sweden with Denmark will bring a swathe of environmental destruction around the southern suburbs of Copenhagen and around Malmo. The Channel Tunnel will 'Brennerise' the motorways through Kent, trans-Pyrenean motorways will destroy unique habitats and ecologies, the east–west highway through central Andalusia linking Seville, Granada and Baza will generate vast amounts of traffic with dire environmental consequences and the former territory of the German Democratic Republic will receive its swathe of motorways in the pursuit of an elusive economic utopia. The EC intends to add 1200km of motorway to the present 3700km in the next ten years (Transport Europe, 1992a). Of the new routes, 40% will be established in Greece, Ireland, Portugal and Spain so that these countries can be incorporated more successfully into the system of large producers and long distance travel to the detriment of more local production and consumption. This plan is costed at 120 billion ECUs and comes from the same stable as the car-free city concept and the green book on the urban environment. Clearly there is some inconsistency in EC policy.

On balance the EC is a force for environmental destruction whose perception of transport is something totally dominated by its role in making the single market work and encouraging development everywhere where there is not enough of it already. The consequences of such a short-sighted view of transport grafted on to national transport policies with similar myopia are disastrous.

The EC has the potential to deliver a system that encourages local autonomy (true subsidiarity) whilst providing funding instruments and setting standards for water quality, noise, air quality etc. Since this is not going to be popular with the national governments running the EC it is unlikely to make any progress.

Europe is at a crossroads. The present pattern of transport consumption and motorised vehicle dependence has destroyed much that is valuable and is not showing any signs of abatement. It has the potential to destroy much more but can be converted into a force that nurtures environment, health and community. The ways in which this can be done are not difficult to design but there are important structural obstacles in the way. Sustainability and its implications offer one way of converting these obstacles into facilitators but is itself already being subverted into a defence of the status quo. If significant progress is to made with global issues of environment and development then a major shift in European patterns of consumption is now due. A phased reduction in dependence on motorised transport and a gradual shift in the organisation of land uses and activities will deliver material rewards as well as dramatic increases in health, psychological well-being and employment.

A commitment by the developed nations to existing patterns of consumption and their health- and community-destructive tendencies will continue to deprive children of independent mobility and all of us of clean air and will signal to the rest of the world that every utterance about rainforests, ozone, global warming etc is pure self-seeking rhetoric to ensure the perpetuation of global inequalities and exploitation by continuing to corner and consume increasingly larger shares of a declining resource base.

APPENDIX 1: CHEMICALS PRESENT IN VEHICLE EXHAUSTS

'A' denotes petrol vehicles; 'D' denotes diesel vehicles; 'V' denotes petrol vapour (from: Ball, Brindlecombe and Nicholas, 1991).

Inorganic compounds

hydrogen	A		
ammonia	A		
nitric oxide	A	D	
nitrogen dioxide	A	D	
hydrogen sulphide	A		
sulphur dioxide	A	D	
sulphur trioxide	A		
sulphuric acid	A		
hydrogen chloride	A		
hydrogen bromide	A		
ammonium chloride; lead bromochloride	A		
diammonium chloride; lead bromochloride	A		
lead bromochloride	A		
carbon monoxide	A	D	
carbon dioxide	A	D	

Alkanes

methane	A	D	
ethane	A	D	
propane	A	D	
butane	A	D	
isobutane	A	D	
2,2-dimethylbutane	A		V
2,3-dimethylbutane	A		V
2,2,3-trimethylbutane	A		
pentane	A	D	V

isopentane	A	D	V
2-methylpentane	A		V
3-methylpentane	A		
2,2-dimethylpentane	A		
2,3-dimethylpentane	A		V
2,4-dimethylpentane	A		V
3,3-dimethylpentane	A		
2,2,3-trimethylpentane	A		
2,2,4-trimethylpentane	A		V
2,3,3-trimethylpentane	A		V
2,3,4-trimethylpentane	A		V
hexane	A	D	V
2-methylhexane	A		
3-methylhexane	A		V
2,2-dimethylhexane	A		V
2,3-dimethylhexane	A		
2,4-dimethylhexane	A		
2,2,5-trimethylhexane	A		V
2,3,5-trimethylhexane	A		V
heptane	A	D	V
2-methylheptane	A		V
3-methylheptane	A		V
4-methylheptane	A		
2,4-dimethylheptane	A		
2,4-dimethylheptane	A		
octane	A	D	V
2-methyloctane	A		V
nonane	A		V
decane	A	D	
3-methyldecane		D	
3-methylundecane		D	
tetradecane		D	
3-methyltetradecane		D	
pentadecane		D	
2-methylpentadecane		D	
hexadecane	A	D	
heptadecane	A	D	
octadecane	A	D	
nonadecane	A	D	
eicosane	A	D	
heneicosane	A	D	
docosane	A	D	
tricosane	A	D	
tetracosane	A	D	
pentacosane	A	D	
hexacosane	A	D	
heptacosane	A	D	
octacosane	A	D	

nonacosane	A	D
tricontane	A	D
hentriacontane	A	D
dotriacontane	A	D
tritriacontane	A	D
hexatriacontane	A	

Alkanes and alkynes

acetylene	A	D	
ethene	A	D	
propene	A	D	
propadiene	A	D	
propyne	A		
1-butene	A	D	V
2-methyl-1-butene	A		V
3-methyl-1-butene	A	D	
2,3-dimethyl-1-butene	A		
2,3,3-trimethyl-1-butene	A		
2-ethyl-1-butene	A		
isobutene	A	D	V
1,3-butadiene	A	D	
isoprene	A		V
cis-2-butene	A	D	V
trans-2-butene	A	D	V
2-methyl-2-butene	A	D	V
2,3-dimethyl-2-butene	A		
1-pentene	A	D	V
2-methyl-1-pentene	A		
4-methyl-1-pentene	A	D	
3,4-dimethyl-1-pentene	A		
2,4,4-trimethyl-1-pentene	A		
3-ethyl-1-pentene	A		
cis-2-pentene	A	D	V
trans-2-pentene	A		V
2-methyl-2-pentene	A		V
3-methyl-2-pentene	A		
4-methyl-2-pentene	A		
3,4-dimethyl-2-pentene	A		
2,4,4-trimethyl-2-pentene	A		
1-hexene	A	D	
4-methyl-1-hexene	A		
5-methyl-1-hexene	A		
2-ethyl-1-hexene	A		
cis-2-hexene	A		
trans-2-hexene	A		
5-methyl-2-hexene	A		

2,3-dimethyl-2-hexene	A		
cis-3-hexene	A		
trans-3-hexene	A		
1-heptene	A	D	
cis-2-heptene	A		
trans-2-heptene	A		
3-heptene	A		
2,6-dimethyl-3-heptene	A		
1-octene	A	D	
cis-2-octene	A		
trans-2-octene	A		
1-nonene	A	D	
1-docecene	A		
1-tetradecene		D	
1-heptadecene		D	

Cyclic hydrocarbons

cyclopentane	A		V
methylcyclopentane	A		V
cyclopentene	A		
1-methylcyclopentane			V
cyclohexane	A		
methylcyclohexane	A	D	V
cic-1,2-dimethylcyclohexane	A		
trans-1,2-dimethylcyclohexane	A		
ethylcyclohexane	A		
dodecylcyclohexane	A		
1-methylcyclohexene	A		
4-methylcyclohexene	A	D	

Aromatic hydrocarbons

benzene	A	D	V
toluene	A	D	V
o-xylene	A	D	V
m-xylene	A	D	V
p-xylene	A	D	V
1,2,3-trimethylbenzene	A		V
1,2,4-trimethylbenzene	A		V
1,3,5-trimethylbenzene	A	D	
1,2,3,5-tetramethylbenzene		D	
ethylbenzene	A	D	V
o-ethyltoluene	A		V
m-ethyltoluene	A		V
p-ethyltoluene	A		V

ethyldimethylbenzene	A	V
1,3-diethylbenzene	A	
[alpha]methylstyrene		D
n-propylbenzene	A	V
1-methyl-2-propyl-benzene	A	
cumene	A	V
m-cymene	A	
n-butylbenzene	A	
sec-butylbenzene	A	
tert-butylbenzene	A	D
methylindane		D
dimethylindane		D
trimethylindane		D
biphenyl		D
trinaphthene benzene	A	
naphthalene	A	D
1-methylnaphthalene	A	D
trimethylnaphthalene		D
1-ethylnaphthalene		D
2-isopropylnaphthalene		D
undecylnaphthalene	A	
1,2-dihydrotrimethylnaphthalene		D
tetralin	A	D
methyltetralin		D
dimethyltetralin	A	D
trimethyltetralin		D
decahydronaphthalene		D
acenaphthalene		D
dimethylcyclopentacenaphthalene	A	
diphenylacenaphthalene	A	
acenaphthylene		D
[beta,beta]binapthyl		D

Polynuclear aromatic hydrocarbons

fluorene	A	D
dimethylfluorene		D
trimethylfluorene		D
ethylfluorene		D
isoamylfluorene	A	
benzo[b]fluorene	A	
phenanthrene	A	D
tetrahydrophenanthrene	A	
octahydrophenanthrene	A	
perhydrophenanthrene		D
2,5-dimethylphenanthrene		D
4,5-dimethylperhydrophenanthrene		D

dimethylbenzophenanthrene   A
benzo[l]phenanthrene   A
dibenzo[b,h]phenanthrene   A   D
anthracene   A   D
benz[a]anthracene   A   D
3-methylbenz[a]anthracene   A
dibenz[a,h]anthracene   A
fluoranthene   A   D
benzo[b]fluoranthene   A
benzo[ghi]fluoranthene   A
benzo[j]fluoranthene   A
benzo[k]fluoranthene   A   D
indeno[1,2,2-cd]fluoranthene   A
pyrene   A   D
cyclopent[cd]pyrene   A   D
benzo[a]pyrene   A   D
methylbenzo[a]pyrene   A
benzo[e]pyrene   A   D
methylbenzo[e]pyrene   A
dibenzo[a,b]pyrene   A
dibenzo[a,e]pyrene   A
dibenzo[cd,jk]pyrene   A   D
indeno[1,2,3-cd]pyrene   A   D
chrysene   A   D
naphthacene   A
dibenzo[a,l]naphthacene   A
perylene   A   D
benzo[ghi]perylene   A   D
methylbenzo[ghi]perylene   A
dibenzo[b,pqr]perylene   A
coronene   A   D

Aldehydes

formaldehyde   A   D
acetaldehyde   A   D
propanal   A   D
n-butanal   A   D
isobutanal   A   D
2-ethylbutanal   A
n-pentanal   A   D
isopentanal   A   D
neopentanal   A
hexanal   A   D
heptanal   A   D
octanal   D
decanal   A   D

acrolein	A	D
methacrolein	A	
crotonaldehyde	A	D
tiglaldehyde	A	
furfural		D
5-methylfurfural		D
furfural alcohol		D
benzaldehyde	A	D
2-methylbenzaldehyde	A	D
3-methylbenzaldehyde	A	
4-methylbenzaldehyde	A	
dimethylbenzaldehyde	A	D
ethylbenzaldehyde	A	
ethyltetramethylbenzaldehyde		D
propylbenzaldehyde		D
butylbenzaldehyde		D
cinnamaldehyde		D
salicylaldehyde	A	D
hydroxylallylbenzaldehyde		D
anisaldehyde		D
phthalaldehyde		D
terephthalaldehyde	A	
4-formylbenzoic acid	A	
piperonal		D
vanillin		D
1-naphthal		D
methylnapthal		D
methoxylnapthal		D

Ketones

acetone	A	D
hydroxypropanone		D
butanone	A	
methylbutanone	A	
dimethylbutanone	A	
2-pentanone	A	
4-methyl-2-pentanone	A	
4-hydroxy-2-pentanone		D
3-pentanone	A	
3-heptanone		D
4-heptanone		D
3-butene-2-one	A	
3-methyl-3-butene-2-one	A	
4-methyl-3-pentene-2-one	A	
1,3-dimethylcyclohexan-5-one		D
methylcyclohexanedione		D

[gamma]-valerolactone		D
[delta]-valerolactone		D
acetophenone	A	D
dimethylacetophenone		D
p-hydroxyacetophenone		D
dihydroxyacetophenone		D
phenylvinylketone		D
diethylphthalate	A	
dibutylphthalate	A	
diisobutylphthalate	A	
dioctalphthalate	A	
butylbenzylphthalate	A	
1-indanone		D
dimethyl-1-indanone		D
3,3-dimethyl-5-tert-butylindanone		D
hydroxyindanone		D
methylhydroxyindanone		D
trimethylhydroxyindanone		D
tetramethylhydroxyindanone		D
methoxyindanone		D
2-indanone		D
indenone		D
dimethylindenone		D
pentamethylindenone		D
hydroxyindenone		D
methylhydroxyindenone		D
dimethylhydroxyindenone		D
1-tetralone		D
methyltetralone		D
methoxytetralone		D
acetonapthone	A	D
2,6-napthoquinone		D
methylnapthoquinone		D
fluorenone		D
9,10-anthroquinone	A	D
benz[a]anthrone	A	
benz[de]anthracene-7-one	A	
2-coumarin		D
3-coumarin		D

Carbolic acids

acetic acid	D
propionic acid	D
butanoic acid	D
pentanoic acid	D
hexanoic acid	D

crotonic acid		D
benzoic acid		D
benzoic acid	A	
phenylacetic acid	A	

Esters

methyl formate	A	
ethyl napthoate	A	

Alcohols

ethanol	A	
1-propanol	A	D
2-propanol	A	
2-butanol	A	
5-pentadecanol	A	
2-buten-1-ol	A	
3-methyl-1-pentyl-3-ol		D
cyclopentanol		D
phenol	A	D
o-cresol	A	D
m-creso	A	D
p-cresol	A	D
2,3-xylenol	A	D
2,4-xylenol	A	D
2,5-xylenol	A	D
2,6-xylenol	A	
3,4-xylenol	A	
3,5-xylenol	A	
2,4,6-trimethylphenol	A	D
tetramethylphenol		D
o-ethylphenol	A	
m-ethylphenol	A	
o-ethylphenol	A	
propylphenol	A	
2,6-di-tert-butyl-4-methylphenol	A	D
chavicol		D
o-phenylphenol		D
m-phenylphenol		D
p-phenylphenol		D
phenylprocatechol	A	
hydroquinone		D
methoxyphenol		D
methylmethoxyphenol		D
benzyl alcohol	A	D

methylbenzyl alcohol   A
dimethylbenzyl alcohol   A
indanol   D

Ethers

ethylene oxide   A   D
propylene oxide   A   D
2,2,4,4-tetramethyltetrahydrofuran   A
furan   A   D
2-methylfuran   D
2,5-dimethylfuran   A   D
methylfuroic acid   D
benzofuran   A   D
hydroxybenzofuran   D
dimethylbenzofuran   D
anisole   A   D
p-methylanisole   D
dimethylanisole   D
trimethylanisole   D
anethole   D
1,2-dimethoxybenzene   D
methoxybiphenol   A

Nitriles

hydrogen cyanide   A   D
cyanogen   A
acrylonitrile   A

Nitro compounds

nitromethane   A   D
nitroethane   A

Heterocyclic nitrogen compounds

2,4-dimethylpiperazine   D
benz[c]acridine   A

Sulphides

carbonyl sulphide   A

Heterocyclic sulphur compounds

trimethylthiophene	D
dimethylbenzothiophene	D

Organometallic compounds

methylmercury	A	
tetramethyllead		V
ethyltrimethyllead		V
dimethyldiethyllead		V
methyltriethyllead		V
tetraethyllead		V

APPENDIX 2: AIR POLLUTANT FACT SHEETS

These Fact Sheets are reproduced from the *Handbook for Urban Air Improvement* which was prepared for ERL for the Commission (DG-XI) and published in 1991 (ERL 1991a).

Pollutant fact sheet: CO

Description

Carbon monoxide (CO) is a colourless, odourless, tasteless gas that is slightly lighter than air.

Occurrence in air

Natural background levels of CO fall in the range $0.01-0.23mg/m^{-3}$. Levels in urban areas are highly variable, depending upon weather conditions and traffic density. Eight-hour mean values are generally less than $20mg/m^{-3}$ but can be as high as $60mg/m^{-3}$.

Major sources

CO is an intermediate product through which all carbon species must pass when combusted in oxygen. In the presence of an adequate supply of O_2, most CO produced during combustion is immediately oxidised to CO_2. However, this is not the case in spark ignition engines, especially under idling and deceleration conditions. Thus, the major source of atmospheric CO is the spark ignition combustion engine. Smaller contributions come from all other processes involving the combustion of organic matter (for example in power stations, industry, waste incineration). In the indoor environment, tobacco smoking can be a significant source of CO.

Atmospheric behaviour

Once emitted to the atmosphere, CO is oxidised to CO_2.

Human health effects

When CO is inhaled it can enter the bloodstream and disrupt the supply of essential O_2 to body tissues. The health effects of CO result principally from its ability to displace O_2 in haemoglobin, forming carboxyhaemoglobin (COHb). (The normal function of haemoglobin is to transport O_2 from the lungs to all body tissues.) The consequent reduced O_2 availability (hypoxia) can give rise to a wide range of health effects (depending on how much the flow of oxygen to the body is impeded).

These health effects are usually related to blood levels of COHb (expressed as a percentage), which can in turn be related to exposure (as a function of exposure time as well as concentration). The 'no-observed-effects' level is about 2% COHb which can be related to an eight-hour exposure (moderate activity) to $15-20mg/n^{-3}$.

Certain neurobehavioural effects can be expected at about 5% COHb (moderate activity for eight hours in $40mg/m^3$) that can be related to observable ambient concentrations. These include: impaired learning ability, reduced vigilance (ability to detect small changes in the subject's environment), decreased manual dexterity, impaired performance of complex tasks, and disturbed sleep activity. There is suggestive but not conclusive evidence that drivers in fatal road accidents often have elevated COHb levels. (There is no evidence as to the significance of this.)

In addition, increased risk of certain effects on the cardiovascular system can be expected to begin at levels close to peak ambient conditions. These effects include: local myocardial ischaemia (in which a part of the heart muscle is deprived of O_2), aggravation of angina pectoris, myocardial infarction (heart attack including those leading to sudden death), reduced exercise and physical work capacity, enhanced development of arteriosclerosis and coronary artery disease.

Elevated COHb levels can also reduce the availability of O_2 to the central nervous system (CNS), including the brain. High levels may cause strokes, involving (depending on the duration of the O_2 deficit): unconsciousness and convulsing, brain swelling and protrusions, death to part of the brain or even the death of the individual. Repeated episodes of impaired O_2 supply would be expected to damage the blood–brain barrier and possibly cause structural damage resulting in the reduced ability of the CNS to transmit information.

Individuals most at risk to the effects of CO include those with existing cardiovascular or chronic respiratory problems, the elderly, young children and foetuses.

Other environmental effects

There are few, if any, other significant environment effects. Plants both produce and metabolise CO and are only harmed by prolonged exposure to very high levels. (The lowest levels of which significant effects on vegetation have been reported is 115mg/m^{-3} for 3 to 35 days.)

Pollutant fact sheet: NO_x

Description

NO_x is a collective term used to refer to two species of oxides of nitrogen: nitric oxide (NO) and nitrogen dioxide (NO_2). (Other members of this species exist, but are not included in the definition of NO_x.) These two oxides are grouped together because most NO_2 from anthropogenic oxygen derives from emissions of NO. Because this transformation occurs quite rapidly, NO_2 is generally regarded as being more important from the point of view of human health. Consequently, data on health risks, ambient concentrations and standards and guidelines are generally expressed in terms of NO_2 rather than NO_x.

Nitrogen dioxide (NO_2) is a reddish-brown gas. It is a strong oxidant and soluble in water.

Occurrence in air

Annual mean concentrations in urban areas are generally in the range $20–90\mu\text{g/m}^{-3}$. Levels vary significantly throughout the day, with peaks generally occurring twice daily as a consequence of 'rush-hour' traffic. Maximum daily and ½-hour means can be as high as $400\mu\text{g/m}^{-3}$ and $850\mu\text{g/m}^{-3}$ respectively.

Major sources

Globally, quantities of nitrogen oxides produced naturally (by bacterial and volcanic action and by lightning) far outweigh anthropogenic emissions. These given rise to low level background atmospheric concentrations. Anthropogenic emissions are mainly due to fossil fuel combustion from both stationary sources (heating, power generation) and transport (internal combustion engines).

In most cases, atmospheric nitrogen is oxidised to NO during combustion and then oxidised to NO_2 when emitted into the atmosphere. This process is temperature dependent, with less 'thermal' NO being produced in lower temperature combustion processes. (Nitrogenous compounds in coal, and to a lesser extent in oil, also make a contribution to the total quantity of NO emitted.) The atmospheric oxidation of NO to NO_2 is caused by reaction with O_3 and other oxidants, such as the hydroperoxy radical HO_2. This occurs rapidly even when there are relatively low concentrations of NO and oxidants in the atmosphere.

Other atmospheric contributions come from non-combustion processes. (For example, nitric acid manufacture, welding processes and the use of explosives.) Indoor sources of NO_2 include tobacco smoking and the use of gas fired appliances and oil stoves.

Atmospheric behaviour

When NO is emitted into the atmosphere, most of it is rapidly oxidised to NO_2 by O_3 or other oxidants such as HO_2:

$$NO + O_3 = NO_3 + O_2$$

$$NO + HO_2 = NO_2 + OH$$

In polluted atmospheres, other oxidating reactions take place involving hydrocarbons, aldehydes, CO and other compounds. NO also combines with OH radicals to produce nitrous acid HNO_2.

Once formed, the atmospheric residence time of NO_2 is of the order of one day. It is then converted to nitric acid (HNO_3) by reaction with OH radicals. Most HNO_3 is then removed from the atmosphere by wet deposition, and to a lesser extent, by dry deposition.

Human health effects

A variety of respiratory system effects have been reported to be associated with exposure to short- and long-term NO_2 concentrations less than $3.8 mg/m^{-3}$ in humans and animals, including: (1) altered lung function and symptomatic effects observed in controlled human exposure studies and in community epidemiological studies, (2) increased prevalence of acute respiratory illness and symptoms observed in outdoor community epidemiological studies and in indoor community epidemiological studies comparing residents of gas and electric stove heated homes, and (3) lung tissue damage, development of emphysema-like lesions in the lung, and increased susceptibility to infection observed in animal toxicology studies. Certain human health effects may occur as a result of exposures to NO_2 concentrations at or approaching recorded ambient NO_2 levels.

Human pulmonary function effects of clear health concern resulting from single, short-term exposures of less than three hours duration have been unambiguously demonstrated only at concentrations (greater than $1.9mg/m^{-3}$) well in excess of ambient exposure levels typically encountered by the public. More subtle health effects that were of uncertain health significance, such as mild symptomatic effects, had been reported for some asthmatics after a single two-hour exposure to about $1mg/m^{-3}$.

Young children and asthmatics are the groups at greatest risk from ambient NO_2 exposures. Chronic bronchitis and individuals with emphysema or other chronic respiratory dieases may also be sensitive to NO_2 exposures. In addition, there is reason to believe that persons with cirrhosis of the liver or other liver, hormonal and blood disorders, or persons undergoing certain types of drug therapies may also be more sensitive to NO_2.

Other environmental effects

Other environmental effects of NO_2 and NO_x compounds include increased acidic deposition and vegetation effects.

Visible injury to vegetation due to NO_2 alone occurs at levels which are above ambient concentrations generally occurring within the USA and Europe, except around a few point sources. For long-term exposures, such as a growing season, the lower concentration reported to depress growth is approximately $0.5mg/m^{-3}$. Interactive effects with SO_2 may however be important.

Pollutant fact sheet: particulates

Description

Particulate matter is a complex mixture of organic and inorganic sustances, present in the atmosphere as both liquids and solids. Coarse particles can be regarded as those with an aerodynamic diameter greater than 2.5μm, and fine particles less than 2.5μm. Coarse particles usually contain earth crustal materials and fugitive dust from roads and industries. Fine particles contain the secondarily formed aerosols combustion particles and recondensed organic and metallic vapours. The acid component of particulate matter generally occurs as fine particles.

A wide range of terminology is applied to particulate matter, reflecting measuring methods (eg total suspended particulates), site of deposition in humans (eg inhalable, thoracic particles) or physical characteristics (eg PM_{10} which refers to an aerodynamic diameter of less than 10 microns).

A further distinction that can be made is to classify particulates as either 'primary' or 'secondary', according to their origin. Primary particulates are those emitted directly to the atmosphere while secondary particulates are those formed by reactions involving other pollutants. In the urban context, most secondary particulate matter occurs as nitrates formed in reactions involving NO_x.

Occurrence in air

Reported concentrations vary accordingly to the sampling techniques. In urban areas, typical annual mean values are 10–40μg/m^{-3} (black smoke method) or 50–150μg/m^{-3} (gravimetric method). Corresponding peak values are 100–250μg/m^{-3} (blacks moke method) and 200–400μg/m^{-3} (gravimetric method). Background levels in rural areas range from 0–10μg/m^{-3} (black smoke method).

Major sources

Particulate matter is emitted from a wide range of sources including power plants and industrial processes, vehicular traffic, domestic coal burning and industrial incineration. Natural sources are less widespread and less important. These include volcanoes and dust storms. Particulate matter can also be formed by the transformation of gaseous emissions such as oxides of sulphur and nitrogen, and VOCs.

Atmospheric behaviour

Particulate matter is removed from the atmosphere by both wet and dry deposition.

Human health effects

Short term health effects of exposure to combined SO_2, black smoke and particulates include increased mortality, morbidity and deficits in pulmonary function. Some of the 'lowest-observed effect' levels for short term exposure to particulate matter are: exccess mortality – $500\mu g/m^{-3}$ (smoke); increased acute respiratory morbidity (adults) – $250\mu g/m^{-3}$ (smoke); decrements in lung function (children) – $180\mu g/m^{-3}$ (total suspended particulates)/$110\mu g/m^{-3}$ (thoracic particles). Smoke levels of up to $1500\mu g/m^{-3}$ occurred in the 1952 London smog (see also SO_2).

In addition, exposure to air pollutants and especially particulates may give rise to feelings of discomfort, which may cause annoyance. This subjective response has been widely reported in studies of Swedish cities.

Other environmental effects

Other environmental effects include the soiling of exposed surfaces, impairment of visibility, potential modification of climate and contribution to acid deposition.

Pollutant fact sheet: SO_2

Description

Sulphur dioxide (SO_2) is a colourless gas. It reacts on the surface of a variety of airborne solid particles, is readily soluble in water and can be oxidised within airborne water droplets.

Occurrence in air

Annual mean concentrations in most major European cities are now below $100\mu g/m^{-3}$, with daily mean values in the range 25–$50\mu g/m^{-3}$. Hourly peak values can be 1000–$2000\mu g/m^{-3}$. Natural background levels are about $5\mu g/m^{-3}$.

Acid aerosol (most of which is formed from SO_2) occurs in concentrations of the order of 0–$20\mu g/m^{-3}$ (measured as sulphuric acid) in North America and Europe.

Major sources

The most important sources of emissions of SO_2 are fossil fuel combustion, smelting non-ferrous ores (mainly copper, lead, nickel and zinc), manufacture of sulphuric acid, conversion of wood pulp to paper, incineration of refuse, production of elemental sulphur. Coal burning is the single largest source of atmospheric SO_2, accounting for about 50% of annual global emissions in recent years, with oil burning accounting for a further 25–30% of emissions.

Atmospheric behaviour

SO_2 is the principal pollutant associated with the problem of acid deposition, after having been oxidised to sulphuric acid. The most likely first step in a chain of reactions to the oxidation of SO_2 by OH is:

$$SO_2 + OH(+M) = HSO_3(+M)$$

(Where M is a molecule of oxygen, nitrogen or other neutral gas which carries off the excess energy, thereby preventing the immediate reversal of the reaction.)

Oxidation reactions involving O_2, O_3 and the hydroperoxy radical (HO_2) are so slow as to be insigificant. Oxidation reactions with organic peroxy radicals (RO_2) can become significant in highly polluted atmospheres.

The subsequent reactions of the transient HSO_3 are still uncertain, although ultimately it is transformed to sulphuric acid (H_2SO_4). The most likely mechanism is thought to be:

$$HSO_3 + O_2 = SO_3 + HO_2$$
$$SO_3 + H_2O = H_2SO_4$$

This sulphuric acid is finally removed from the atmosphere by either wet or dry deposition.

Human health effects

Concentrations of more than $10000\mu g/m^{-3}$ SO_2 can give rise to severe effects in the form of bronchoconstriction, chemical bronchitis and chemical tracheitis. Concentrations in the range $2600–2700\mu g/m^{-3}$ give rise to immediate clinical symptoms with bronchospasm in asthmatics.

Epidemiological studies indicate the following effects after short term

SO_2 exposures: possible small reversible declines in children's lung function ($250-450\mu g/m^{-3}$); aggravation of bronchitis (about $500\mu g/m^{-3}$); increased mortality ($500-1000\mu g/m^{-3}$).

Sulphuric acid and other sulphates also have human health effects. Respiratory effects have been reported for concentrations of $350-500\mu g/m^{-3}$ sulphuric acid with a lowest-demonstrated-effect level of $100\mu g/m^{-3}$ for exercising adolescent asthmatics. The odour threshold for sulphuric acid is in the range $750-3000\mu g/m^{-3}$.

High concentrations of SO_2 ($>1000\mu g/m^{-3}$) together with suspended particles are believed to have been responsible for high mortality levels during London smogs (the December 1952 smog was associated with 4000 excess deaths).

Other environmental effects

There is evidence that some species of plant are affected by SO_2 concentrations of the order of $50-100\mu g/m^{-3}$, although concentrations in most agricultural regions in Europe are unlikely to affect cereal yields. Various species of tree have exhibited effects at concentrations of less than $50\mu g/m^{-3}$ however, interpretations of all of these studies are complicated by the presence of other pollutants (O_3, NO_x, acid deposition and heavy metal soil contamination).

Acid deposition (to which sulphur compounds are the greatest contributors) can affect both terrestrial and aquatic ecosystems. Terrestrial ecosystem impacts can be either direct above-ground effects or indirect as a result of changes in soil characteristics. Aquatic ecosystems, especially lakes, most at risk are those with low levels of alkalinity. (Acid deposition liberates aluminium from the catchment area of lakes. Once in the water, aluminium hydroxide is formed, which is then responsible for the observed fish-kills.)

SO_2 also has an important role to play in deterioration of stonework and metal corrosion.

Pollutant fact sheet: benzene

Description

Benzene is a colourless, clear liquid with a boiling point of 80.1°C. It is fairly stable chemically, but highly volatile (that is, it readily evaporates).

Occurrence in the air

Ambient concentrations of benzene are typically between 3 and 160μg/m^{-3}. Levels close to major emission sources (for example, petrol stations) can be as high as several hundred μg/m^{-3}.

Major sources

About 80% of anthropogenic emissions of benzene comes from petrol fuelled cars. This results from both the benzene content of petrol and the pyrolysis (thermal breakdown) of petrol. A further 5% of emissions comes from the handling, distribution and storage of petrol, and about 1% comes from oil refining. Significant emissions also come from benzene producing and handling industries, involving such processes as the catalytic reforming of naphtha and toluene hydrodealkylation. The burning of wood and other organic material also results in an appreciable release of benzene. Some emissions also come from the use of benzene as a laboratory reagent and in sample collection, preparation and extraction. Cigarette smoking may be a significant source of benzene for smokers, especially in the indoor environment. Another source in the indoor environment is the use of benzene in glues, adhesives and solvents.

Atmospheric behaviour

Benzene is removed from the atmosphere by both wet deposition and chemical transformation in the atmosphere (principally in reaction with the hydroxyl radical OH). The half life for chemical transformation is about five days. Deposition to the soil usually leads to degradation by bacterial action or re-evaporation (owing to benzene's high vapour pressure).

Human health effects

Benzene is known to have both carcinogenic and toxic effects. At levels of occupational exposure (several hundred mg/m^{-3}) there is a clear excess incidence of leukaemia. No case of leukaemia has been confirmed following regular and repeated occupational exposure to benzene in air at concentrations below 320mg/m^{-3}.

Early manifestations of toxicity are anaemia, leucocyotopenia or thrombocytopenia (literally, 'poverty' of leucocytes or thrombocytes).

Persistent exposure to toxic levels of benzene may cause injury to the bone marrow, resulting in pancytopenia. Exposure to high levels ($>3200\text{mg/m}^{-3}$) of benzene causes neurotoxic symptoms. No adverse effect on blood formation in humans has been confirmed following regular and repeated occupational exposure to benzene in air concentrations below $80\text{--}96\text{mg/m}^{-3}$.

Other environmental effects

Benzene is generally toxic to biota, but there are not significant effects at ambient levels.

REFERENCES

Ackermann, U. et al (1987) Luftverschmutzung und Gesundheit: Erste Ergebnisse der Studie uber Atemwegs-erkrankungen bei Kleinkindern in den Kantonen Basel-Stadt und Zurich, research report, University of Berne

Adams, J. (1981) *Transport Planning: vision and practice*, Routledge and Kegan Paul, London

—— (1985) *Risk and Freedom: the record of road safety regulation*, Transport Publishing Projects, Cardiff

—— (1992) Towards a sustainable transport policy, in Roberts et al (1992) 320–33

Albrecht, H. and Huss, H.U. (1990) Electricity and hydrogen as alternative fuels, in 'The Route Ahead'. Proceedings of the WWF conference on road transport and the greenhouse effect, World Wide Fund for Nature UK, 101–14

American Lung Association (1990) *The Health Costs of Air Pollution: a survey of studies published 1984–1989*, Washington, DC

Apel, D. (1988) *Zweiter Bericht für die AG 'Flache' der Enquete Kommission Bodenverschmutzung, Bodennutzung und Bodenschutz-Verkerhsflachen*, Deutsches Institut fur Urbanistik, Berlin

Appleyard, D. (1981) *Livable Streets*, University of California Press, Berkeley

Appleyard, D. and Lintell, M. (1969) The environmental quality of city streets: the resident' viewpoint, *Journal of the American Planning Association*, 35, 84–101

Arbeitskreis Verkehr (1988) *Lärm-Minderung durch prinzipielle Verkehrs-Beruhigung*, Berlin

Ashton, J. (1992) *Healthy Cities*, Open University Press, Milton Keynes

Ball, D.J., Brimblecombe, P. and Nicholas, F.M. (1991) *Review of Air Quality Criteria for the Assessment of Near-field Impacts of Road Transport*, Contractor Report 240, Transport and Road Research Laboratory, Crowthorne, Berks

Barde, J.-P. and Pearce, D. (1991) *Valuing the Environment: six case studies*, Earthscan, London

Barrett, S. (1991) Global warming: economics of a carbon tax, in Pearce, D. (ed) *Blueprint 2*, 31–52, Earthscan, London

Bayley, S. (1986) *Sex, Drink and Fast Cars: the creation and consumption of images*, Faber & Faber, London

Benetou-Marantidou, A., Nakou, S. and Micheloyannis, J. (1988) Neuro-behavioural estimation of children with life-long increased lead exposure, *Archives of Environmental Health*, 43(6), 392–5

Berkman, L.F. and Syme, S.L. (1979) Social networks, host resistance and mortality: a nine year follow up of Almeda County residents, *American Journal of Epidemiology*, 109, 186–204

Berry, W. (1987) *Home Economics*, North Point Press, San Francisco

Bhopal, R., Moffat, S., Phillimore, P. and Foy, C. (1992) *The Impact of an Industry on the Health of a Community: the Monkton Coking Works study*, University of Newcastle upon Tyne, Division of Epidemiology and Public Health

Blair, S.N., Kohl, H.W., Paffenbarger, R.S. et al (1989) Physical fitness and all-cause mortality, *Journal of the American Medical Association*, 262, 395–401

Blazer, D.G. (1982) Social support and mortality in an elderly community population, *American Journal of Epidemiology*, 115, 686–94

Bleijenberg, A.N. and Sips, H.W. (1989) *Indirect Taxes and the Environment*, Centre for Energy Conservation and Environmental Technology, Delft

Blumer, W., Blumer, L. and Scherrer, L. (1989) Messungen von feinstem Teerstaub an einer Autostrasse mit hoher Krebsmortalität, *Medicina Generalis Helvetica*, 9(1), 19–21

Blumer, W. and Reich, T. (1980) Leaded gasoline – a cause of cancer, *Environment International* 3, 465–71

BMA (1992) *Cycling: towards health and safety*, British Medical Association, London

Bowers, J. (1990) *Economics of the Environment: the conservationists' response to the Pearce report*, British Association of Nature Conservationists

Bowling, A. (1991) *Measuring Health: a review of quality of life measurement scales*, Open University Press, Milton Keynes

Bracher, T. (1988) Radwege – van der Chance zur Illusion. Fahrradplanung aus der Sicht der Radfahrer, in Muller, A.K. *Symposium Fahrradzukunft*, Technische Universität, Berlin

Bremener Strassenbahn AG (1990) Informationsmaterial zur Tagung 'Umwelt und Stadtentwicklung' Perspektiven einer konzertierten Aktion in der Europäischen Gemeinschaft, 24–26 January, Bremen

Brown, L. (1990) *The State of the World*, Worldwatch Institute/Norton, New York

——— (1992) *State of the World*, Earthscan, London

Buchanan, K. (1967) *The Southeast Asian World*, Bell, London

Campbell, G.W. (1992) *A Survey of Nitrogen Dioxide Levels in the UK using Diffusion Tubes*, LR893, Warren Springs Laboratory, Stevenage

Church, A. (1992) London's transport system, *Geography*, 334(77), part 1, 84–7

Cleary, J. (1992) Benign modes: the ignored solution, in Whitelegg (1992d), 153–68

Climate Network Europe (1991) *Global Warming and the EC Budget: Recommendations to the European Parliament in the debates on the 1992 budget*, Brussels

Cooper, J. (1989) *The Social and Economic Consequences of Freight Deregulation in Three Countries: the UK, Australia and USA*, Polytechnic of Central London

——— (1990) Freight needs and transport policy, Discussion paper no.15, Rees Jeffreys Road Fund, Transport and Society Programme, Transport Studies Unit, Oxford University

Cooper, J. et al (1991) *European Logistics*, Blackwell Business, Oxford

Coronary Prevention Group (1987) *Exercise, Heart, Health*, CPG, London

Davey Smith, G. and Morris, J.N. (1992) Assessment of physical activity and physical fitness in population surveys, *Journal of Epidemiology and Community Health*, 46(2), 89–91

Davis, R. (1993) *Death on the Streets: cars and the mythology of road safety*, Leading Edge, Hawes, N. Yorks

Daly, H. (1991) *Steady State Economics*, Island Press, Washington DC

Department of the Environment (1991) *The Potential Effects of Climate Change in the UK*, HMSO, London

Department of Transport (1986) *Road Accidents Great Britain, 1985*, HMSO, London

—— (1989) *National Traffic Forecast*, HMSO, London

—— (1991) *Road Accidents Great Britain 1990: the casualty report*, HMSO, London

DocTer (1990) *European Environmental Yearbook*, Milan

EC (1988a) The Economics of 1992. *European Economy*, 35(March), Brussels

—— (1988b) *Research on the Costs of Non-Europe: basic findings*, Vol. 1, *Executive Summaries*, Brussels

—— (1989a) *Freight Transport 1987, Road*, Eurostat, Brussels

—— (1989b) *Official Journal of the European Community*, C 318, 20 December 1989, p7, Brussels

—— (1990a) Green paper on the urban environment, COM(90) 218 final, Brussels, 27 June 1990, Brussels

—— (1990b) Economic and fiscal incentives as a means of achieving environmental policy objectives. Hearing of the Committee on the Environment, Public Health and Consumer Protection, 21/22 June in Brussels. European Parliament, Directorate General for Research, Research and Documentation Papers, Series: *Environment, Public Health and Consumer Protection*, 16

—— (1991) Forecast of emissions from road traffic in the European Communities, Report EUR 13854, Environment and Quality of Life, Brussels

—— (1992a) COM(92) 46 final, Green Paper on the impact of transport on the environment. A community strategy for sustainable mobility 20 February 1992, Brussels

—— (1992b) *Official Journal of the European Community* 15 September 1992, No C 236/6–18 and COM(92) 231 final, Transport Infrastructure, Brussels

—— (1992c) *The Future Development of the Common Transport Policy: a global approach to the construction of a Community framework for sustainable mobility*, Communication from the Commission, COM(92) 494 final, 2 December, Brussels

ECMT (1991) *Transport and Spatial Distribution of Activities*, European Conference of Ministers of Transport, Round Table 85, OECD, Paris

Economist (1992) Planes, trains and automobiles, 12 September 1992, 91–2

Edinburgh District Council (1991) *An Investigation into Nitrogen Dioxide Levels in the City of Edinburgh, October 1990–October 1991*, City of Edinburgh District Council, Environmental Health Department

Ehrlich, P. and Ehrlich, A. (1990) *The Population Explosion*, Simon and Schuster, New York

Ekins, P. et al (1992) *Wealth Beyond Measure: an atlas of new economics*, Gaia, London

Ende, M. (1984) *Momo*, Penguin, London

ERL (1991a) *Handbook for Urban Air Improvement*, ERL. London

—— (1991b) *Integrated Noise Policy at European Community Level*, Oxford Environmental Consultants Ltd, Oxford

—— (1991c) *Research and Technology Strategy to Help Overcome Environmental Problems in relation to Transport (SAST Project No.3)* Study 1, *Local Pollution* (Interim Report), Environmental Resources, London

ERR (1989) *Atmospheric Emissions from the use of Transport in the UK*, Vol. 1, *The Estimation of Current and Future Emissions*, Earth Resources Research (ERR) and World Wide Fund for Nature (WWF), London

—— (1990) *Atmospheric Emissions from the use of Transport in the UK*, Vol. 2, *The Effect of Alternative Policies*, Earth Resources Research (ERR) and World Wide Fund for Nature (WWF), London

Feanby, D. (1992) Underreporting of pedestrian road accidents, *British Medical Journal*, 304, 422

Fergusson, J.E. (1986) *Lead: Petrol Lead in the Environment and its Contribution to Human Blood Levels*, The Science of the Total Environment, 50, 1–54

Flowerdew, R., Pooley, C. and Whitelegg, J. (1992) *A Baseline Health Survey of Heysham (Lancashire)*, Environmental Epidemiology Research Unit, Department of Geography, University of Lancaster

Fox, A.J. and Goldblatt, P.O. (1982) *OPCS Longitudinal Study. Sociodemographic Mortality Differentials 1971–75, England and Wales*, HMSO

French, H.F. (1990) *Clearing the Air: A Global Agenda*, Worldwatch Paper 94, Worldwatch Institute, Washington DC, USA

Friends of the Earth (1991a) *Climate Change. A Briefing on the Science and Impacts of Global Warming*, Friends of the Earth, London

Friends of the Earth (1991b) *Air Quality and Health*, Friends of the Earth, London

Gleissner, E. (1987) *Gemeinwirtschaftliche Bewertungsmaßstabe im öffentlichen Personennahverkehr (Vorstudie)*, Hans-Bockler Stiftung, Düsseldorf

Godlee, F. (1991) Air Pollution: II – road traffic and modern industry, *British Medical Journal*, 303, 1539–43

—— (1992) Transport: a public health issue, *British Medical Journal*, 304, 48–50

Goyer, R. (1990) Lead toxicity from overt to subclinical subtle health effects, *Environmental Health Perspectives*, 86, 177–81

Group Transport 2000 Plus (1990) *Transport in a Fast Changing Europe*. Vers un Reseau Europeen des Systemes de Transport, European Commission, Brussels

Hagerstrand, T. (1975) Space, time and the human condition, in Karlquist, A., Lundquist, L., and Snickars, F. (eds) *Dynamic Allocation of Urban Space*, Saxon House, Lexington, MA

Haigh, N. (1991) *EEC Environmental Policy and Britain*, (2nd edn), Longman, Harlow

Hajer, M.A. (1991) Environmental performance review as instrument of ecological modernisation: a contextual analysis. Paper for the international symposium Environmental Performance Review: a new tool?, The Fridtjof Nansen Institute, Oslo, 28–31 May

Hamer, M. (1987) *Wheels Within Wheels: a study of the road lobby*, Routledge & Kegan Paul, London

Hillman, H., Adams, J. and Whitelegg, J. (1990) *One False Move: a study of children's independent mobility*, Policy Studies Institute, London

Holgate, S.T. (1992) Asthma and our environment, *Medical Research Council News*, December

Holman, C. (1989) *Air Pollution and Health*, Friends of the Earth, London

Holzapfel, H. (1992) Violence and the car, unpublished manuscript, University of Kassel

Houghton, R.A. and Woodwell, G.M. (1989) Global climatic change, *Scientific American*, April, 36–44

Hughes, P. (1991) The role of passenger transport in CO_2 reduction strategies, *Energy Policy*, 19(2), 149–60

——— (1992) A strategy for reducing emissions of greenhouse gases from personal travel in Britain, PhD thesis, Open University, Energy and Environment Research Unit

Huntley, B. (1990) Lessons from climates of the past, in Leggett, J. (ed) *Global warming: the Greenpeace report*, Oxford University Press, Oxford, 133–48

Illich, I. (1974) *Energy and Equity*, Marion Boyars, London

ILS (1992) *Autofreies Leben*, Institut fur Landes- und Stadtentwicklungsforschung des Landes Nordrhein–Westfalen, Dortmund

International Union Of Railways (1987) *Charging Surface Transport Operators for the use of the Infrastructure: the case for basing the charges on the marginal social cost*, International Union of Railways, Paris

IPCC (1990) Scientific Assessment of Cliamtic Change, Report of Working Group 1, Intergovernmental Panel on Climatic Change, World Metereological Organization, Geneva

Ippen, M., Fehr, R. and Krasemann, E.O. (1989) Krebs bei Anwohnern verkehrsreicher Strassen, *Versicherungsmedizin*, 2, 39–42

IUCN, UNEP, WWF (1991) *Caring for the Earth: a strategy for sustainable living*, Earthscan, London

Jacobs, J. (1961) *The Life and Death of American Cities*, Pelican, London

Janelle, D.G. (1968) Spatial reorganisation: a model and concept, *Annals of the Association of American Geographers*, 58, 348–64

Jensen, R.A. and Laxen, D.P.H. (1987) The effect of the phase-down of lead in petrol on levels of lead in air, *The Science of the Total Environment*, 59, 1–8

Johnson, C.E. and Henshaw, J. (1991) *The Impact of NO_x Emission from Tropospheric Aircraft*, AEA-EE-0127, Modelling and Assessments Department, AEA Environment and Energy, Harwell Laboratory, Oxfordshire

Jones, P. (1992) What the pollsters say, in Whitelegg (1992d), 11–32

Just, U. (1992) Local transport strategies in North Rhine–Westphalia, in Whitelegg (1992d), 51–70

Keyfitz, N. (1992) Population growth can prevent the development that would slow population growth, in Mathews, J.T. (ed) *Preserving the Global Environment*, Norton, New York, 39–77

Kuck, H.A. (1990) Technical solutions to reduce greenhouse gas emissions, in 'The Route Ahead', proceedings of the WWF conference on road transport and the greenhouse effect, World Wide Fund for Nature UK, 101–14

Lamb, K.L., Brodie, D.A., and Roberts, K. (1988) Physical fitness and health related fitness as indicators of a positive health state, *Health Promotion*, 3, 171–82

Lents, J. (1990) The South California air quality management plan in World Wide Fund For Nature – UK, *The Route Ahead: proceedings of the WWF conference on road transport and the greenhouse effect*, 201–9, WWF, London

Loske, R. (1991) Ecological taxes, energy policy and greenhouse gas reductions: a German perspective, *The Ecologist*, 21(4), 173–6

Lowe, M. (1989), The bicycle: vehicle for a small planet. Worldwatch Paper 90, Worldwatch Institute, Washington DC

MacKenzie, J. and Walsh, M.P. (1990) *Driving Forces*, World Resources Institute, New York

Marchetti, C. (1988) Building bridges and tunnels: the effect on the evolution of traffic, Document SR-88-01, International Institute for Applied Systems Analysis, Vienna

Meadows, D.H. et al (1972) *The Limits to Growth*, Universe, New York

Meadows, D.H., Meadows, D.L. and Randers, J. (1992) *Beyond the Limits: confronting global collapse, envisioning a sustainable future*, Chelsea Green, Vermont

Mogridge, M. (1990) *Travel in Towns*, Macmillan, London

Navarro, R.A., Heierli, U. and Beck, V. (1985) *Alternativas de Transporte en America Latina: la bicicleta y los triciclos*, SKAT, Centro Suizo de Technologia Apropiada, St Gallen, Switzerland

Nelson, P.M. (1989) The impact and control of vehicle noise, Working Paper WP/VE&D/89/61, Transport and Road Research Laboratory, Crowthorne, Berks

Netherlands Agency for Energy and the Environment (1989) *The Netherlands Travelling Clean: towards a trend breach scenario*, Sittard, The Netherlands

New, S.J. and Senior, M.L. (1991) 'I don't Believe in Needles': qualitative aspects of a study into the uptake of infant immunisation in two English Health Authorities, *Social Science and Medicine*, 33(4), 509–18

Nieper, N. (1991) *Der steuerbegünstigte Lungenkrebs, Raum & Zeit*, Ehlers Verlag, Munich

OECD (1988) *Transport and the Environment*, OECD, Paris

——— (1991) *The State of the Environment*, OECD, Paris

O'Riordan, T. and Rayner, S. (1991) Risk management for global environmental change, *Global Environmental Change*, 1(2), 91–108

Owens, S. (1991) *Energy Conscious Planning: the case for action*, Council for the Protection of Rural England, London

Owens, S., Anderson, V. and Brunskill, I. (1990) *Green Taxes*, Institute for Public Policy Research, London

Oxford Institute of Retail Management (1989) *Responding to 1992: key factors for retailers*, OIRM, Oxford

Pearce, D., Markandya, A. and Barbier, E.B. (1989) *Blueprint for a Green Economy*, Earthscan, London

Pfundt, K., Eckstein, K. and Meewes, V. (1989) Zonen-Geschwindigkeits Beschrankung, Beratungstelle fur Schadenverhutung des HUK-Verbandes/ Innenministerium Baden-Wurtemberg

Planco (1990) Externe Kosten des Verkehrs. Schiene, Strasse, Binnenschiffahrt. Gutachten im Auftrag der Deutschen Bundsbahn. Zusammenfassung. Planco, Lilienstrasse 44, 4300 Essen

Polino, M.-N. (1993) The French TGV since 1976: a few hints for historical research, in Whitelegg, Hulten and Flink (1993), 38–47

Pollution Probe (1991) *The Hidden Costs of the Car: a study of the environmental and social costs associated with private car use in Ontario*, Pollution Probe, Toronto

Renner, M. (1988) Rethinking the role of the automobile, Worldwatch Paper 84, Worldwatch Institute, Washington, DC

Reutter, U. (1989) *Welche Erkentisse liegen der Landesregierung uber Gesundheitsgefahren durch Reifen und Bremsbelagabriebe*, ILS, Dortmund

Roberts, J. (1989) User-friendly cities: what Britain can learn from mainland Europe, in TEST

—— (1992) Trip degeneration, in Whitelegg (1992d), 135–52

Roberts, J. et al (1992) *Travel Sickness: the need for a sustainable transport policy for Britain*, Lawrence and Wishart, London

Rothengatter, W. (1991) Development of Transport flows in Europe with a special focus on problems, plans and possible solutions for Germany, in *New Strategies for European Freight Transport '91*, proceedings from a conference, October 29–30, Hamburg, TFK and VTI Transportforschung GmbH, Hamburg, 20–42

Rowell, A., Holman, C. and Sohi, S. (1992) *Breathing is a Risky Business: populations at risk from air pollution*, Greenpeace, London

Sachs, W. (1992) *For the Love of the Automobile: looking back into the history of our desires*, University of California Press, Berkeley

Savitz, D.A. and Feingold, L. (1989) Association of childhod cancer with residential traffic density, *Scandinavian Journal of Work and Environmental Health*, 15, 360–3

Schmidt, M., Mampel, U. and Neumann, U. (1987) Gesundheitschaden durch Luftverschmutzung, IFEU Bericht no 47, Wunderhorn, Heidelberg

Schneider, S. (1990) The changing global climate, *Scientific American*, 261(3), 38–47

Schramm, G. and Warford, J.J. (1989) (eds) *Environmental Management and Economic Development*, World Bank/Johns Hopkins University Press, Baltimore

Schulz (1989) *The Social Costs of Car Traffic*, Federal Environment Office, Berlin

Schumacher, E.F. (1973) *Small is Beautiful*, Abacus, London

Seifried, D. (1990) *Gute Argumente: Verkehr, Beck'sche Reihe*, Beck, Munich

Senatsverwaltung für Stadtentwicklung und Umweltschutz (1992) Luft- und Lärmbelastungen in der Berliner Innenstadt durch den KFZ-Verkehr, Nr 15

Sharp, C.H. (1973) *Transport Economics*, Macmillan, London

Siemiatycki, J. et al (1988) Associations between several sites of cancer and ten types of exhaust and combustion products, *Scandinavian Journal of Work and Environmental Health*, 14, 79–90

Simonis, U.E. (1990) *Beyond Growth: elements of sustainable development*, Wissenschaftszentrum fur Sozialforschung, Berlin

Stadt Köln (1989) *Verkehrsberuhigung auf dem Prufstand*, Stadterneuerung, Köln

Statistisches Bundesamt (1990) *Verkehersunfälle, 1989*, Metzler-Poeschel, Stuttgart

Stephens, J. (1988) Physical activity and mental health in the United States and Canada: evidence from four population surveys. *Preventive Medicine*, 17, 35–47

Steven, H. (nd) Beurteilung der Auswirkung verschiedener Massnahmen zur minderung des Verkehrslärms, FIGE GmbH, Forschungsinstitut Gerausche und Erschutterungen, Aachen

Task Force (nd) *'1992': the environmental dimension*, Task Force report on the environment and the internal market.

TEST (1991) *Wrong Side of the Tracks: impacts of road and rail transport on the environment – a basis for discussion*, Transport and Environment Studies, 177 Arlington Rd, London

Teufel, D. (1989) *Gesellschaftliche Kosten des Strassen-Güterverkehrs: Kosten Deckungsgrad in Jahr 1987 und Vorschläge zur Realisierung des Verursacherprinzips*, Bericht Nr 14, Umwelt und Prognose Institut, Heidelberg

Teufel, D. et al (1988) *Ökosteuern als marktwirtschaftsliches Instrument im Umweltschutz – Vorschläge fur eine ökologisches Steuerreform*, Umwelt und Prognose Institut, Heidelberg

Tolley, R. (1990) (ed) *The Greening of Urban Transport: planning for walking and cycling in Western cities*, Belhaven, London

Townsend, P. and Davidson, N. (1982) *Inequalities in Health: the Black Report*, Penguin, Harmondsworth

Transport and Health Study Group (1991) *Health on the Move: policies for health promoting transport*, Public Health Alliance, Birmingham

Transport Europe (1992a) *The Community Framework: infrastructure*, Transeuropean network: implementation of Maastricht treaty, No 18, May, Europe Information Service, Brussels

Transport Europe (1992b), as above, No 19

UBA (1988) *Lärmbekampfung '88, Tendenzen, Probleme, Lösungen*, Umweltbundesamt, Berlin

UITP (1992) *Assessments of Mobility in Europe*, Union Internationale des Transports Publics, Brussels

Umweltbundesamt der BRD (1986) Umweltauswirkung von Tempo 30, Berlin

Vahrenholt, F. (1984) (ed) *Tempo 100. Soforthilfe fur die Wald?* Spiegel-Buch, Rowohlt, Hamburg

Verkehrs-Club der Schweiz (1991) *Transit durch Granit*, Herzogenbuchsee, Switzerland

Von Weizsäcker, E.U. (1988) *Regulatory Reform and the Environment: the case for environmental taxes*, Institute for European Environmental Policy, Bonn

——— (1990), Prices should tell the ecological truth, paper presented at a conference on sustainable development – science and policy, Bergen, 8–12 May, 1990, European Institute for Environmental Policy

Von Weizsäcker, E.U. and Jesinghaus, J. (1992) *Ecological Taxation Reform: a policy proposal for sustainable development*, Zed, London

Waller, H. (1988) *Noise Abatement in The Netherlands*, Ministry of Housing, Physical Planning and Environment, The Hague

Walsh, M.P. (1990) Trends in vehicle use and emissions control approaches worldwide, in World Wide Fund for Nature – UK, *The route ahead: proceedings of the WWF conference on road transport and the greenhouse effect*, 131–46, WWF, London

Waters, M.H.L. (1990) *UK Road Transport's Contribution to Greenhouse Gases: a review of TRRL and other research*, Contractor Report 223, Transport and Road Research Laboratory, Crowthorne, Berks

Watkins, S.M. (1984) *Cycling Accidents* (final report of a survey of cycling and accidents), Cyclist' Touring Club, Godalming, Surrey

Welin, L. et al (1992) Social networks and activities in relation to mortality from cardiovascular diseases, cancer and other causes: a 12 year follow-up of the study of men born in 1913 and 1923, *Journal of Epidemiology and Community Health*, 46, 127–32

Whitelegg, J. (1982) *Inequalities in Health Care: problems of access and provision*, Straw Barnes Press, Retford, Notts

—— (1983) Road safety: defeat, complicity and the bankruptcy of science, *Accident Analysis and Prevention*, 15(2), 153–60

—— (1988) *Ein Vergleich von Strassenverkehrsunfällen und Verletzen in Köln und Manchester*, Institut für Landes- und Stadtentwicklungsforschung des Landes Nordrhein–Westfalen, Dortmund

—— (1990a) *Auswirkungen der EG-Politik auf den Gütertransport und die Folgen für Nordrhein–Westfalen*, Institut für Landes- und Stadtentwicklungsforschung des Landes Nordrhein–Westfalen, Dortmund

—— (1990b) Traffic calming: a green smokescreen? in *Traffic Calming: ways forward* (report of a conference held at the London Borough of Ealing, 21 January 1990), Town Planning and Building Control, Ealing

—— (1990c) European instruments for an environmental transport policy. Paper presented at hearings organised by European Parliament Committee on the environment, consumer protection and public health, 'Economic and fiscal incentives to promote environmental policy objectives', Brussels, 21–22 June

—— (1990d) The principles of environmental traffic management in Tolley (1990), 75–87

—— (1991) Freight transport implications of 1992: why economic growth and industrial restructuring are bad news for the environment, in Moyes, A. (ed) *Companies, Regions and Transport Change*, Transport Geography Study Group, Aberystwyth

—— (1992a) Cutting corners, *Commercial Motor*, 1(7) (October), 26–7

—— (1992c) Till the pips squeak: ecological taxation reform in Whitelegg (1992d), 169–85

—— (1992d) (ed) *Traffic Congestion: is there a way out?*, Leading Edge, Hawes, N. Yorks

Whitelegg, J. and Holzapfel, H. (1993) The conquest of space by the destruction of time, in Whitelegg, Hulten and Flink (1993), 203–12

Whitelegg, J., Hulten, S. and Flink, T. (1993) *Fast track to the future: high* speed trains and society, Leading Edge, Hawes, N. Yorks

WHO (1958) *The First Ten Years: the health organization*, Geneva, World Health Organization

────── (1987) *Air Quality Guidelines for Europe*, World Health Organisation, Regional Office for Europe, Copenhagen

────── (1990) *Environment and Health – the European Charter and Commentary*, World Health Organisation, Regional Office for Europe, Copenhagen

Wicke, L. (1987) Soziale Nutzen und Soziale Kosten des Automobils- eine positiv Bilanz? Referat auf der Internationalen Automilausstellung an 18 September in Franfurt am Main

Wolff, S. (1992) Correlation between car ownership and leukaemia: is non-occupational exposure to benzene from petrol and motor vehicle exhaust a causative factor in leukaemia and lymphoma? *Experientia*, 48, 304–10

World Commission on Environment and Development (1987) *Our Common Future* (The Bruntland Report), Oxford University Press, Oxford

WWF (1991) *Aircraft Pollution: environmental impacts and future solutions*, World Wide Fund for Nature Research Paper, Godalming, Surrey

INDEX

AA 156
Aachen 97, 129, 160
accessibility 60, 83, 96
accidents 35, 56, 69, 70, 85, 86, 87,
    89–92, 97, 99, 109–13, 116, 127,
    128, 130–2, 134, 135, 141, 153 see
    also fatality rates
acidification 138
ADAC 156
Africa 3, 11, 155
agriculture 20, 142, 151
air
    industry 50
    pollution 1, 5, 9, 22, 29, 32, 36–59,
        60, 71, 72, 75, 77, 90, 114, 115,
        116–25, 128, 131–4, 136, 138,
        139, 143, 148, 153, 155, 157, see
        also carbon monoxide, nitrous
        oxides, ozone etc
    quality 30, 32, 40–3, 46, 50, 54, 75,
        116, 122, 125, 136, 137, 154, 156,
        161
    Quality Guide-lines for Europe 38
    transport 19, 22, 57, 58, 127, 153,
        157
    travel 92, 94
aircraft 19, 20, 21, 60, 64
airports 60, 72, 78, 137, 154
Alabama 77
alcohol fuels see fuels, biomass
    see also ethanol, methanol
Alpine transit routes 161
alternative technology see technology,
    alternative
aluminium 45
American Lung Association 123, 136
Amsterdam 46, 97, 159, 160
Andalusia 161
angina 114, 117
    see also cardiovascular disease

Aosta 160
Arbeitskreis Verkehr 69
asbestos 37, 45, 115, 120
Asia 13
asthma 43, 114, 115, 117, 118, 121,
    125, 137
Australia 3, 124, 125, 151

Baden-Würtemberg 70
Bangladesh 11, 13
Basel 122
Bath 160
Baza 161
beer 149
Belgium 112
benzene 36–8, 45, 48, 97, 121, 139
benzo-α-pyrene 49
benzopyrene 124
Berlin 136
bicycle 9, 13, 25, 35, 74, 81, 83, 106,
    109, 156, 160
    see also cycling
Billingham 47
biodiversity 127
biomass fuels see fuels, biomass
blood creation, impairment of 124
Bologna 97, 160
brain damage 115
Brazil 13, 29
Bremen 130, 136
Brenner Pass 161
British Medical
    Association 109
    Journal 97
Broken Hill 125
bronchitis 114–16
Bruntland Report 7
Brussels 46, 48, 60, 78
buses 9, 50, 57, 59, 65, 79, 83, 85, 94,
    105, 106, 144, 156

by–pass 127, 128, 161

cabotage 148, 149, 153
cadmium 38, 45
caesium 31
California 9, 11, 29, 30, 32, 122, 123,
　137, 156, 159
Canada 122, 139
cancer 115, 116, 120, 121, 122, 124
car
　clean 6, 31, 140
　company 25, 32
　-free cities 71, 97, 129, 160, 161
　industry 130, 138, 158
　ownership rates 5, 6, 10, 11, 16, 30,
　　60, 69, 121, 128, 137, 138, 155
　prices 147, 158
carbon
　dioxide 6, 14–25, 27, 29–35, 38, 43,
　　50, 57, 58, 67, 69, 97, 127, 134,
　　141, 143
　monoxide 14, 23, 29, 31, 32, 36–8,
　　40, 43, 45–7, 49, 50, 52–4, 57,
　　58, 97, 114, 117, 123, 143
　tax 15, 140–2, 174–6
carcinogen- 28, 31, 37, 38, 45, 114,
　115
cardiovascular disease 83, 108, 114–16,
　121, 138
　see also circulatory problems
car-parks 9, 77, 78, 83, 160
catalytic converters 9, 22, 31, 45, 46,
　49, 50, 53, 54, 96, 126, 139–41, 154
Channel Tunnel 161
chest discomfort 123
　see also respiratory disease,
　　bronchitis etc
children 9, 10, 38, 43, 83, 85, 98, 99,
　104–7, 109, 110, 112, 114, 121–6,
　129, 162
China 5, 10, 13, 155
chlorofluorhydrocarbon (CFC) 14, 17,
　20, 139
Christian Salvesen 150
chrome 45
chromium 139
circulatory problems 114, 115
　see also cardiovascular disease
Clean Air Act 29
climatic change 5, 14, 18, 127
　see also global warming
cloud formation 21

coal 29, 30, 32, 36, 141
cobalt 45
Colorado 121
commercial vehicles *see* lorries
community 23, 76, 78, 80, 92, 96, 98,
　104, 106, 112, 121, 123, 126, 128,
　155, 156, 159, 160, 162
　destruction 9, 31, 78
　disruption 1, 69, 85, 142
　severance 97
commuters 129
commuting 10, 30, 31
Confederation of Independent States
　155
congestion 22, 49, 69, 78, 80, 82, 83,
　128, 132, 136, 143, 144, 159
construction industry 130
Copenhagen 38, 161
Coronary Prevention Group 108
cost
　-benefit analysis 94, 111, 127,
　　137
　recovery 2, 142
coughing 114, 123
　see also bronchitis, respiratory
　　disease etc
crime reduction 99
cycleway 108
cycling 10, 13, 16, 25, 35, 49, 59, 60,
　69, 73, 77, 98, 108, 109, 111, 129,
　136, 143, 144
cyclists 9, 46, 75, 79, 85, 89, 95, 96,
　109, 110, 112, 113, 128

Daimler Benz 88
deaths *see* fatalities
　see also mortality rates
dengue 18
Denmark 26, 108, 111, 112, 161
Denver 121, 137
Department of Transport 112
deregulation 147, 151, 153
diesel 25, 27–9, 31, 38, 39, 65, 67, 75,
　114, 115, 122
disease 18, 106, 121, 158
　heart *see* heart disease
　respiratory *see* respiratory
　　disease
　see also bronchitis, asthma etc
drunk driving 112
dual-use vehicles 29
Düsseldorf 3, 60

Earth Resources Research (ERR) 21, 24, 27, 28, 31, 32, 34, 50, 53, 54, 56
Earth Summit *see* Rio Summit
ecological taxation 2, 140
  reform (ETR) 131, 141–5
economic
  development 35, 160
  growth 2, 3, 5, 11, 140, 146–8, 158
  incentives 25
  policy 143, 153
Edinburgh 36, 43, 46
elderly 83, 98, 104, 110, 126, 129
electric vehicles 9, 25, 31, 32, 45, 126, 154
electricity 9, 12, 30–2, 156
electronic road pricing (ERP) *see* road pricing, electronic
Elmira 139
emphysema 114–16
employment 11, 76, 97, 98, 122, 142, 147, 162
encephalitis 18
encephalopathic symptoms 119, 124
energy 11, 14, 35, 139, 142–4
  conservation 13, 143
  consumption 7, 9, 12, 13, 32, 58, 59, 80, 92, 94, 125, 134, 136, 140, 141, 156
  conversion 83
  costs 138
  efficiency 83
  -intensive societies 95
  renewable 6
  use 16, 34, 57–9
engine size 25, 26, 29, 32, 89
Enquete Kommission 16
Environment Commissioner 147
environmental
  auditing 139
  consequences 78, 161
  control 46
  cost 57, 138, 140
  damage 9, 12, 34, 80, 130, 131, 133–5, 140, 143, 149, 157
  degradation 147, 151
  destruction 161
  disbenefits 128
  disturbance 159
  economists 128, 139
  efficiency 37, 142
  groups 97

impact 2, 4, 8, 9, 11, 22, 31, 133, 137, 139, 147, 148, 154, 156
  improvement 2, 6
  objectives 42, 43, 130, 159
  policies 2, 3, 37, 42, 49, 147, 158
  problems 1, 9, 12, 14, 36, 42, 46, 60, 77, 80, 85, 129, 142, 146, 149
  Protection Agency 121
  quality 1, 2, 3, 69, 136, 144, 146
  systems management 139
  taxation *see* ecological taxation
  technology 143
  valuations 137
epidemiological data 41, 43, 45, 46, 122, 123, 157
erythrocyte changes 119
ethanol 11, 29, 30
EURET research programme 152
Europe 2, 3, 11, 18, 34, 36, 38, 43, 48, 72, 80, 107, 111, 130, 131, 142, 143, 146–58, 161, 162
  Eastern 5, 6, 16, 158
  Mediterranean 158
  Southern 16, 48, 150, 152, 157, 161
European
  Community 2, 3, 11, 15, 34–6, 38, 41, 42, 47, 49, 59, 60, 111, 112, 130, 141, 146–61
    directive 38–40
    regulation 71–5
    see also Single European Market
  Parliament 60, 131
Exel Logistics 150
exercise 98, 106, 108, 109
eye irritation 114, 118, 119, 123, 137, 138

fatality rates 85, 86, 87, 110, 113, 123, 127
  see also accidents; mortality
Federal Noise Ordnance 73
Fehr 122
Finland 141
Florence 160
food
  crops 11
  industry 149, 151
forecasts
  air pollution 48–56
  road traffic 21, 22, 33, 34, 37, 48, 49, 53, 152

forests 11, 15
  see also rainforests
formaldehyde 36, 49, 114, 118
fossil fuels *see* fuels, fossil
France 2, 48, 72, 78, 112
Frankfurt 48, 71
free radicals 31
freight 1, 2, 3, 5, 6, 13, 34, 35, 54,
  56–9, 64, 130, 133, 143, 146,
  147–53, 157, 159
  industry 150
  rates 151
  transfer 25, 64, 75
  see also lorries
Friends of the Earth (FOE) 116
fuel 127, 133, 142, 144
  alternative 25, 29, 138
  biomass 11, 20, 30, 31
  cell technology 23, 30
  clean 141
  consumption 9, 22, 25–9, 31, 32,
    49, 69, 88, 89, 141
  economy 25, 29
  efficiency 9, 22, 35, 67
  fossil 12, 30, 32, 141, 142,
    143
  new 45, 126
  tax 135, 140, 150
German Democratic Republic (GDR)
  (former) 6, 10, 161
Germany 4, 10, 11, 16, 26, 43, 48,
  62–4, 69, 73, 78, 89, 108, 111, 112,
  129–33, 136, 139, 149, 150, 152,
  153, 156, 158, 160
Gesamtverkehrsplan 43
Glasgow 47
Global Environmental Monitoring
  System (GEMS) 48
global warming 1, 14–35, 38, 126,
  128, 138, 140, 141, 155, 162
Goodyear 139
Gothard Pass 154
Gourdon 48
Granada 161
Granby Hall project 94
Greece 2, 112, 124, 150, 161
'green growth' 8–10
Green Paper 146
greenhouse
  effect 16, 127
  gases 1, 6, 14, 15, 17–19, 32, 34,
    35, 140, 142, 155

  see also carbon dioxide,
    chlorofluorcarbons, methane,
    nitrous oxides etc

Hagersville 139
Hamburg 84, 85, 87, 122
Hannover 84
harmonisation *see* Single European
  Market
haulage *see* freight
hayfever 114
headaches 114, 115, 123
health 1, 2, 6, 9, 10, 36–8, 97–126,
  130, 138, 140, 154–6, 162
  audit 157
  costs 137, 138
  damage 13, 22, 43, 60, 128, 132,
    136, 138, 142
  effects 31, 38, 83, 139
  hazard 14, 36, 139
  problems 12, 45
  risks 31, 38
hearing damage 115
heart disease *see* cardiovascular disease
heavy
  goods vehicles (HGV) *see* lorries
  metals 37
Heysham 108
high speed train (HST) 2, 3, 42, 78,
  80, 85, 92, 94, 130, 154
hospitals 76, 83
Hungary 10
hydrocarbons 14, 23, 37, 48, 50, 53,
  54, 56, 97, 114, 115, 123
  polycyclic 122
hydrochlorocarbons 143
hydrogen 30, 31
hydroplant 32
hydroxyl radicals 14
hyperactivity 115
hypermarket 77

impairment of vigilance 117
in-car navigation 84, 144
India 5, 6, 10, 155
inland waterways 133
Intergovernmental Panel on Climatic
  Change (IPCC) 15–18, 24, 155
intermediate technology 13
International Institute for Applied
  Systems Analysis 18
International Union of Railways 133

internationalisation 151, 152
Ippen 122
Ireland 2, 112, 161
isolation 99, 106, 110
Italy 72, 112, 149, 152, 160
IUNC (World Conservation Union) 7, 14, 19

Japan 15, 146

Kassel 84
Kent 161
kidney damage 115, 124
Köln 69, 70, 84, 90–2, 111–13
Krasemann 122
Kuwait 10, 137

Lancaster 36
land take 34, 78, 134, 153
land-use 1, 10, 13, 16, 25, 35, 49, 94, 98, 128, 139–41, 144, 148, 154, 157, 158, 160, 162
landfill 139
lead 36, 38, 39, 41, 43, 45, 49, 50, 97, 115, 118, 124, 125, 137–9
-free petrol 9, 140
legislation 37
see also EC directive; EC regulation
Leicester 94, 95
leishmaniasis 18
leisure 10, 78, 105, 160
Leq measurement 60, 61, 64
leukaemia 121
liberalisation 148, 153
liver damage 124
light rail see tram; metro
London 4, 46–8, 94, 149, 159
Air Pollution Monitoring Network 46
lorries 1, 9, 10, 14, 16, 25, 26, 39, 48, 50, 56, 64–7, 71, 72, 116, 128, 131–3, 136, 143, 154, 161
operators 142, 144, 148
see also freight
Los Angeles 29, 30, 32, 43, 48, 77, 121, 122
Louvain 160
Lübeck 71, 97, 129, 160
lung
cancer 115, 120, 122
disease see respiratory disease
see also American Lung Association

Luxembourg 112
Lyon 94

Maastricht Treaty 2, 146, 159
Madrid 48
Madyha Pradesh 13
malaria 18
Malmo 161
Manchester 47, 94, 111–13, 161
Meana, Carlo Ripa de 147
Mediterranean 18, 157
mesothelia 115, 120
methane 14, 17, 18, 20, 30, 57, 58
methanol 11, 29, 30
metro 57, 79
Milan 48
Ministry of Transport (North Rhine Westphalia) 3
modal
shift 33
split 25, 29, 35, 43
'Momo' effect 80, 83
monetarisation 95, 128
Montreal 122
mortality rate 98, 104, 108, 115, 137
motorcycle 57, 64, 65
motorcyclists 112, 113
motoring organisations 10, 130, 156
see also AA; ADAC; RAC
motorisation 13, 35, 77, 82, 95, 133
motorway 2, 10, 34, 45, 78, 80, 92, 130, 136, 158, 160, 161
Munich 46

Naples 160
National Environmental Policy Plan Plus 43, 72
natural gas 30–2, 141
nausea 114
nervous system damage see neurological damage
Netherlands 26, 43, 72, 108, 111, 112, 141, 143
Agency for Energy and the Environment 43
Netstal 121
neurological damage 115, 118, 138
neuropsychologic effect 124
New York 121
nickel 45
nitrogen dioxide 36, 39–41, 46, 48–50, 88

nitrogen oxides 14, 19, 21, 23, 31, 32, 37, 38, 43, 45, 46, 49–51, 53–5, 57, 58, 97, 114–17, 121, 123, 143
nitrosamine 139
nitrous oxide 17, 20, 36
noise 1, 5, 38, 56, 60–75, 77, 89, 90, 94, 97, 99, 108, 110, 125, 127–34, 136, 137, 139, 141, 153, 154, 156–8, 161
  Abatement Act 72
North Rhine Westphalia 3, 43, 69, 158
nuclear power 30, 32, 141, 143

OECD 7, 37, 38, 61
oil 10, 29, 32, 130, 137, 139, 141
Ontario 10, 139
Orange County 122
out-of-town shopping centres 9, 77, 160
Owen Sound 139
Oxleas Wood 139
ozone 14, 20, 21, 37, 38, 41, 48, 49, 97, 115, 119, 121–3, 138, 140, 162

PAH 38
PAN 38
Paris 47, 78, 93
particulates 28, 39, 42, 45, 49, 114–16, 118, 122, 123, 137, 139
pasta 149
PCB 139
pedestrians 9, 46, 74, 75, 78, 79, 84, 85, 89, 94–6, 99, 109, 111–13, 128, 160,
  see also walking
Pembrokeshire 2
petrol 30, 31, 39, 121, 124, 125, 133, 135, 138–40
  see also lead-free petrol
  vehicles 25, 27–9, 38, 39, 49, 50, 65, 67, 88, 126
phenol 139
photochemical smog 48
platinum 31, 46
pneumonia 114
Poland 10
'polluter pays' principle 37, 140, 141
pollution *see* air pollution; carbon dioxide; noise; time pollution etc
Pollution Probe 139
polonium 31

polycyclic hydrocarbons 122
population 5, 7, 8, 11, 17, 18, 56
  growth 11–13
Portugal 2, 112, 150, 161
poverty 6, 12
power stations 6, 20
precautionary principle 19
pregnancy, complications of 115
pregnant women 42, 121
propane 30
public transport 16, 33–5, 49, 74, 77, 80, 83, 85, 96, 98, 108, 133, 135, 136, 138, 141, 143, 144, 156, 158, 160
pyrene 36
Pyrenees 147, 161

quality of life 54, 69, 75, 76, 106, 138, 147, 156, 157
Queensland 124
'Quiet Heavy Vehicle' project 67
quiet zones 72

RAC 156
radio-nuclides 31
rail 31, 35, 57–9, 62, 64, 72, 75, 92, 94, 127, 128, 130, 133, 135, 143, 151, 153, 156
  privatisation 94
rainforest 13, 162
rare metals 31, 46, 126
Reading 36
recreation 76, 82, 97, 98, 106, 160
refineries 20
Regional Human Exposure Model (REHEX) 122, 123
regulatory impact analyses (RIA) 124, 137
Renault 88
reproductive system damage 115
respiratory disease 1, 83, 114, 116, 121, 122, 137, 138
  see also asthma; bronchitis; emphysema; pneumonia
retailing 151, 152
  see also shops
retardation 124
rickshaws 13
Rio Summit 1, 156
risk compensation 69
Riverside County 122

road
   construction 4, 9, 49, 59, 78, 94, 95,
      125, 130, 135, 137, 144, 147, 153,
      154, 156
   pricing 49, 127, 128, 144
      electronic (ERP) 84, 96
   safety 89, 109, 128, 138, 150
   schemes 82, 94, 95, 111
   space 4, 84, 128, 136, 144
   surfaces 66, 67, 74
   traffic accidents (RTA) *see* accidents
   see also motorway
Rotterdam 46
rubber 139
Ruhr area 139

Sagar 13
San Bernadino 122
San Francisco 100–3
Scandinavia 64
schistosomiasis 18
school 76, 83, 98, 99, 104, 106, 142
sea levels 17–19
Second World Climate Conference 16
Seville 161
shipping 20, 127
shops 76–8, 82, 83, 97, 98, 110, 142
   see also out-of-town shopping
shorelines, recession of 18
Single European Market (SEM) 3,
   136, 146, 147, 151, 153, 159
skin
   damage 138
   irritant 114
smoke 40, 41, 50
smoking 122, 123
Snowdonia National Park 2, 147
social
   interaction 99, 102, 104, 111, 141,
      157
   support networks 97, 98, 106, 108,
      109
soot 36
sore throat 123
South Africa 29
South America 11, 155
South Coast Air Quality Management
   29, 43, 122, 123
Soviet Union (former) 10
space 1, 5, 16, 78–80, 84, 85, 92, 94,
   95, 112, 125, 126, 139, 144, 156
   economy 142, 143, 159

Spain 2, 112, 161
spatial restructuring 2, 152, 153
speed 23, 26, 64–6, 69, 70, 76, 78, 79,
   81–3, 85, 86, 88, 89, 95, 96, 109,
   112, 125, 126
   limits 9, 10, 25–7, 32, 69–71, 74,
      85, 87, 89, 90
Stockholm 7, 78
street (as social space) 98–104, 106,
   111
stress 97, 110, 111, 128, 138
subsidiarity 159, 161
subsidy 37, 130, 142, 144, 156
substitution measures 25
sulphur 39
   dioxide 29, 38–43, 45, 47–50, 114,
      118, 137, 141
'Sustainable Development of the
   Biosphere' programme 18
Sweden 141, 161
Switzerland 16, 72, 73, 121
synergistic effects 45

Task Force report 152
taxation 26, 127, 130, 131, 135, 140–5,
   156
   see also ecological taxation reform
taxes 37, 129, 141, 143, 144, 147, 150
taxis 32
technological solutions 15, 25, 35, 66,
   69, 70
technology 6, 8, 22, 46, 126, 144, 154
   alternative/intermediate 13
telecommuting 30
temperature rise 14, 16–19
Third World 5, 6, 8, 11, 12, 13, 15
time 1, 128, 137–9
   pollution 76–96
toluene 45
Toronto conference 21, 24
tourism 82, 94, 160
traffic
   calming 25, 69, 70–2, 89, 144, 158
   management 25, 33, 74
tram 57, 79
Transport and Environmental Studies
   (TEST) 116, 155, 156
Transport and Health Study Group
   report 97, 98, 108, 110
Transport and Road Research
   Laboratory (TRRL) 28
'Travelling Clean' report 43

trees 69
trip degeneration 154
trishaws 13
trucks *see* lorries
tunnels 60, 73, 130, 142
Turin 125
tyres 9, 10, 29, 45, 66, 67, 139

unemployment 143
Uniroyal 139
United Kingdom 2, 4, 12, 16, 18, 19,
    24, 25, 33, 34, 36, 43, 44, 46, 50,
    67, 70, 72, 94, 108, 110–12, 116,
    121, 124, 125, 130, 150–2, 155, 158,
    159
United Nations 7
    Environmental Programme (UNEP)
        7, 14, 16, 19, 48
United States of America 3, 10–12,
    15, 26, 29, 34, 76, 121, 123, 124,
    136, 137, 146, 151
unleaded petrol *see* lead-free petrol
urban planning 69, 85, 108
urbanisation 148

valuation of life 111, 137
value added tax (VAT) 140, 147
vehicle excise duty (VED) 140
Verkehrsberuhigung *see* traffic calming
Verkehrsentwicklungsplanung 43
vibration 56, 72, 97
Vienna 18
viral infections 114
volatile organic compounds (VOC) 38,
    43, 50, 57, 58, 115
VW Golf 28, 88

walking 10, 13, 16, 25, 35, 49, 59, 60,
    69, 77, 95, 98, 108, 111, 129, 136,
    143, 144
    see also pedestrians
Walsall 47
Warsaw 48
Washington 121
waste 9, 11, 16, 138, 142–4
water
    emissions 21
    pollution 131, 132, 136, 138, 139,
        143, 144
    quality 161
    supplies 18
    transport 58, 127
White Paper 34, 147
Winchester 139
women 83, 85
    see also pregnant women
work *see* employment
World Commission on Environment
    and Development 5, 7
World Conservation Strategy 7
World Health Organisation (WHO)
    36–8, 40–2, 47, 48, 106, 117, 155
World Meteorological Organisation 16
Worldwatch Institute 1, 121
Worldwide Fund for Nature (WWF)
    7, 14, 19
Wroclaw 48

Zagreb 48
zero-emission vehicle 9, 11, 32, 123,
    125, 156
zinc 45
Zürich 74, 122, 158, 159